The United Arab Emirates has become the fulcrum for Middle East business and is an important crossroads for East-West trade. It welcomes all companies and entrepreneurs to share in it's growth.

The UAE offers many business opportunities in all sectors, especially for companies willing to establish a physical presence and bring technology to this market. The UAE government is committed to a free market economy and continues to nurture an environment which encourages innovative ideas.

The Al Masaood Group is continually evolving its business to meet demands and competitiveness of the Middle East, contributing to the development of t[illegible]rcial and industrial diversity of the UAE.

You will find this book "[illegible]E" both informative and helpful, [illegible]ment of the Al Masaood Group are always w[illegible] give further local advice and support to new entrants entering into the market.

المسعود

AL MASAOOD

محمد بن مسعود واولاده
MOHAMMED BIN MASAOOD & SONS

Al Masaood Group Presence in the UAE

Core Business

Al Masaood Automobiles

Najda - T: 971-2-6772000 F: 971-2-6776689

Al Masaood Bergum

T: 971-2-6742100 F: 971-2-6720588
Email: bergumad@emirates.net.ae

MBM Diesel Engineering Division

T: 971-2-5542700 F: 971-2-5544116

MBM Marine Products & Services Division

T: 971-2-6760999 F: 971-2-6768167
Email: mpsdiv@emirates.net.ae

MBM Marine Transport Division

T: 971-2-6767919 F: 971-2-6767114

MBM Projects & Engineering Services

T: 971-2-6771688 F: 971-2-6770840
Email: mbmpesd@emirates.net.ae

MBM Property Division

T: 971-2-6761510 F: 971-2-6762019

Sharjah Grand Hotel

T: 971-6-5285557 F: 971-6-5282861
Email: sales@sharjahgrand.com

MBM Trucks & Heavy Eqpt. Division

T: 971-2-6424602 F: 971-2-6425375

MBM Tyres & Accessories

T: 971-2-6425148 F: 971-2-6425106
Email: mbmtyres@emirates.net.ae

MBM Engineering Products Division

T: 971-2-6424222 F: 971-2-6424111
Email: mbmepdad@emirates.net.ae

Associates

Masaood John Brown LLC

T: 971-2-6767560 F: 971-2-6767580
Email: mjbadsc@emirates.net.ae

Masaood/KSB Fluid Systems

T: 971-2-6772095 F: 971-2-6727539
Email: amarex@emirates.net.ae

Masaood Mowlem

T: 971-2-6726224 F: 971-2-6727223

MTU Middle East Service Centre

T: 971-2-5542700 F: 971-2-5544116

Affilliates

Advanced Group

T: 971-2-6778813 F: 971-2-6770451
Email: advgroup@emirates.net.ae

Al Masaood Farms

T: 971-3-7721408

Al Masaood OISS

T: 971-2-6267666 F: 971-2-6273422
Email: masoil@emirates.net.ae

Al Masaood Travel & Services

T: 971-2-6212100 F: 971-2-6325323
Email: masaoodt@emirates.net.ae

Avenue Retail/Interiors

T: 971-2-6740402 F: 971-2-6745670
Email: avenurt@emirates.net.ae
Email: avenuein@emirates.net.ae

Harley Davidson UAE

T: 971-4-3391909 F: 971-4-3391317
Email: hddubai@emirates.net.ae

Horse & Course

T: 971-4-3361339 F: 971-4-3361317
Email: horsecou@emirates.net.ae

Indigo

T: 971-2-6765598 F: 971-2-6767882
Email: goindigo@emirates.net.ae

Specialist Project Management

T: 971-2-6742545 F: 971-2-6722554
Email: spmaduae@emirates.net.ae

Timco

T: 971-3-7215848 F: 971-2-7210652
Email: timco@emirates.net.ae

Al Masaood Group - Regional Offices

Abu Dhabi - T: 971-2-6722300 F: 971-2-6791541
Dubai - T: 971-4-2829119 F: 971-4-2829229
Al Ain - T: 971-3-7219999 F: 971-3-7216547

Email: masaood@emirates.net.ae

المسعود
AL MASAOOD

Doing Business with the United Arab Emirates

Doing Business with the United Arab Emirates

Consultant Editors:
Philip Dew
Anthony Shoult

TRADE
PARTNERS UK
www.tradepartners.gov.uk

المسعود
AL MASAOOD

KOGAN
PAGE

Publishers' note

Every possible effort has been made to ensure that the information contained in this handbook is accurate at the time of going to press and neither the publishers nor any of the authors can accept responsibility for any errors or omissions, however caused. No responsibility for loss or damage occasioned to any person acting, or refraining from action, as a result of the material in this publication can be accepted by the editor, the publisher or any of the authors.

This book is intended as a general guide only. Its application to specific situations will depend upon the particular circumstances involved. The environment for foreign direct investment in the UAE continues to be subject to rapid change. It is therefore important to be aware that the information given in this book is time sensitive and should not be relied upon as a substitute for obtaining professional advice.

First published in 2000

Kogan Page Limited
120 Pentonville Road
London N1 9JN

Web site: www.kogan-page.co.uk

British Library Cataloguing in Publication Data

ISBN 0 7494 31717

Typeset by Saxon Graphics Ltd, Derby
Printed and bound in Great Britain by Bell and Bain Limited

Front cover image provided by the Government of Dubai, Department of Tourism and Commerce Marketing

Contents

Literature review? – Kuda mad?

List of Contributors

Arthur Andersen & Co.
Arthur Andersen & Co., a member of the Andersen Worldwide group of companies, is a leading accountancy firm in the UAE. A full range of financial, taxation, audit, accountancy and business advice and services is offered.

John Simpkins and Robert Peake are based in the firm's Dubai office.

ASA Consulting
ASA Consulting is a UK-based independent marketing-focused consultancy specialising in the Middle East region. The firm provides a wide range of consultancy services across industrial sectors, either directly or through affiliated organisations, to both international and local public and private sector agencies and organisations. The services provided include assistance to investors in specific areas such as market research and investigations for technical and industrial products and services and techno-economic feasibility studies to the highest standards.

Brian Cave LLP
Brian Cave LLP has one of the largest and most well-established legal practices in the Arabian Gulf, with more than 20 years experience in the region and with offices in each of the UAE (Abu Dhabi and Dubai), Saudi Arabia and Kuwait – each of which is staffed with resident American and/or British as well as Arab attorneys. A broad base of international and local companies, financial institutions, government agencies and individuals are represented to whom legal advice is provided across a broad spectrum which includes joint venture formation, agencies, franchises, distributorships, partnerships, limited liability and joint stock companies; banking and financial representations (including Islamic banking); US and GCC government contracts and tenders; offset matters; corporate and project finance (including privatisation initiatives); local and foreign (especially US) regulatory advice (including tax issues and trade regulations); technology and intellectual property licensing; employment and labour issues; and Shari'ah Law and litigation matters.

Clifford Chance
Clifford Chance LLP is the world's first top tier global law firm. It now has 30 offices covering all major financial centres. The firm's focus is on business and finance law and it has pre-eminent international practices in relation to banking and finance, projects and corporate law. Its international network of offices enables Clifford Chance lawyers to advise on aspects of local law in their respective jurisdictions, including in the UAE, as well as on international and cross-border considerations.

Alastair J. McNair W.S., is on secondment from Clifford Chance to Hadef Al-Dhahiri & Associates in Abu Dhabi

Caroline O'Hare is a partner with Clifford Chance and heads up their banking and finance practice in the Gulf region. She specialises in conventional and Islamic financing and is based in their regional office in Dubai.

Cluttons

Cluttons, a firm of Chartered Surveyors and Property Consultants, is some 235 years old, having been established in 1765. Their head office in London is complemented with three other London offices, as well as 16 regional offices throughout the United Kingdom. Since 1975, Cluttons has established a strong real estate presence within the Middle East. There are now six integrated offices in the Gulf region including three in the UAE (Abu Dhabi, Dubai and Sharjah). Cluttons specialise in property management, leasing, valuation and feasibility studies and corporate consultancy.

Ian Albert is an associate partner based in Cluttons Dubai office.

Emirates Industrial Bank

Emirates Industrial Bank is a specialised financial institution founded in 1982. Owned by the UAE government and local banks and companies, the Bank's objectives are the promotion of economic growth in the UAE by diversifying the country's sources of income and assisting in the development of its industrial base. The Bank aims both to aid the establishment of new industries and to consolidate and strengthen existing factories.

Hadef Al Dhahiri & Associates

Hadef Al Dhahiri & Associates is one of Abu Dhabi's oldest and most established commercial law firms, with strong connections into the Abu Dhabi business community, public sector and international companies with a presence in Abu Dhabi. The firm has grown significantly in recent years and now has a substantial presence, with both local and international expertise, servicing a broad range of clients. The firm has strong links with Clifford Chance of London and Dubai and offers a broad range of services in the commercial area, also having a strong litigation and arbitration practice. The firm's senior lawyers are Dr Faraj Ahnish (Managing Partner) and Alastair J. McNair, W.S., who is seconded to them by Clifford Chance. A second Clifford Chance secondee joined the firm early in 2000.

Handshaikh

Handshaikh Ltd, which is owned by Jeremy Williams OBE, who has spent more than 14 years in five Gulf locations: Sharjah, Dubai, Riyadh, Abu Dhabi and Bahrain, is based near Winchester in England and in Dubai in the UAE. Handshaikh offers induction seminars, advice and negotiation training that focus on the cross-cultural aspects of life and work in the countries of the Gulf. More than 200 companies have been counselled.

Hay Management Consultants
The Hay Group is one of the leading management consultancy firms worldwide which specialises in providing advice and assistance to clients on the organisation, development and management of people. Founded in Philadelphia in 1943, the firm has 7000 clients worldwide. The Middle East is managed from Dubai. Hay has the largest Middle East database for evaluated jobs and associated levels of compensation covering thousands of positions.

Martin Mankowski is the Middle East Director for Hay Management Consultants based in Dubai.

Jack Pearce Associates
Jack Pearce Associates is the Middle East public relations affiliate of Saatchi & Saatchi. The practice's owner, Jack Pearce, has over 19 years public relations, journalism and marketing experience in the UAE and is located in Dubai.

Middle East Research and Consultancy (MERAC)
MERAC, based in Dubai, is one of the largest full-service ad hoc marketing research companies in the region, operating throughout the Arabian Peninsular, Lebanon, Jordan, Syria and Egypt. MERAC was established in 1980 and became part of NFO Worldwide Inc. in 1997. MERAC has a specialist knowledge of the Arabian Gulf and surrounding markets providing added-value research solutions to a wide range of international clients, especially in consumer packaged goods, dairy and tobacco products and financial services.

Stuart Campbell-Morris is the Regional Managing Director, Middle East and Africa for MERAC WLL, an NFO Worldwide company and is based in Dubai.

Norwich Union
Norwich Union's first office in the Gulf was opened in 1950. Today the company has a well-developed regional network of offices covering Bahrain, Saudi Arabia (Riyadh, Jeddah and Al Khobar), the UAE (Abu Dhabi, Dubai, Jebel Ali and Sharjah) & the Sultanate of Oman (Muscat). A full range of commercial, industrial, marine and healthcare insurances are written at each location as well as the provision of risk management services.

Paul Hawkins
Paul Hawkins has been a senior banking executive with international banks in South America, New York, Europe and since 1985 the Middle East. He has developed into one of the Gulf's foremost writers on banking and technology issues and his second book is due for publication in June. The first *The Key to Productivity and Performance* is one of the few management books based purely on management experiences in the Middle East. He is based in Dubai.

Redwood Partners
Redwood Partners is a Dubai-based independent corporate finance firm which focuses exclusively on the GCC markets. The three principal areas of activity are: advisory work for public companies; financial advice to private

companies; and private equity. Redwood advised BP Middle East Limited in public flotation and listing of BP's Oman operations on the Muscat Securities Market. The Redwood principals were responsible for the region's first management buyout.

David Knights is a partner of Redwood. He has worked at Saudi International Bank and at Bahrain International Bank, where he was General Manager, Bahrain responsible for the bank's corporate finance business, including its corporate advisory, fund management and private equity operations in the Gulf

Richards Butler

Richards Butler is an United Kingdom registered legal practice which has maintained a locally-associated office in Abu Dhabi for more than 20 years under then name Al-Sayegh Richards Butler. The primary focus of the Abu Dhabi office is the provision of advice to local interests and international companies on corporate and business matters in the UAE and Gulf region.

Anthony Trew has been a partner in the British international law firm, Richards Butler for more than 25 years. For 21 of them, he has been their resident partner in Abu Dhabi where he advises many international companies and leading UAE interests on corporate and business matters connected with the UAE and the Gulf region. He is currently chairman of the British Business Group Abu Dhabi and a governor of Al Khubairat Community School – the British school there.

Saadiyat Market

The Saadiyat Project, including Saadiyat Market, was given full backing by the Government of Abu Dhabi in July 1996 when Saadiyat Island was declared a free trade zone pursuant to Abu Dhabi Executive Council Law No.6. This law also provided for the creation of the Abu Dhabi Free Zone Authority to act as the sole regulator for the island. Located off the coast of Abu Dhabi, Saadiyat Island is being developed as a city of the future where financial and commodities services will be provided using the latest e-technology and telecommunication services in an environment regulated to the highest international standards

Sarah Lloyd

Sarah J. Lloyd is the Senior Correspondent for the Middle East for Platt's which is a leading energy news service. Over the past decade she has written extensively on oil and natural resource-related issues for the Caucasus, Central Asia and Middle East. She has also worked in London for the Energy Intelligence Group and in Moscow for the Russian Petroleum Investor. She has a BA in Middle Eastern history and politics and an MA in Middle Eastern studies from the School of Oriental and African Studies, University of London. Her publications include: 'The Caspian" in Standard & Poor's Old Oil, *New Rules, Strategies for the 21st Century* (McGraw-Hill Co, 2000); 'Pipelines to Prosperity?" In *The International Spectator* (Rome: Istituto Affari

Internazionali, Jan-Mar 1997); 'Land-locked Central Asia: Implications for the Future" in the *Geopolitics and International Boundaries Journal* (London: Frank Cass, Summer 1997).

Stafford Associates

Stafford Associates is headquartered in Dubai and works throughout the Gulf Region. As well as consulting in market research and market development, Stafford is also well known as the leading postgraduate centre in the Gulf, offering masters and now doctoral programmes from Leicester, Sheffield and Exeter Universities. Stafford offers other consulting skills, a psychometric service and recently became the UAE centre for Dale Carnegie Training.

Philip Marsh is the Managing Director of Stafford Associates and Julius Fernandes is a Marketing Consultant.

The Philip Dew Consultancy Limited

The Philip Dew Consultancy Limited was founded in 1982 to support local and international principals in the comprehensive development of their businesses in the Middle East. Since that time assignments have been fulfilled for over 200 companies, many of them well-known international names. The basic services provided include: identification, investigation and evaluation of market opportunities; market research and feasibility studies; identification of partners, principals, and associates; due diligence enquiries; development of marketing and business strategies; business generation on behalf of principals; and on-the-ground support and assistance to market entrants, including the provision of background and cultural information. The consultancy is owned and managed by Philip Dew who has over 30 years experience of working and living in the Middle East (Bahrain, the UAE, Saudi Arabia and Lebanon), is an Arabic speaker and who acted as consultant editor for *Doing Business with the UAE*

Philip Dew is located in Bahrain from where he covers the whole Middle East.

Thomas Hussain

Thomas Hussain has covered the UAE as a journalist and analyst since 1993. During that period, he served first as chief reporter and then deputy managing editor of the Abu Dhabi-based daily, *Emirates News*. He was also theSenior Gulf Correspondent of United Press International, and has justfinished an assignment as news editor of Dubai Television and Radio. He continues to write in a freelance capacity for a wide range of specialist publications and news wires, including the Economist Intelligence Unit and the Associated Press. Thomas has been a consultant for ANZ Grindlays Bank, the Dutch defence electronics manufacturer Hollandse Signaalapparaten, and British naval shipbuilder, Vosper Thornycroft.

Foreword

The United Arab Emirates is a young and dynamic country which is developing with dizzying speed. It has a distinct identity as a regional hub for communications and trade which is attractive to foreign entrepreneurs and investors as a stable and friendly base. The economy is buttressed by the wealth derived from Abu Dhabi's enormous oil and gas reserves and Dubai's flourishing trade interests and burgeoning tourist industry.

The Emirates are home to the largest British expatriate community in the Middle East. In 1998 Britain exported £1.5 billion of goods to the UAE. It is now the 21st largest market for British exports in the world. British companies and individuals are engaged in every kind of business and are particularly prominent in financial and other services, civil engineering, oil and petrochemicals and tourism. At the many trade exhibitions held in the UAE every year, British companies are usually the largest group of exhibitors. So Britain has a high profile in the Emirates.

The UAE is a rapidly changing market ready to embrace new ideas and new technology. There are many opportunities for companies and individuals to work with local partners. I hope that this comprehensive business guide will assist them in promoting even closer business ties between the United Kingdom and the United Arab Emirates.

H. E. Mr Patrick Nixon
Her Majesty's Ambassador to the United Arab Emirates

Foreword

The United Arab Emirates has been witnessing significant socio-economic developments since it was formed in 1971. These have been reflected by the achievement of high and rapid growth rates on the macro and sectoral levels, leading to a continual rise in the standards of living and per capita income for the population.

Gross Domestic Product (GDP) has been accelerating noticeably in spite of some fluctuations in certain years due mainly to the dramatic changes in the international oil markets. GDP is anticipated to reach US$55.6 billion by the end of 2000, an increase of 7.1 per cent from its 1999 level. In turn, per capita income is expected to rise to US$15,700. At the same time, the non-oil sectors are projected to grow by three per cent.

These considerable economic achievements have been the result of prudent economic policies, political stability in the UAE and statesmanship of the UAE's leadership.

The strategic policy of endorsing a free and open economic system has been adopted in the UAE since its inception. A hallmark of this long-standing policy is minimal governmental intervention. Another feature is the implementation of a liberalised trade policy, reflecting the UAE's rich experience in trade on the local and international levels. Simultaneously, and in order to reduce dependence on oil revenues, the UAE has opted to diversify its economic base through a comprehensive strategy to develop its commodity and services sectors.

The private sector has been encouraged to undertake a greater role in the economy through both reducing the government's participation in economic activities and carrying out a serious privatisation programme. In addition, a host of business and commercial laws and regulations have been issued to organise business activities in all economic sectors and to protect consumers, producers, and national and foreign investors.

Recognising the vital importance of investments as the engine for growth, and in order to create a favourable business environment, various investment incentives are being created and granted by the government to national and foreign investors; namely: providing pre-investment incentives, sophisticated industrial areas and free zones, modern infrastructure, import duties exemptions, zero taxes, and subsidised public services. The success of this investment strategy has been reflected by the continuously rising number of local and foreign companies and enterprises operating in the country. For example, the number of foreign companies in the UAE has increased from 536 in 1991 to about 1200 in 1999.

In light of the UAE's long-standing liberalised trade policy and the present international endeavours towards globalisation, the UAE joined the World Trade Organisation in March 1996 to be an effective member in the new world economic order.

Moreover, the UAE has always been keen to strengthen its regional economic cooperation with Gulf Cooperation Council (GCC) states and other Arab countries. The planned unification of GCC customs by the year 2005 along with the UAE's membership in the grand Arab free trade area which is expected to be completed by 2007 will facilitate this cooperation further. As a member of this free trade area, the UAE has already applied a 20 per cent reduction on tariffs on products of Arab origin.

One cannot over emphasise the fact that the UAE is a gateway to both the East and the West and to the huge neighbouring markets such as Iran, Pakistan, the CIS, the Arab world and East Africa, a market representing more than one billion customers.

In this context, I would like to assure investors and businessmen that these pro-business policies and investment incentives will continue in the future, and to encourage the investors to seize the tremendous investment opportunities, which are abundantly available in the UAE.

Finally, I believe that this publication will be of great value to the potential investors and interested parties as it provides comprehensive information and insight about the UAE's dynamic and flourishing economy.

H.E. Sheikh Fahim bin Sultan Al-Qasimi
Minister of Economy and Commerce

Foreword

Despite the tremendous progress made in promoting awareness of the United Arab Emirates' attractions for international business in recent years, there is still much to be done to disseminate authoritative, relevant and accessible information to a wider global audience.

Likewise, the sheer pace of the UAE's economic growth and development calls for a constant updating of existing information in the public domain.

I am therefore delighted that such a well-known and respected publisher as Kogan Page has decided to produce *Doing Business with the UAE*, which I am sure will prove highly valuable in addressing both these issues.

In particular, in helping to spread the word internationally about the UAE, its economy and business climate, this book directly complements and enhances the activities of the Dubai Government's Department of Tourism and Commerce Marketing (DTCM) in our worldwide promotion of investment, trade and tourism.

Doing Business with the UAE should also make an important contribution to the broader goal of fostering international goodwill, by helping to make the country and its culture more widely understood in the global community.

Besides being a valuable reference source for organisations interested in developing their business within the UAE and Gulf states, the book should also convey a taste of the outstanding prospects that the country offers as a gateway into some of the exciting new and emerging markets of the surrounding region. These include Iran, the Indian sub-continent, East and North Africa, the Levant and CIS/Central Asia.

We believe the UAE offers an unrivalled range of attractive opportunities both as a trading partner and as a base for regional offices, distribution centres and manufacturing facilities. But life is not all business, and *Doing Business with the UAE* also looks into the country's emergence in recent years as one of the world's most rapidly developing upmarket tourist destinations. Whether on business or pleasure, I sincerely hope that readers will be inspired to pay us a visit and experience the country and its attractions at first hand.

Khalid A bin Sulayem
Director General, Department of Tourism and Commerce Marketing
Government of Dubai

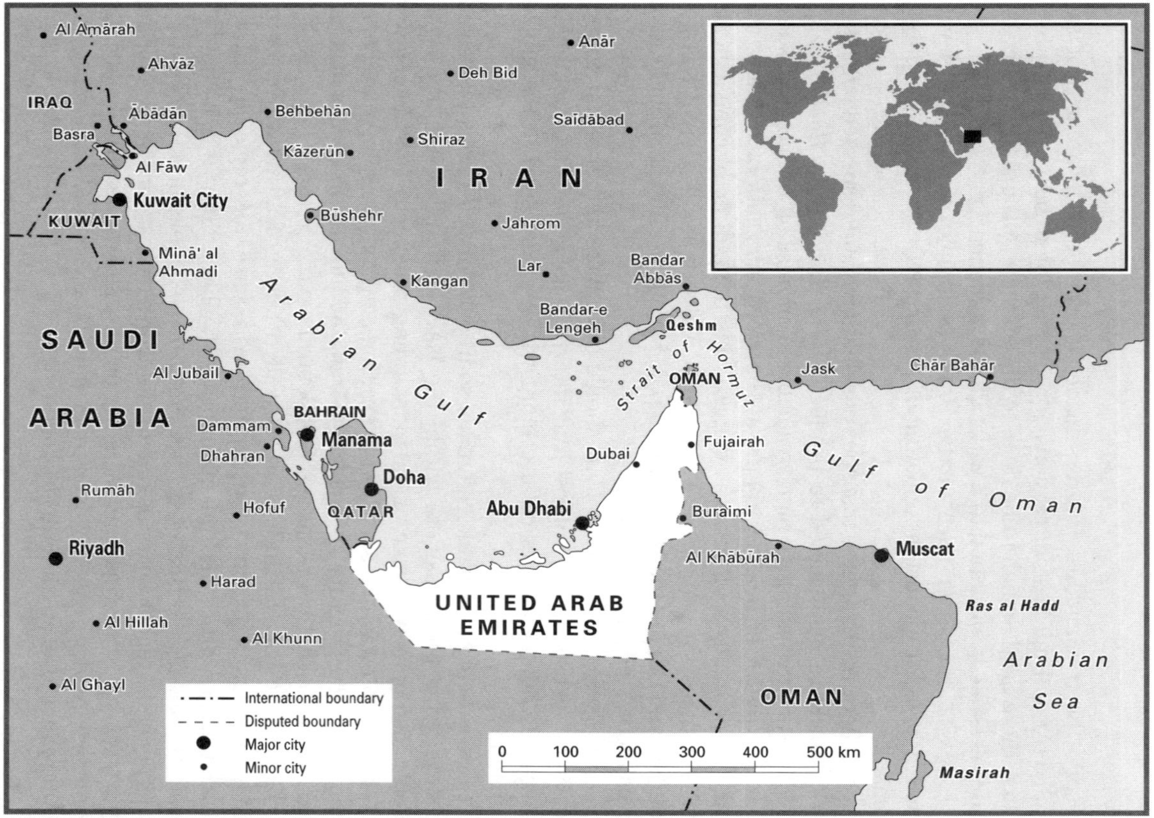

The UAE and its neighbours

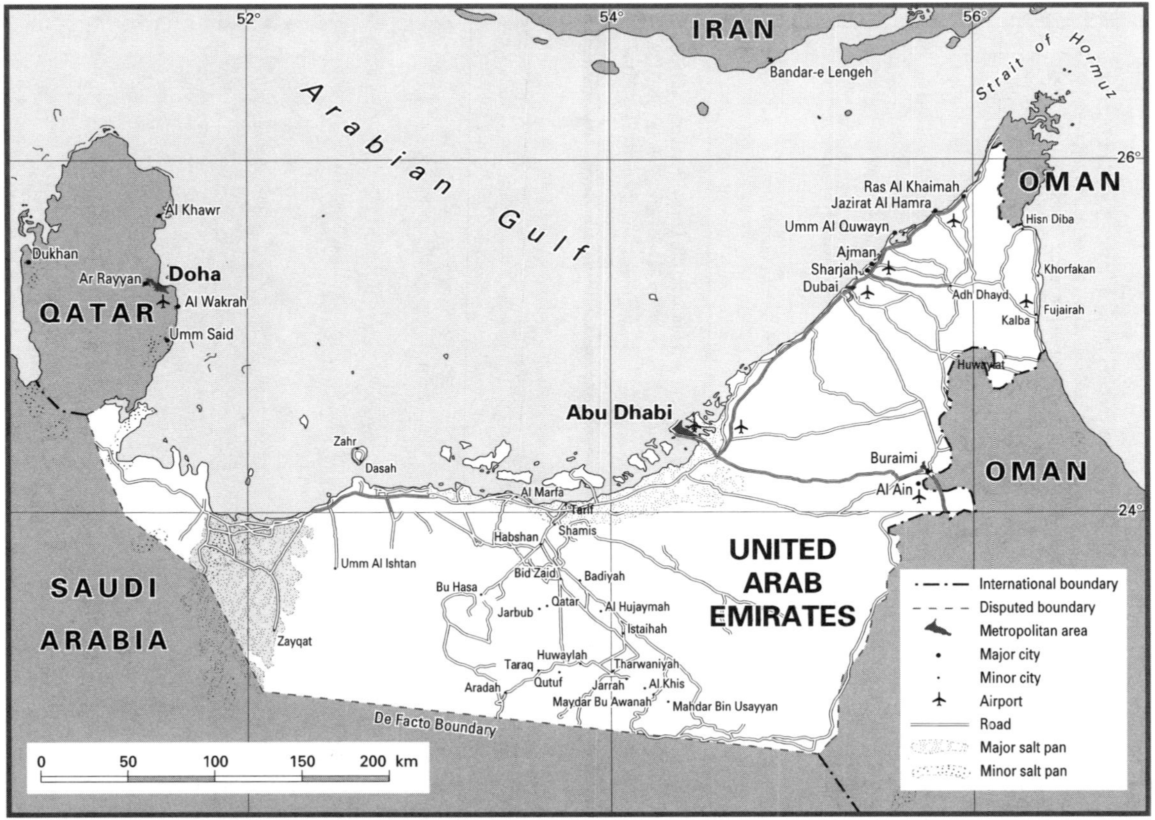

The Infrastructure of the UAE

Part 1

The Background

1.1

Background Information

Philip Dew, Philip Dew Consultancy Limited, Bahrain

The United Arab Emirates (UAE), formerly known as the Trucial States, is a federation of seven emirates, Abu Dhabi, Dubai, Sharjah, Ajman, Umm AlQuwain, Ras alKhaimah and Fujairah.

Since these emirates came together in late 1971 and early 1972, the UAE has witnessed remarkably rapid economic development, having maximised the benefits to be derived from the country's substantial oil wealth. Today, however, the Emirates are no longer totally dependent on oil, having also found large quantities of natural gas and by diversifying their economies into trade, tourism and industry.

Integral to the country's economic growth has been the desire of the federal government and of the governments of the individual emirates to develop a sophisticated infrastructure and an open commercial environment conducive to both local and foreign investment.

Their success in providing such an attractive business environment is best expressed in the large number of international companies which have now made their regional bases in the country. But this is not the end of the story, as the UAE has the ambition to enhance yet further its reputation as a place in which to do business and to relax as a tourist long into the twenty-first century.

Geography

The UAE stretches for more than 650 kilometres along the southern coast of the Arabian Gulf and is bordered to the east by Oman and the Gulf of Oman; to the south by Saudi Arabia; and to the west by Qatar and Saudi Arabia. Six of the emirates lie along the Arabian Gulf coast, with the seventh, Fujairah, being sited on the Gulf of Oman.

The total area of the country approximates to 84,000 square kilometres, with the largest emirate, Abu Dhabi, comprising 75,000 square kilometres (90 per cent) of the total, although most is barren desert. In the Musandam Peninsula, which reaches up in the north east to the Straits of Hormuz across from Iran, there are many natural creeks and inlets, which have traditionally provided large natural harbours for the emirates of Dubai, Sharjah and Ras alKhaimah.

Ras alKhaimah nestles at the foot of the Hajar Mountains which extend through Oman to the very east of the Arabian Peninsula. The highest peak within the UAE rises to some 2500 metres. To the west, and largely within Abu Dhabi, is a sand and gravel desert interspersed with oases, such as AlLiwa and AlAin, which contain numerous villages fed by underground water reserves. To the very south are high sand dunes, which stretch away into the wastes of the so-called Empty Quarter.

Overall, natural vegetation is sparse, with the exception of land close to oases and the Hajar Mountains and the vast areas afforested in recent years within Abu Dhabi.

The climate within the UAE is generally hot and dry, although along the coastal plain high humidity is frequently experienced. Temperatures range between an average minimum in January and February of 10°C to 14°C and an average maximum in July and August of 48°C to 50°C. In the AlHajar Mountains temperatures are considerably lower, especially at altitude. Average annual rainfall is less than 120mm, although in some mountainous areas it can exceed 350mm. Rain storms, especially along the coast, are not unusual, frequently causing flooding in dry valley beds. Sandstorms, sometimes quite violent, can and do reduce visibility.

Demography

Based on the last census undertaken in 1995 and the officially estimated annual growth rate of 4.0 per cent, the population in late 1999 numbers 2.8 million. Of the total, over 80 per cent reside in the emirates of Abu Dhabi, Dubai and Sharjah. Only some 25 per cent are UAE nationals, with 50 per cent being from the Indian sub-continent and the balance made up of Asians, other Arab nationals and Europeans and Americans.

A substantial majority of the population is Muslim and the main languages are Arabic, the official language of the UAE, Persian, English, Hindi and Urdu.

History

The early history of what is now the UAE remains subject to speculation, but archaeologists suggest excavations have unearthed signs of human habitation dating back over 7000 years. Certainly evidence has been found that in about 2300BC there were connections with Mesopotamia and the Indus Valley and that over at least two millennia a sophisticated society flourished in the vicinity of AlAin and nearby Hilli. By the time Islam reached the area in the late AD 630s evidence suggests that there were a number of permanent settlements both inland and along the coast, with Julfar, today's Ras alKhaimah, being used as a port both by the Muslim armies and as an outlet for trade.

Somewhat later the Portuguese succeeded in attaining a commercial monopoly within the Arabian Gulf, but between the sixteenth and eighteenth centuries their influence gave way first to the Dutch and subsequently to the British. During the early years of British influence European and Arab piracy was rife in the region, to overcome which a number of treaties were signed with the principal local sheikhs, which led over time to the UAE being known as the Trucial Coast.

Late in the nineteenth century other countries, including France, Germany and Russia, began to show increasing interest in the Gulf. To protect its interests, and its trade routes to India, Great Britain then entered into exclusive treaties with all the sheikhs along the Gulf coast, under which they undertook not to enter into any relationship or cede any territory to any foreign government other than Great Britain, without the latter's consent, in return for British protection from outside attack.

This situation prevailed until 1968, when Britain announced its intention to withdraw troops from the area. At that time a federation of the states of the Trucial Coast was proposed, including both Bahrain and Qatar which subsequently chose separate independence from Britain. On implementation of the proposal in 1971 just six of the Trucial States became part of the UAE, with the seventh, Ras alKhaimah, joining early the next year.

Government

The UAE is a Federal Sovereign State bound by a constitution under which the Supreme Council of the Federation, which is comprised of all the rulers of the seven member emirates, is the highest political authority, including being responsible for the election of The President and the Vice-President of the country. The Prime Minister is appointed by the President, with the consent of the Supreme Council, and is responsible for recommending Federal Ministers.

The Federal National Council, comprising members of each emirate, is the UAE's legislative body. The Council is responsible for drafting all Federal Laws prior to their referral to the Supreme Council for enactment, discussing issues of public import and for monitoring the conduct of the Federal Government.

1.2

The Constitutional Structure

Alastair McNair, (on secondment from Clifford Chance) Hadef Al Dhahiri and Associates, Abu Dhabi

The United Arab Emirates is comprised of a number of Emirates which were collectively known as the Trucial States. Prior to the British pull-out each of the Trucial States had Protectorate arrangements with Britain. The individual Emirates are:

- Abu Dhabi
- Dubai
- Sharjah
- Ras AlKhaimah
- Ajman
- Fujairah
- Umm Al Quwain

Until the formation of the UAE, each Emirate was regarded as a sovereign state. The UAE as a Federal State came into being on 2 December 1971 with the withdrawal of Britain from the Gulf. The UAE is the only Federal State in the Arab World. Each Emirate retains jurisdiction over some matters, whilst certain other matters have been ceded by the individual Emirates to the Federal Authorities and Government under the Constitution. The UAE is governed by a Constitution which was originally executed in provisional form by the Rulers of each of the Emirates on 18 July 1971.[1] This became permanent in the middle in 1996. Under the UAE constitution, the present structure is as follows:

President (Sh. Zayed Bin Sultan Al Nahyan, Ruler of Abu Dhabi)
Vice President (Sh. Maktoum Bin Rashid Al Maktoum, Ruler of Dubai, also the present Prime Minister)

[1] Ras Al Khaimah only acceded on 10 February 1972

The Supreme Council of Rulers (the UAE's senior policy-making body in which the Rulers of each Emirate have involvement)
The Cabinet (or Council of Ministers). This is the apex of the Federal Governmental Structure and is presided over by the Prime Minister.
The Prime Minister is chosen by the President and his colleagues in the Supreme Council of Rulers.
The Federal National Council with 40 members drawn from each of the Emirates on the basis of population, thus:

- Abu Dhabi, eight members
- Dubai, eight members
- Sharjah, six members
- Ras Al Khaimah, six members
- Fujairah, four members
- Umm Al Quwain, four members
- Ajman, four members

The Judiciary (headed by the Federal Supreme Courts, with the Courts of Appeal and First Instance below).

The Supreme Council of Rulers

The Supreme Council of Rulers is ultimately involved, after an elaborate but substantially informal consultative process, in approving all Federal legislation. Each of the seven Emirates is represented there by their respective Rulers.

The Cabinet or Council of Ministers

This is the apex of the Federal Government structure.

Assigned to the Federal Authorities under the Constitution (Articles 120 and 121) were the areas of:

- foreign affairs
- security and defence
- nationality and immigration
- education
- public health
- currency
- posts and telecoms
- air traffic control and communications
- labour and social affairs
- banking
- delineation of the territorial seas
- the extradition of criminals

The promulgation and follow-up on Federal legislation are largely dependent on the initiatives of the Council of Ministers and its Legislative sub-committee. The Council of Ministers provides continuity and control of the Federal Ministries and Public Agencies and meets on a weekly basis. There are 26 members, each Emirate enjoying significant representation on it.

These are represented in the various Federal UAE Ministries and Public Agencies which are invariably based in Abu Dhabi and include:

- The General Postal Authority
- The Ministry of Agriculture & Fisheries
- The Ministry of Communications
- The Ministry of Economy & Commerce
- The Ministry of Electricity & Water
- The Ministry of Finance & Industry
- The Ministry of Foreign Affairs
- The Ministry of Health
- The Ministry of Information & Culture
- The Ministry of Interior
- The Ministry of Justice
- The Ministry of Labour & Social Affairs
- The Ministry of Islamic Affairs & Endowments
- The Ministry of Petroleum & Mineral Resources
- The Ministry of Public Works & Housing
- The Civil Service Commission
- The Ministry of Youth & Sports
- The UAE Armed Forces
- The UAE Central Bank
- The UAE Securities and Commodities Commission
- The UAE State Audit Institution
- The UAE University

Powers not covered by Federal Authorities are held at a local Emirate level: Article 122 of the Constitution specifically states that:

The Emirates shall have jurisdiction in all matters not assigned to the exclusive jurisdiction of the Federation in accordance with the preceding provisions.

The Federal National Council

This takes the form of a Consultative Council and is responsible under the Constitution for examining and (if it wishes) amending Federal (as distinct from Emirate) legislation. It does not, however, have the power to propose legislation. The Federal National Council may summon federal ministers to explain the performance of the Ministry for which they are responsible. The Federal National Council is presided over by a Speaker or either of two Deputy Speakers elected from amongst their overall membership.

The judiciary

The independence of the judiciary is specifically guaranteed by the UAE Constitution. There exists a federal court structure which is as follows:

- The Federal Supreme Court
  (this only hears appeals on points of law and has particular responsibility for disputes involving administrative law aspects.)
- The Court of Appeal
  (which may hear appeals on the basis of points of law or fact.)
- The Court of First Instance
  (which is, in commercial terms, the Court of original jurisdiction.)

This has divisions for: civil/commercial matters; criminal matters; Sharia matters (this deals with criminal cases involving muslims and family/consistorial/property matters).

Dubai and Ras Al Khaimah are not within the federal judicial system and have their own similarly structured court systems, not being involved in the (Federal) Supreme Judicial Council. This is because certain Emirates reserved some matters to themselves at the time of accession to the Constitution (1971–72)

Abu Dhabi Emirate

As noted above, the local Emirate authorities retain jurisdiction which has not been specifically afforded to the federal authorities by the UAE Constitution. The individual Emirates retain the power to promulgate and implement legislation in non-federal areas in the form of Emiri Decree. In Abu Dhabi the Emirate's structure is thus:

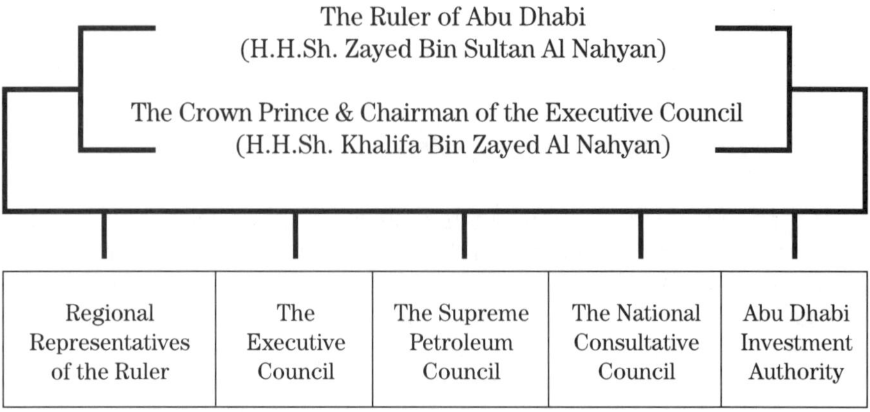

Regional Representatives of the Ruler

The Regional Representatives or Chairmen of the concerned Municipalities of the Ruler are responsible to the Ruler for the overseeing of governmental functions in:

- Western Region (Liwa and Rhuwais)
- Eastern Region (Al Ain)
- Das Island
- Abu Dhabi Municipality
- Al Ain Municipality

The Executive Council

The Executive Council is chaired by H. H. Sh. Khalifa Bin Zayed Al Nahyan and is responsible for the supervision of all areas and aspects of the Government of Abu Dhabi. In essence this is the apex of the Abu Dhabi Governmental structure.

Abu Dhabi government departments

The administration of the Emirate of Abu Dhabi is implemented by a number of local departments including:

- The Amiri Flight
- The Civil Aviation Department

- The Cultural Foundation
- Customs
- The Economic Department
- The Environment Research and Wildlife Development Agency
- The General Industries Corporation
- The Planning Department
- The Directorate General of Police
- The Public Works Department
- The Purchasing Department
- The Seaports Authority
- The Department of Social Affairs and Commercial Buildings (also sometimes known as the 'Khalifa Committee')
- The Water and Electricity Department

Over and above these various entities, there are a number of companies in which the Emirate of Abu Dhabi enjoys a significant and often controlling stake, for example, the National Bank of Abu Dhabi, Union National Bank, Abu Dhabi Investment Company, Abu Dhabi National Hotels Company and Abu Dhabi Aviation Services.

The Supreme Petroleum Council

The Supreme Petroleum Council is responsible for the Emirate of Abu Dhabi's oil and gas industry and the setting of its policy in this area. It is chaired by Sh. Khalifa Bin Zayed Al Nahyan and is effectively run by H. E. Yousef Omeir Bin Yousef. ADNOC and its group are responsible to the Supreme Petroleum Council and include:

- ADGAS
- ADCO
- ADCAP
- FERTIL
- GASCO
- ADNATCO
- ADMA-OPCO
- NPCC

- ZADCO
- ADNOC FOD
- National Drilling Company

The National Consultative Council

The National Consultative Council comprises 50 members drawn from amongst the most prominent families in Abu Dhabi. Its membership includes prominent family members, technocrats and influential merchants. Its role is similar to that of the Federal National Council. In the past the National Consultative Council (which is chaired by Sh. Khalifa Bin Zayed Al Nahyan) has been a vocal source of suggestions for the introduction and revision of Federal legislation.

The Abu Dhabi courts

The Abu Dhabi courts fall under the federal courts system – unlike those in Dubai. There are special courts in the following areas – civil courts (which encompass most commercial matters including debt collection), criminal courts and Sharia courts (mainly to do with personal property matters concerning nationals and believers in Islam). Only UAE national lawyers can now appear in and follow cases before the Abu Dhabi courts.

1.3

The UAE Economy

Thomas Hussain

In the grander scheme of global economics, the United Arab Emirates is admittedly a small player. Its gross domestic product was worth just US$46.3 billion (170 billion dirhams) in 1998. That is minuscule in comparison to the trillion-dollar-plus sums boasted by most of the Group of Seven industrialised countries. Yet this federation of seven small emirates on the north-eastern tip of the Arabian Peninsula have just earned a rare honour. The UAE will in 2003 become the first country in the Middle East to host a joint meeting of the World Bank and International Monetary Fund.

The reasons are simple enough. It has the strongest fiscal position of any country in the region, its economy is the most diversified and it is the most friendly to foreign investors. In figure terms, the federal budget deficit is a very manageable US$676.3 million (2.48 billion dirhams), inflation hovers between 1.5–2 per cent and the non-oil economy now accounts for about 78.3 per cent of GDP.

However, these statistics cannot hide the fact that oil remains the driving force behind the UAE economy. The hydrocarbon sector accounted for US$10.07 billion (36.95 billion dirhams) or 21.7 per cent of GDP during 1998, despite it being a year in which the international price for Abu Dhabi's marker Murban grade plummeted to as low as US$10.25/barrel. In a better year such as 1997, oil made up more than 29.6 per cent of GDP. It should come as no surprise that the oil price slump of 1998 had a major effect on the UAE's payments position. The value of crude exports was down 27.3 per cent to US$9.73 billion (35.7 billion dirhams), which in turn forced down export earnings by 10.7 per cent. This was largely responsible for the country's trade surplus falling by nearly 57.5 per cent to US$3.15 billion (11.55 billion dirhams). It was also reflected in a 71.7 per cent dive in the current account surplus.

This was always going to pop pop into a major economic downturn. Indeed, the UAE's GDP did shrink by 5.8 per cent in nominal terms, and 7 per cent in real terms, during 1998. The oil price slump was the main culprit for a 24 per cent slump in state revenues to US$11.6 billion (42.7 billion dirhams).Yet state spending actually rose by 11.2 per cent to US$19.5 billion (71.6 billion dirhams) during this recessionary period, encouraging the consolidated deficit of the federal and seven local governments to explode by 352 per cent, to nearly US$7.9 billion (28.9 billion dirhams). This meant that the deficit constituted 17 per cent of GDP in 1998, up from just 5.1 per cent the previous year.

In practically any other country, this would have been a recipe for fiscal disaster. In the UAE, the ability to increase spending during a year such as 1998 was a testament to the country's financial depth. Its largest member emirate, Abu Dhabi, is widely recognised as having an overseas investment portfolio of in excess of US$160 billion. This figure is supplemented by Dubai's additional US$35 billion. To put things in perspective, it should be noted that draw-downs routinely top US$6.5 billion (23.9 billion dirhams) annually. That is precisely why the Central Bank was able to declare, during a year of such economic adversity, that the UAE's budget was 'financed entirely by returns on government investments'.

Table 1.3.1 Key UAE economic data, 1997–98 (in billion UAE dirhams, unless stated; US$1: Dh3.67)

	1997*	1998**
GDP, of which:	180.63	170.07
oil	53.51	36.95
non-oil	127.12	133.12
GDP growth at current prices (%)	3.6	-5.8
Population (million)	2.62	2.76
GDP per capita (dirhams)	68,838	61,640
Labour force (million)	1.33	1.38
Consolidated government revenues	56.19	42.69
Consolidated government expenditure	64.39	71.63
Consolidated government deficit	8.2	28.94
Inflation (%)	2–3	1.5–2.0
Total exports (including re-exports), of which:	124.86	111.45
oil	49.1	35.7
re-exports	38.25	39.15
Total imports	97.7	99.9
Trade balance	27.16	11.55
Net services	8.5	7.8
Net transfers	12.5	-12.8
Current account surplus	23.16	6.55
Capital account deficit	-21.96	3.79
Balance of payments surplus	1.2	2.76

* revised

** preliminary

Source: Central Bank of the UAE 1998 Annual Report

However, it would be foolish for the UAE to have dismissed the economic impact of the oil price slump as a temporary problem. It had severe repercussions for the non-oil economy, the growth of which was reduced sharply to about 4.7 per cent from over 7.1 per cent in 1997.

Worst hit was the manufacturing sector, which watched in anguish as the 12.85 per cent growth it recorded in 1997 was turned into a reversal of 0.2 per cent, with a net value of US$5.5 billion (20.19 billion dirhams). The reason: most of the UAE's major re-export markets are oil-dependent economies less diverse than itself. Prime examples are Iran, Saudi Arabia and Kuwait.Other non-oil sectors also had a difficult year, although their pain was comparatively minor. The growth of the wholesale and retail sector – the largest segment of the non-oil economy, worth nearly US$5.6 billion (20.5 billion dirhams)– slowed to under 5.2 per cent in 1998, from over 7 per cent the previous year. Similarly, the value of the real estate and construction sector was up 4.5 per cent to almost US$9.4 billion (34.45 billion dirhams), against the 5.1 per cent growth recorded in 1997.

Table 1.3.2 UAE GDP at factor cost and by economic sector (in billion dirhams; US$1: Dh3.67)

Sector	1996	1997	1998
Agriculture, livestock & fishing	5.05	5.5	5.83
Mining & quarrying, of which:	57.7	54.12	37.59
crude oil	57.12	53.51	36.95
Manufacturing	17.93	20.23	20.19
Electricity, gas & water	3.47	3.73	4.14
Construction	14.49	15.61	16.24
Wholesale, retail trade & repairing services	18.20	19.48	20.49
Restaurants & hotels	2.9	3.11	3.33
Transport, storage & communications	11.18	11.65	12.31
Financial institutions & insurance	9.88	10.41	11.03
Real estate & business services	16.86	17.35	18.21
Social & personal services	2.85	3.15	3.36
Less – inputted bank services	3.66	3.71	3.84
Government services	17.64	18.64	19.7
Domestic (household) services	1.28	1.36	1.49
Total GDP, of which:	175.78	180.63	170.07
non-oil sectors	118.66	127.12	133.12

Source: UAE Ministry of Planning

Beyond its financial depth, there were good reasons behind the UAE's calm reaction to the financial crunch brought on by the low oil prices of 1998.

In Abu Dhabi, steps had already been initiated to transfer the burden of capital expenditure on infrastructure development to the private sector.

The process began in late 1997, with the award of a contract to the US firm CMS Energy for the first semi-independent power plant, namely Taweelah A-2, while two similar projects are currently under evaluation. Operation and management contracts have also been awarded for sewage treatment facilities in Abu Dhabi. It must be noted that these two sectors cost the emirate about US$617.2 million (2.27 billion dirhams) in development expenditure in 1997. The potential savings to the government became all the more obvious in April 1999, when Emirates CMS Power arranged US$556 million in commercial borrowing to finance 75 per cent of the cost of building Taweelah A-2 – money which otherwise would have come from the state coffers.

Abu Dhabi is also using this brand of privatisation to cut down on current expenditure, as has been seen through the disbandment of its utilities department. A similar downsizing of inefficient bureaucracy is under way in the health sector, with a four-year US$109 million (400 million dirhams) management contract for the capital's new Sheikh Khalifa Medical Complex having been awarded to Canada's InterHealth. This approach is due to be expanded to all new facilities under the federal government, which budgeted the health sector at US$1.3 billion (4.8 billion dirhams) in 1998. Even the military is getting in on the act, by awarding in November 1999 a US$2.8 billion, 14-year contract for the management and development of its medical facilities to a local/US joint venture.

There are also clear signals that Abu Dhabi intends to use partial privatisation to help pay for downstream oil projects, including such as the Ruwais refinery expansion project. Commercial borrowing is under consideration for the emirate's first major petrochemicals project, the Abu Dhabi Polymers Company (a joint venture with the Scandinavian firm, Borealis).

Abu Dhabi has adopted privatisation largely as a means of freeing up funding for the further development of its oil and gas reserves. It is currently in the midst of implementing a five-year programme which will increase crude production capacity to 3 million barrels/day by the end of 2001. The emirate estimates that it can sustain this level of production for up to 150 years.

On the other hand, Dubai's oil reserves are fast dwindling and production is already down around the 230,000 barrels/day mark. The government is, therefore, focusing on the development of public bodies as revenue generators. Prime examples are Dubai Aluminium, Dubai Ports Authority and the Jebel Ali Free Zone. These and other state organisations are having to use internal finances to pay for developments such as the US$540 million expansion of Dubai International Airport.

But the emirate still has some way to go before it can survive without oil, which still accounted for 37.7 per cent of the government's estimated US$2.17 billion (7.95 billion dirhams) in 1998. That is why Dubai is leading the charge for the lifting of restrictions on foreign investment. It began this in 1987 with the establishment of the Jebel Ali Free Zone, where foreign investors were allowed 100 per cent ownership of commercial ventures. And in October 1999 it announced that companies investing in a planned new information technology free zone, Dubai Internet City, would be granted 50-year renewable land leases. This was a major concession to foreign investors who had been demanding this, but had been denied it because of demographic concerns. UAE nationals make up less than 20 per cent of the country's population, so the country's rulers have been at pains to ensure the population does not lose control of its economy. The concessions made to foreign investors in the free zones of Dubai and other emirates may, in time, be extended to the country as a whole.

But there will be a price to pay. To date, the burden of providing jobs for UAE nationals has been shouldered by the state, particularly the federal government, which is the largest employer of citizens from the poorer northern emirates – Ajman, Fujairah, Ras alKhaimah, Sharjah and Umm AlQuwain. That is a situation which is now fast changing. Banks are already implementing a programme under which they will increase the proportion of national employees from the current average of 12 per cent to 40 per cent by 2006.

The government is soon expected to expand the scheme to sectors such as insurance, tourism and industry. In other sectors, private firms will have to comply with a positive discrimination regime under which they will only be able to hire expatriate staff if national candidates are unavailable.

It would be irrational for the private sector not to toe the line. The alternative would be for the government to dispense with its practice of not levying taxation on foreign individual and corporate earnings, a move which would prove harmful to both sides in the long run.

1.4

Oil and Gas in the UAE

Sarah J. Lloyd, Senior Correspondent, Middle East, Platt's

Historical background

The Emirate of Abu Dhabi granted its first oil concession in January 1939 to Petroleum Development Trucial Coast Ltd (PDTC), which was a subsidiary of the Iraq Petroleum Company (IPC). The concession, which was based on a payment of royalties to the host country, covered all of the Emirate's onshore and part of its offshore acreage for a period of 75 years. PDTC made its first significant oil discovery at the Murban field at Bab in 1960. Two years later the company made its first commercial find at Bu Hasa, after which it changed its name to the Abu Dhabi Petroleum Company (ADPC). In 1965, the company's exploration agreement was amended so that it had to relinquish part of its acreage every two years.

In 1953, Abu Dhabi granted a concession for its remaining offshore acreage to the D'Arcy Exploration Company, which was later transferred to a new company called Abu Dhabi Marine Areas (now known as Adma-Opco). Adma was largely owned by CFP (now France's Totalfina Elf), and British Petroleum, which sold 45 per cent of its stake in 1972 to a Japanese consortium called Japan Oil Development Company (Jodco). That same year the government of Abu Dhabi acquired a 25 per cent stake in Adma, which was later raised to 60 per cent, making it a majority shareholder. In 1958, the company discovered oil in commercial quantities at Umm Shaif and as a result, a processing centre and export terminal were established at Das Island. Abu Dhabi's first shipment of crude left the island in 1962. Substantial reserves were subsequently discovered at the Zakum field which went into production in 1967. Adma later relinquished its rights over part of the field, retaining what is known as Lower Zakum. Upper Zakum was developed by the Zakum Development Co (Zadco) and is today owned by the Abu Dhabi National Oil Co (ADNOC) and Jodco.

The withdrawal of the British from the Persian Gulf at the end of 1971 led to the formation of the United Arab Emirates. In line with other regional oil producing states, the UAE set up its own national oil company, ADNOC, to operate at all levels of the oil industry. Soon thereafter, the government of Abu Dhabi took a 25 per cent stake in ADPC through its new national oil company, which was increased to 60 per cent in 1974. In 1978, the Abu Dhabi Company for Onshore Oil Operations (ADCO) was established, replacing ADPC. Shareholders in ADCO include: BP, Shell, Total (each with a 9.5 per cent stake), Exxon and Mobil (4.75 per cent stake each) and Partex (2 per cent stake). Since February 1979, ADCO has been responsible for operations in the onshore concession area, which after relinquishments now covers more than 21,000 sq kms.

While Abu Dhabi was making great strides towards becoming a significant oil producer, exploration activities were being conducted in the other emirates but with much less success. The first commercial discovery in Dubai was made by a subsidiary of the US company Conoco at the offshore Fateh field in 1966. Conoco had picked up the acreage in 1963 after ADPC had relinquished it. A few other minor discoveries were made in the 1970s, followed by a major find in 1981 of a gas and condensate field at Margham.

In nearby Sharjah, Crescent Petroleum Co made the emirate's only commercial find in 1972 at the offshore Mubarak oilfield. However, significant reserves of gas were later found onshore. Ras al-Khaimah is the only other emirate to have made a discovery in commercial quantities. In 1983, the small gas and condensate field of Saleh was discovered.

According to the UAE's constitution, each emirate is responsible for its own oil and gas affairs. In Abu Dhabi, a Supreme Petroleum Council was set up in June 1988 which is responsible for policy making and directly manages the affairs of ADNOC. The SPC is currently headed by Sheikh Khalifa bin Zayed al-Nahyan, the Crown Prince and Chairman of the Abu Dhabi Executive Council.

Oil

According to the *BP Statistical Review of World Energy* for 1999, the UAE's proven oil reserves stood at 97.8 billion barrels at the end of 1998, which accounts for 9.5 per cent of the world's total reserves. Abu Dhabi has approximately 92 billion barrels of reserves, representing 94 per cent of the country's total, while Dubai contains an estimated four billion barrels of crude reserves, followed by Sharjah and Ras al-Khaimah, with 1.5 billion and 100 million barrels respectively. Hence, Abu Dhabi accounts for almost all of the UAE's current crude production of two million barrels per day (b/d). Meanwhile, Dubai's output has been steadily declining over the past decade and has dropped from 270,000 b/d in 1996 to 225,000 b/d in 1999. Abu Dhabi is likely to continue to make up for the fall in Dubai's output through its spare production capacity, which is currently at 2.5 million b/d.

Table 1.4.1 Abu Dhabi's Oil Production and Exports

('000 b/d)

Year	Total	Onshore	Offshore	Exports
1988	706	442	264	524
1989	1338	549	789	1204
1990	1716	774	942	1544
1991	2040	990	1050	1836
1992	2000	991	1009	1795
1993	1900	900	100	1650
1994	1805	920	886	1614
1995	1788	950	838	1573
1996	1900	975	925	1665
1997	1950	960	990	1685
1998	2050	950	1100	1785

Source: Abu Dhabi Department of Planning, Arab Oil & Gas Directory estimates

Like other regional producers, the UAE has been expanding its production capacity to meet the growing world demand for OPEC crude. In January 2000, ADNOC signed a memorandum of understanding with the Japanese National Oil Corp (JNOC) to boost production capacity at the offshore Zakum field. However, given that the UAE already has plenty of spare production capacity, the government is in no rush to invest heavily in new expansion plans. In mid-1999, the maximum crude oil production capacity for the UAE as a whole was estimated at 2.7– 3.0 million b/d.

The UAE's output, however, will continue to be constrained by adherence to collective decisions taken by OPEC. In an effort to boost prices, which had hit record lows in 1998 as a result of the Asian crisis, an unseasonably mild winter in the Northern Hemisphere and excess supplies of crude on the world market, the UAE joined other producers in slashing its production. The country cut its output from 2.366 million b/d in November 1997 to two million b/d in March 1999. Unlike some other OPEC members, the UAE has maintained a good record for compliance to its pledged cuts. By sticking to the cutbacks, compliance is around 85–90 per cent, and OPEC has regained its credibility in the market, which is reflected in the rise in crude prices. Benchmark North Sea Brent is currently hovering around $24 per barrel.

There is a concern among OPEC nations that if prices reach $30 per barrel for Brent for an extended period of time, they will lose their market share to non-OPEC producers, which will find it profitable to conduct operations in marginal areas. It is therefore plausible that if prices are sustained at such a level, OPEC will increase its production. However, this will not occur before the current cutback agreement expires in March 2000.

Based on future world demand forecasts, Platt's has estimated that the UAE's production will increase to 2.18 million b/d in 2000 and reach 3.7 million b/d in 2020.

Table 1.4.2: UAE's production forecast to 2020

Year	Output in millions of barrels per day
1998	2.24
2000	2.18
2005	2.65
2010	3
2015	3.35
2020	3.7

Source: *Oil Market Outlook Long-term Forecast* (October 1999), Platt's Analysis and Consulting Group

The UAE is one of the world's major crude oil exporters, with more than 80 per cent of its production sold abroad. The majority of the crude is considered light, with API gravities ranging from 32 degrees to 44 degrees. The two main types of export crudes are Abu Dhabi's Murban (39 degrees API) and Dubai's Fateh blends (32 degrees API). The Japanese market accounts for nearly 60 per cent of the UAE's crude exports.

Refining

The UAE's two main refineries are operated by ADNOC and are located in Abu Dhabi at Ruwais and Umm al-Nar. Ruwais is the country's largest refinery with a capacity of 126,000 b/d. It produces light products mainly for export, while the fuel oil is both sold as bunkers and used in the power generation sector. ADNOC is planning on upgrading the refinery to produce naphtha and feedstocks for petrochemical plants by adding two condensate splitters, each with a capacity of 140,000. Both splitters are due onstream in the first half of 2000 and will in effect boost the refinery's capacity to over 400,000 b/d. There are no current plans to upgrade the 85,000 b/d Umm al-Nar refinery.

In Dubai, the Emirates National Oil Co brought onstream its 120,000 b/d condensate refinery this year which produces naphtha, jet fuel, diesel, gasoline and liquified petroleum gas (LPG).

There are two other refineries in the UAE that are not operational at present. The 80,000 b/d Metro refinery in Fujairah went into liquidation in February 1998 after Metro Trading International filed bankruptcy. The refinery had been processing Texaco's Ratawi crude from the Neutral Zone as well as crude owned by the trading house Glencore. Glencore has claimed that Metro Trading International owes it some seven million barrels of refined products, a loss equal to around $175 million. The creditors are currently in negotiations for a settlement, which is rumoured to be close at hand. If the talks continue to go well, the start-up date for the refinery is said to be March 2000.

The other refinery is located in Sharjah and is run by the privately-owned FAL group. The $200 million refinery was due to go onstream in October 1997 but ran into technical and financial difficulties. It has a capacity of 80,000 b/d and is designed around three mothballed refineries imported from Canada. At present, there is no set start-up date.

The UAE also has a 50 per cent stake in the Hyundai Oil Refining Company of South Korea. It was purchased in 1998 through the country's downstream investment company, the International Petroleum Investment Company.

Gas

The UAE is estimated to have 204.9 trillion cubic feet (tcf) of proven natural gas reserves, accounting for 4 per cent of the world's total reserves. About 90 per cent of the country's production and reserves is concentrated in Abu Dhabi, which has an estimated 188.4 tcf. The emirate's offshore non-associated Khuff reservoir is one of the largest gas bearing structures in the world and has yet to be fully developed.

In 1998, Abu Dhabi produced around 3.25 billion cubic feet/day (bcf/d) of gas and exported some eight million metric tonnes of liquified natural gas (LNG) and LPG. Abu Dhabi began exporting LNG in the 1970s from its Das Island liquefaction plant. The country's next largest source of gas is Sharjah, which has maintained its gas output at just under one bcf/d.

One of the UAE's main energy objectives is to expand its gas sector, particularly in Abu Dhabi. The primary reasons for this are: to meet rising domestic demand, the restrictive OPEC oil output quotas which in turn limit production of associated gas, the need for gas for oilfield injection in enhanced oil recovery schemes, and to raise export revenues through the expansion of its LNG export capacity.

There are three gas development projects currently underway in Abu Dhabi. Two of them are concentrated onshore at the Bab and Asab fields, while the last one involves the futher development of the Khuff reservoir under the Abu al-Bukhoosh and Umm Shaif fields. Initially the Khuff project was designed to feed Dubai with 500 million cubic feet per day (Mcf/d) starting in 2001, but the project has recently been restructured and now the gas will be piped to Das Island primarily for export. However, ADNOC still retains an agreement with Dubai to deliver 500 Mcf/d of gas.

Dubai has been unable to produce enough gas to meet its domestic requirements since the mid-1980s. In addition to its own supplies from the Margham field, which averaged 140 Mcf/d in 1998, Dubai has been

importing gas from neighbouring Sharjah. However, Sharjah's main priority is to meet its own domestic demand, which is on the rise. It is therefore highly unlikely that Sharjah will maintain the same level of exports to Dubai, which were 400 Mcf/d in 1998 out of a production rate of 600 Mcf/d.

With gas consumption rising at an annual rate of 7 per cent per year, Dubai is desparately seeking alternative supplies.

Table 1.4.3: UAE Gas Demand Projection

(Mcf/d)

	1998	2000	2005
Dubai	600	800	1100
Abu Dhabi	3100	4200	6300
N. Emirates	390	420	520

Source: Qatar General Petroleum Corp, March 1999

Perhaps the most publicised gas supply project to Dubai is the $8–10 billion Dolphin project, which is being spearheaded by the UAE Offsets Group. Dolphin envisages piping 300,000–500,000 Mcf/d of Qatari gas from the North Field through an 800km sub-sea line with a capacity of three Bcf/d to the Abu Dhabi coast. From there the gas will be piped to Dubai, Oman and on to Pakistan. Offsets has estimated that a further $2–3 billion will be needed to take the gas to Pakistan.

In June 1999, the Dubai Supply Authority signed a Memorandum of Understanding to purchase between 200–700 Mcf/d of gas from Dolphin. The group has also signed a Statement of Principle with the Qatar General Petroleum Corp and MOUs with the governments of Oman and Pakistan. More recently it signed an MOU with the Abu Dhabi Water and Electricity Authority. According to the latter MOU, 'Dolphin shall be the exclusive supplier of gas to meet all of ADWEA's requirements except in the Western Region, in addition to the quantities of gas as contracted between the government of Dubai and ADNOC after obtaining the approval of the government of Dubai'.

Although the group has made great strides in securing MOUs, the project is still at a preliminary stage and some of the fundamental issues have yet to be discussed. The group has yet to work out the purchase price of the gas from Qatar, which is in a monopoly position. Moreover, as the UAE's main utilities are subsidised, there is a question as to how outside investors will be able to recoup their investments. If the scheme does not get off the ground, Dubai may face a more serious gas shortage in the near future.

Bibliograpy

Arab Oil & Gas Directory 1999, Arab Petroleum Research Center (Paris, 1999)
World Energy Service, Africa/Middle East 1999, Platt's Analysis & Consulting Group (Lexington, MA, 1999)
Country Profile – United Arab Emirates, Centre for Global Energy Studies, (London, Vol 10, Issue 2, Mar-Apr 1999)
United Arab Emirates, United States Energy Information Administration (Dec 1999)
Perspective on the United Arab Emirates, eds. Edmund Ghareeb and Ibrahim al Abed (Trident Press, London, 1997)

1.5

The Commercial Environment – Internationalisation Boosts non-Oil Sector Diversification

Patrick Macdonald, Department of Tourism and Commerce Marketing, Dubai

While oil revenue remains the lifeblood of the UAE's prosperity and growth, the dominant economic trend over the past ten years has been the rapid development of the non-oil sector.

This has resulted in a significant and healthy diversification of the nation's economy, well illustrated by the fact that crude oil contributed less than 22 per cent of gross domestic product in 1998. Even though this low figure was partly a reflection of the oil price slump during that year, it nevertheless underlines the substantial progress being made towards the creation of a stable, well-rounded economic structure.

Wholesale and retail trade accounted for 12.05 per cent of the UAE's gross domestic product (GDP), followed by manufacturing with 11.87 per cent, government services 11.58 per cent and real estate and business services 10.71 per cent. The other main GDP components during 1998 were, in descending order, construction (9.55 per cent), transport and communication (7.24 per cent), finance and insurance (6.49 per cent), agriculture (3.43 per cent) and water and electricity (2.43 per cent). This national picture inevitably masks considerable regional variations. In particular, since most economic activity outside Abu Dhabi emirate is not directly attributable to hydrocarbon production, the non-oil sectors of Dubai and the Northern Emirates are correspondingly larger in relative terms.

A key element in the diversification process in recent years has been the internationalisation of the economy through the growth of trade, cross-border investment and tourism.

In the ten-year period 1988 to 1997, the UAE's non-oil merchandise trade (excluding freight in transit) expanded by nearly 173 per cent to Dh111.3 billion (US$30.3 billion). During 1997, imports amounted to Dh84.2 billion (US$22.9 billion), domestic exports to Dh5.2 billion (US$1.4 billion) and re-exports to Dh21.9 billion (US$6.0 billion).

Dubai, with its twin seaports at Jebel Ali and Port Rashid and purpose-built airfreight terminal (Dubai Cargo Village), accounted for some 80 per cent of total non-oil trade. This dominant position as the country's trading hub is even more pronounced when statistics for the Jebel Ali and Airport Free Zones are factored into the total. On this basis, Dubai and its free zones handled trade worth Dh118.2 billion (US$32.2 billion) in 1997, equivalent to more than US$35,000 per capita. Dubai has long played the role of a regional entrepôt. However, while this was once largely confined to serving the Gulf Cooperation Council (GCC) and Iranian markets, the past decade has seen the city extending its business horizons to a much wider geographical region. These days, its top dozen re-export markets include countries as far afield as India, Afghanistan, Azerbaijan, Turkey, Russia and Libya.

Apart from conventional re-exports, Dubai, Sharjah and other cities in the UAE are also important sourcing centres for professional 'shopping tourists' from surrounding countries where consumer goods are less readily or competitively available. These include Iran, parts of East Africa and the former Soviet Union. Indeed, in the mid-1990s, visitors from the CIS were estimated to be spending more than US$1 billion annually in the UAE, mostly on electronics and other consumer goods to be resold back home, though this trade has since fallen off sharply.

The business generated in the UAE whether by re-export demand or by visitors shopping on a commercial scale has always tended to fluctuate in line with economic, and sometimes political, developments in the markets it serves. The expansion of the country's trading hinterland to include a more diversified region is therefore likely to have positive long-term repercussions by ironing out volatility of demand, for example in response to oil price changes.

Growing international awareness that the UAE's gateway role now extends well beyond the Middle East is duly being reflected in a surge in inward investment. These days, it is by no means unusual for multinationals to use Dubai or Abu Dhabi as their regional headquarters for the Middle East, entire African continent and much of South, West and Central Asia. Likewise, many other international firms, large and small, have set up offices, distribution centres or manufacturing operations in the UAE in recent years. Apart from the largely untapped potential of the emerging markets of Asia and Africa, the attraction for these investors is the UAE's 'win-win' combination of, on the one hand, a highly developed business infrastructure and, on the other, a relatively low cost operating environment.

One of the defining characteristics of the country's economic development has been the government's consistently far-sighted investment in high quality facilities, covering everything from desalination plants and power stations to port and airport developments, highway networks and social and leisure amenities. Coupled with the region's most sophisticated and diversified services sector, the UAE therefore offers incoming investors all the efficiencies of a true 'first world' economy.

In parallel with this, the absence of any corporate or income taxes keeps down the cost of doing business. Likewise, labour (largely expatriate), energy and accommodation costs compare favourably with many international business centres. Many overseas companies investing in the UAE have been attracted to its free zones. In addition to the advantages available elsewhere in the country, these zones give foreign investors the incentive of 100 per cent ownership and control, freedom from import duties and a wide range of administrative support, including pre-built accommodation if required and staff recruitment assistance. There is also the added comfort that the nation-wide absence of income and corporate taxes comes with a renewable 15-year guarantee.

Since it opened in 1985, Dubai's Jebel Ali Free Zone has attracted more than 1,500 companies, from top household-name multinationals to small trading and service firms, while the UAE's other more recently established zones look set to replicate this success.

The latest initiative, announced in the second half of 1999, is Dubai Internet City, the world's first Internet free zone. Its declared aim is to create 'an infrastructure, environment and attitude that will enable Internet-related enterprises to operate globally out of Dubai with significant competitive advantages'. It will incorporate the world's first Internet university specialising in all types of e-business, R&D centre, science and technology park and permanent display facilities.

While the internationalisation of the economy through trade, investment and tourism is expected to be a key driving force in the new millennium, a number of important domestic developments are also transforming the commercial climate.

As throughout the Gulf, the public sector has traditionally played a prominent role in the UAE's economy. This is not confined to investment in the business and social infrastructure or in the operation of utilities, but includes direct holdings in manufacturing, airlines, banks, insurance companies, hotel management and other such businesses.

While this will not change overnight, privatisation is expected to be a growing trend in the years ahead. The long-awaited launch of the official UAE stock market should be a key factor here, not only providing a more efficient mechanism for mobilising private capital, but also helping to keep investment funds within the country. In parallel with this, public sector entities will increasingly be expected to be self-financing and the level of public/private sector collaboration should rise.

Another important priority in the economic management of the country is the need to ease dependence on foreign manpower and to promote emiratisation. The indigenous population has been growing rapidly and the public sector – the preferred employer for many UAE nationals – can no longer absorb the number of young people entering the workforce. Accordingly, while recognising that businesses must continue to import labour and expertise in the foreseeable future, initiatives to encourage greater local participation in the private sector can be expected in the years ahead.

This will mean further rapid structural change. It has been said that the UAE has largely bypassed the industrial revolution, transforming itself from a nineteenth century economy to a twenty-first century economy in the space of a single generation. Certainly, there is some truth in the view that, while a healthy manufacturing industry is vital to the creation of a well-rounded economy, only a service sector, knowledge-based economy can be expected to create sufficient clean, 'white collar' jobs necessary to provide suitable employment for young, well-educated nationals. (Such considerations are of course very much part of the inspiration for the Dubai Internet City project.)

Among other key trends in UAE business life, increased inter-emirate collaboration can be expected, as well as increased cooperation among the member states of the GCC. On the business side, for example, we have seen the Abu Dhabi government become a shareholder in Dubai Cable Company; meanwhile the GCC has recently reached agreement after 18 years on the harmonisation of customs tariffs. In any case, the potential for synergies and need for harmonisation of regulations and their implementation are well understood and further progress is likely.

1.6

Tourism Development: The Dubai Case Study

Patrick Macdonald, Director United Kingdom and Ireland, Government of Dubai, Department of Tourism and Commerce Marketing, Dubai

Background

Tourism has emerged as one of the UAE's most dynamic growth sectors in recent years. This has been evident to a greater or lesser extent in each of the seven emirates, but Dubai has clearly led the way, to the point where the industry has become a major component in the city's economy. Indeed, recent surveys estimate that spending by visitors now accounts for some 13 per cent of the emirate's gross domestic product, higher than the percentage contributed by oil.

While this figure includes substantial expenditure on shopping by visitors from neighbouring regions, international leisure tourism has become the most rapidly growing segment of the industry. So much so that, today, Dubai is widely acknowledged as ranking among the world's leading international resort destinations, having been viewed as little more than a duty free stopover as recently as the late 1980s.

A number of factors have made this remarkable transformation possible. The hospitable and welcoming culture of the region was, in Dubai's case, combined with a long exposure to and familiarity with foreign visitors through the city's trading heritage. Equally important was the vision of the ruling Al Maktoum family in recognising the potential of the emirate's natural tourist assets, including:

- strategic geographical location;
- winter sunshine;
- extensive beaches;
- desert scenery.

Another important element in the successful development of the destination has been investment. Both the public and private sector have collaborated to ensure the creation of a first class tourism infrastructure, encompassing visitor accommodation, aviation, recreational facilities and tourism services. It is no coincidence that Dubai has played a pioneering role in the Middle East in everything from golf course development to the construction of a dedicated cruise terminal.

Naturally, Dubai's success also owes much to the rapid growth of international tourism during the 1990s and to increasingly adventurous travellers seeking new and different destinations offering attractive and interesting experiences. However, the emirate's success in tapping into this worldwide trend was not by chance. Here again, Dubai was the pioneer of the region in terms of its international marketing and promotion initiatives spearheaded by the Department of Tourism and Commerce Marketing and its predecessor organisation, the Dubai Commerce and Tourism Promotion Board.

A brief history

Despite having long attracted visitors from other lands through its seafaring and trading activity, the development of a formalised hotel infrastructure in Dubai is very recent. Sharply increased oil prices in the 1970s were the catalyst, creating the need to accommodate business travellers attracted to the Gulf. Dubai's first luxury hotel opened in 1975. This was quickly followed by a boom in construction activity with the result that, by the early 1980s, the emirate boasted an impressive array of fine hotels.

Even by the mid-1980s, Dubai's hospitality industry was almost exclusively geared to the business traveller, with recreational tourism largely confined to visitors from countries within the Gulf region.

The development of international leisure tourism can be dated from the latter half of the 1980s. This was a period of prosperity and extended vacation entitlements in Europe, and this gave rise to a boom in medium- to long-haul travel. At the same time, increasing familiarity with the more established destinations actively inspired travellers to seek out destinations perceived as being more exclusive and exotic.

Against this background, the climate was set fair for the development of Dubai's tourism sector, and the remainder of the 1980s saw an encouraging growth in business as a number of European tour operators started marketing Dubai holiday packages.

Tourism marketing and administration

In the early days of Dubai's tourism development, a number of organisations were active in promoting the destination, including Emirates airline, the Department of Civil Aviation (notably through publicising Dubai Duty Free) and the hotel sector. However, it was not until the creation of the Department of Tourism and Commerce Marketing's (DTCM) predecessor organisation, the Dubai Commerce and Tourism Promotion Board (DCTPB) in 1989, that international marketing activities were co-ordinated through a single body. Without the authority of a government department, the DCTPB had a straightforward role and mission to promote Dubai's commerce and tourism interests internationally.

Its initial strategy for tourism was to focus on building up business from two core markets – the Arab Gulf Co-operation Council (AGCC) countries and Western Europe – while pioneering the destination in potential future markets, such as the Far East and North America. In the case of the AGCC, familiarity with Dubai, proximity and ease of travel (without visas), made it possible and cost-effective to market the destination directly to the consumer via press and TV advertising.

The DCTPB's approach to Europe and other markets was to concentrate primarily on the travel trade, so as to build up the number of tour operators promoting Dubai holiday packages in their brochures. Accordingly, the marketing strategy was focused on exhibition participation, familiarisation trips, direct sales visits and workshops, all supported by promotional materials of the highest international quality.

As this strategy led to success, the priority shifted more towards supporting the tour operators by promoting public awareness of the destination through media relations and advertising activities. At the same time, the DCTPB extended the scope of its operations to new markets around the world, taking advantage of international trends such as the opening up of markets like Russia, the Indian sub-continent and South Africa.

Besides geographical diversification, Dubai's marketing strategy has also been directed to capitalising on growth trends and niche markets, such as the MICE (meetings, incentives, conferences and exhibitions) sector and special interest tourism (ecotourism, golf packages etc).The success of these efforts was quickly apparent. In the five years before the DCTPB was established, the number of hotel guests had grown by 49 per cent. In the five years after its establishment, the number soared by 153 per cent. This was achieved despite the disruptive effects of the Gulf War and relative difficulty of increasing the growth percentage from a high starting point.

While the DCTPB was successfully carrying out its promotional responsibilities, it was becoming clear that tourism had grown in significance to a point where it merited a fully-fledged government department dedicated to its development and interests. Accordingly Law No 1 of 1997 was promulgated, creating the DTCM with responsibilities extending beyond international promotion to include being the primary authority for planning, regulating and developing the emirate's tourism industry.

Underlining the importance attached to tourism development at the highest level, the DTCM's Chairman is HH Sheikh Mohammed bin Rashid

Al Maktoum, Crown Prince of Dubai and UAE Defence Minister. Its Director General is Khalid A bin Sulayem.

In its marketing role, the DTCM plans and implements an integrated programme of international promotions and publicity activities, incorporating:

- exhibition participation;
- roadshows;
- presentations;
- workshops;
- direct sales calls;
- familiarisation visits;
- advertising;
- the production and distribution of brochures, videos and newsletters;
- media relations;
- enquiry and information services.

The DTCM is also a major player in the planning and implementation of major collaborative promotional projects, such as the Dubai Shopping Festival and Dubai Summer Surprises. Likewise, it actively supports and promotes the many high profile events that help put Dubai on the international map. These range from sporting events like the Dubai World Cup race meeting, the Desert Classic PGA Golf Tournament, the Dubai Open ATP Tennis and World Class One Powerboat Grand Prix to the full calendar of major trade exhibitions and conferences staged in the city.

In addition to its head office, the DTCM takes the Dubai message to the world via a network of 14 overseas offices. These cover: the UK and Ireland; France; Germany; Italy; the Nordic countries; Russia/CIS; North America – East & Central; North America – West Coast; Japan; Far East; Australia and New Zealand; India; South Africa; and East Africa.

The DTCM's administrative responsibilities within Dubai include the licensing and classification of hotels and other visitor accommodation, licensing of tour operators, travel agents and tourist transport companies, and training and licensing of tour guides. It supervises the museums and other tourist, archaeological and heritage sites, tourism conferences and exhibitions, the operation of tourist information services. Meanwhile, the DTCM's first major project since assuming its development role is the construction of a dedicated cruise line terminal, scheduled for completion in October 2000, at Port Rashid.

Growth in Dubai visitors (1989–98)

Tracking the growth of tourism in Dubai is complicated by the fact that available figures do not differentiate between business visitors and leisure travellers. Also, the compilation of statistics has improved over time and figures for earlier years may not be entirely reliable. However, the numbers of hotel (and hotel apartment) guests over the 10 year period from 1989 to 1998 do provide a clear indication of the pace of growth:

Table 1.6.1 Hotel guests over 10 year period

	1989	*1998*
UAE	40,402	220,065
Other AGCC	122,847	546,258
Other Arab	58,995	229,493
Asia & Africa (non-Arab)	245,122	708,184
Europe	146,132	723,871
Americas	14,212	90,483
Rest of world	798	25,741
TOTAL	628,508	2,544,095

Sources: UAE Ministry of Planning, Dubai Department of Economic Development, Dubai Department of Tourism and Commerce

Marketing Dubai's tourist attractions

In promoting the destination internationally, the DTCM is able to highlight the many attractions that Dubai offers the discerning traveller. These include:

The Arabian experience
The Arab world is still relatively undiscovered by international travellers. Dubai provides a taste of Middle Eastern culture and life that is new and fresh to many visitors, yet within the framework of a welcoming and cosmopolitan society.

Sun, sea and sand
Dubai offers virtually guaranteed sunshine all year round, with miles of clean, uncrowded sandy beaches, pools, beach parks and marinas.

High quality accommodation
The hotels are modern and luxurious, with guest rooms and public areas equipped and furnished to the highest standards. Staff service is friendly and efficient and facilities are excellent, especially in terms of the range and quality of food and beverage outlets.

Fine sporting facilities
Recognised as the 'sports capital of the Middle East', Dubai offers outstanding facilities for the active tourist, including golf courses of championship standard and a wide range of watersports.

Tours and safaris
There are a number of highly professional and efficient destination management companies offering a wide range of sightseeing, shopping and adventure tours, including such memorable experiences as desert safaris by four wheel drive vehicle, sand skiing and dhow cruises.

Shopping
As a tax free city with an open market, Dubai is recognised as one of the great shopping centres of the world. Dubai offers a choice of luxurious malls and bustling souks and a wide range of bargains in everything from gold to electronics.

A clean and safe environment
Dubai is a clean, bright, well-tended city, where the tourist can move around freely with no fear of crime.

The future

The future outlook for tourism to Dubai, and the UAE in general, appears very bright. The strong world-wide growth in both leisure and business travel is expected to continue, with the World Travel and Tourism Council projecting an annual increase of 3 per cent over the next few years. Dubai, still a relatively small player in global terms, is well placed to expand its share of the business.

In this regard, the government's commitment to supporting the industry will continue to be important in the face of growing competition from other destinations. This support is evident both in the DTCM's marketing and promotion activities and from the involvement of the public sector in general, led by the DTCM, in building the tourism infrastructure. In parallel with this government support, and encouraged by it, the private sector has adopted a forward-looking approach, building the new hotels and expanding tourism-related services that should sustain the momentum of the industry's development in the twenty-first century.

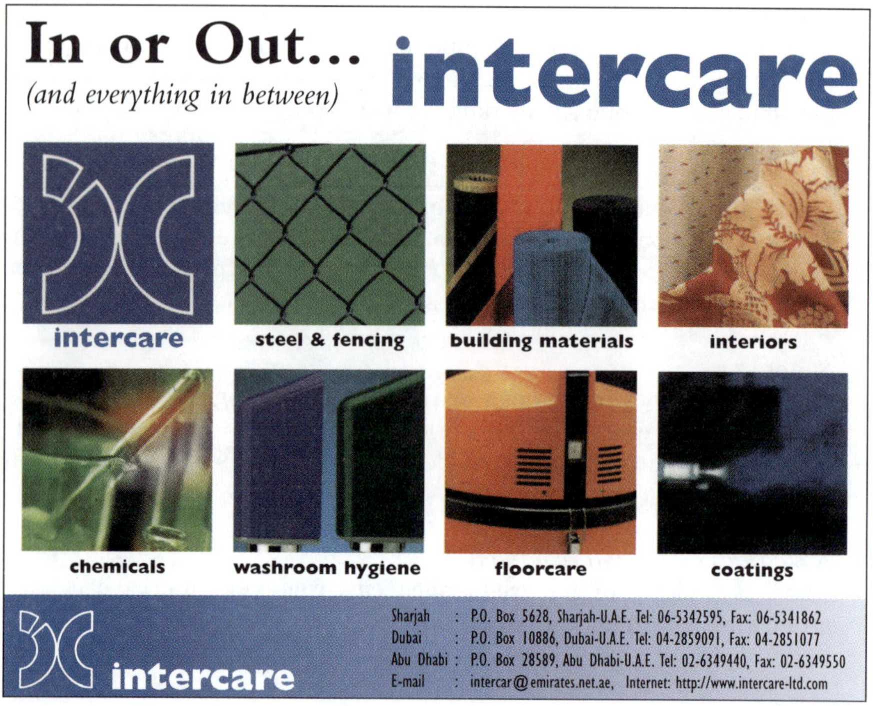

INTERCARE GROUP

Intercare Ltd. has been established in the UAE since late 1974, having local offices in Dubai (two), Abu Dhabi (one) and Sharjah (one). Overseas, it has offices in Cyprus and Switzerland (parent company). Through agents, licensed manufacturers or joint ventures, it operates throughout the GCC, Syria, Lebanon and Jordan.

Its activities are in the following business areas:

Institutional Cleaning

- Washroom Hygiene & Janitorial Supplies (Intercare Washroom Hygiene Division),
- Institutional Cleaning machines and Supplies (Intercare Floorcare Division),
- Manufacture and sale of Cleaning Chemicals (Intercare Chemicals Ltd).

Building Division

- Powder, Wet and Electrostatic spray painting (Intercare Coatings),
- Fabrication and erection of all types of Steel Structures, Security Systems, Gates and Barriers (Intercare Steel Ltd.),
- Specialty Floorings and Entrance Mats (Intercare Building Materials Division),

Building Division

- Manufacture Hospitality Contract Interiors & Refurbishment (Intercare Interiors).
  Contractors for Interior fit-out projects (Intercare Enterprises).

The Intercare Group is well known in the various niche markets it has concentrated upon with various satisfied customers of many years' standing in every sector.

In a number of the Group's activities it enjoys market leadership – no easy feat in an ultra competitive environment such as the Gulf area. This enviable position has been acknowledged for some time by its Multinational Principals – and even its competitors.
Never one to skimp on quality, Intercare's slogan has always been to deliver on its promise.

Part 2

Establishing a Business in the UAE

2.1

Ways in which Foreign Companies can do Business in the UAE

Alastair McNair, (on secondment from Clifford Chance) Hadef Al Dhahiri Associates, Abu Dhabi

There are a number of ways in which foreign (i.e. non-UAE based) companies can do business in the UAE, each one of them different and each one of them particularly suited to certain circumstances. They include the following.

Companies

Public joint stock companies

These are similar to a public company in the UK. There are controls as to the manner and way share capital and debentures may be offered to the UAE public and their minimum share capitalisation is UAE Dhs.10 million. The creation of a public joint stock company is a complicated process.

Banks and insurance companies are required to be public joint stock companies as, in theory, are companies with Federal or individual Emirate government or public agency involvement. At a practical level there are not many public joint stock companies in which foreign capital is invested – out of which most are UAE Offsets Group investments.

Private joint stock companies

These are essentially similar to public joint stock companies except that their minimum share capitalisation is UAE Dh.2 million. The shares are placed privately to a minimum of three 'founders' and cannot be through public subscription.

Limited liability companies

These are essentially similar to the private limited company as it is recognised the world over.

In respect of each of the above types of legal entity, the maximum foreign investment is 49 per cent. In the case of each of the above in theory this may (or may not) be accompanied by 'management' arrangements by which management (and possibly commercial) responsibility is devolved on a foreign company with, at least in theory, particular experience in a given area or areas. To date, by far the bulk of foreign investment in the UAE has been into limited liability companies. All of the above are entities recognised under the UAE Companies Law of 1984 (although only implemented in 1992) (the 'Companies Law'), as also are:

Most joint ventures in corporate form are constituted as limited liability companies. A limited liability company has a board of managers (Directors) and it is possible to build management and other safeguards into their basic documentation. Limited liability companies may not be involved in the areas of banking, insurance and the investment of funds for third parties. A limited liability company may have between two and 50 shareholders. In Abu Dhabi the present minimum capitalisation is US$41,000 and in Dubai US$82,000. There is no concept of authorised share capital in the UAE, all capital being paid up.

Branch offices

This is exactly what its name says it is – that is the branch office of a foreign company. Thus the legal entity in question is a part of the overseas company and it is the local branch office of the overseas company which will be licensed to conduct business in the UAE. Branch offices may conduct trade in the UAE and may earn profit here. The Ministry of Economy and Commerce has however clearly indicated that the creation of new branch offices in the UAE will only now be allowed in certain restricted circumstances. Creation of these may be difficult and time consuming, dependent on where they are to be located. The creation of a branch office requires the supporting appointment of a UAE national agent. Branch offices are required to maintain and file audited accounts.

Representative offices

In many respects, these are similar to branch offices except that they cannot earn profits in the UAE. The purpose of a representative office is effectively only to provide liaison and support. It might, for example, be set up by an overseas principal who wished to liaise with a number of distributors in the UAE and/or in other parts of the Gulf. Once again, a representative office is actually a part of the overseas company and it is the local office of the overseas company which will be licensed to conduct limited business in the UAE. The creation of a representative office requires the supporting appointment of a UAE national agent. Representative offices are required to maintain and file audited accounts.

All of the above provide a foreign or overseas company with a legitimate presence here in the UAE.

Service companies

These are effectively professional partnerships and are suitable vehicles for professionals providing services (e.g. doctors, dentists, accountants and other recognised professions). These do not confer limited liability protection. This type of entity may be 100 per cent foreign owned. They may also sometimes be referred to as 'work' companies and, in respect of foreign investment, require the appointment of a national agent. The granting of licences in this area may take a fair amount of time.

Limited liability partnerships

Non-UAE nationals may only be 'sleeping' partners in such an enterprise and should under no circumstances be involved in their management, or their limited liability status (as sleeping partners) is likely to be lost. As elsewhere with this type of legal entity, it is represented by the general partner who must be a UAE national; in practice, this type of vehicle is little used.

Free zones

A number of free zones exist in the UAE, the best known of these being Jebel Ali Free Zone in Dubai Emirate. Free zones also exist in Ajman Fujairah and in Umm Al Quwain and at Dubai and Sharjah International Airports. A financial services free zone is in the process of creation in Abu Dhabi, UAE (the Saadiyat Market). Businesses established in the free zone may be 100 per cent foreign owned and are invariably focused not on the UAE market itself but on the Gulf market generally – and in some cases even further afield. Businesses which are not familiar with the UAE and/or Middle Eastern markets may generally be tempted towards free zones, which, because of the infrastructure, provide greater administrative support for businesses operating in the UAE. The free zone concept means that these areas are, for customs purposes, outside the particular Emirate in question – hence customs duty (presently four per cent) is only payable if the product is brought into the Emirate in question. The licensing regime differs marginally from free zone to free zone in the UAE although there are substantial similarities. Businesses based in the various free zones have, as their legal basis, decrees issued by the relevant Emirate's Ruler and are outside the scope of the UAE Companies Law.

Sponsorships

Many companies however, for historical or other reasons, prefer to exist sheltering under the commercial registration/trade licence of their sponsor (a UAE national or a company entirely owned and controlled by UAE nationals) to whom they pay 'sponsorship' fees which are often based on turnover. This type of arrangement is still in widespread use. The actual degree of liability assumed by the sponsor is, to a large extent, dependent upon the type of entity the sponsor selects to use for this purpose. While these arrangements are in widespread use, they are at best of dubious legal origin (being essentially unlawful) and at worst leave both the foreign company in question and the investment with potential exposure. They may also result in the sponsor incurring significant exposure. Sponsorship arrangements such as these are not to be recommended. There is case law in Dubai and legislation in Abu Dhabi, UAE, which suggests that these arrangements are unlawful and, possibly, unenforceable.

Other forms of representation

In the event that the nature of the foreign company's business is such that it does not require an actual presence in the UAE, the foreign company may wish to appoint one of the following.

- **A commercial agent**: this function is to represent foreign companies, keeping them abreast of commercial opportunities here in the UAE. As and when they successfully connect a foreign principal and a customer, a commercial agent would generally earn a commission. A commercial agent may or may not carry stock/inventory.
- **A distributor:** this is a conventional function as exercised the world over. A distributor makes his money in the form of profit upon the sale of stock, etc.

Both commercial agencies and distributorships are governed by the Trade Agencies Law (as amended) (the 'Trade Agencies Law'). If a foreign company wishes to effect sales to UAE government departments, it is the invariable rule (except in relation to military sales, where commission agents are strictly prohibited) that the commercial agency or distributorship in question must be registered in the Trade Agencies Register. To be registered, it requires to be held either in the name of a UAE national or in the name of a company entirely owned and controlled by UAE nationals. Due to the breadth of coverage provided by the Trade Agencies Law, franchises (whether for the sale of products or the provision of services) almost certainly fall within the scope of the Trade Agencies Law.

The Trade Agencies Law builds in substantial protection for the local agent or distributor which, in legal terms, is almost impossible to displace. In many cases (dependent upon the market one is selling into and whom one's main customers are likely to be) it may not be necessary to actually register an agency or distributorship agreement. Considerable effort and research should be put into the appointment of a commercial agent or distributor. The failure of such a relationship can be extremely expensive and may result in the exclusion of one's products from the UAE market for a considerable time and may even result in the seizure of goods in customs.

Additionally to the foregoing, one can have licensing arrangements for such matters as the use of software, intellectual property and process applications; likewise one may license the use of trademarks, patents and copyright.

Companies involved in the areas of manufacturing are required to obtain a National Industrial Licence. Companies involved in the areas of banking and insurance will be subject to further regulatory requirements by the UAE Central Bank and the Ministry of Economy and Commerce respectively. The UAE Central Bank also regulates some financial services areas and it seems likely that its role in these areas will increase over the next few years.

There is, throughout the UAE, presently no corporate or personal taxation, except for that applicable to the branches of foreign banks, and to oil companies. Taxation is a matter dealt with at individual Emirate level.

2.2

Legalities, Policies and Procedures for Doing Business in the UAE

Alastair McNair, (on secondment from Clifford Chance) Hadef Al Dhahiri and Associates, Abu Dhabi

People wishing to do business in the UAE should be aware of the basic regulations concerning the various types of vehicles for doing business in the country. Each of the different types of legal entities will now be described in slightly greater detail.

Public joint stock companies

The shares of public joint stock companies are offered directly to the public. Furthermore, all shares must be of equal value, between Dhs1.00 and Dhs100. There is also a requirement that there be at least ten founder shareholders (unless the company in question is established by the Federal Government or any individual Emirate Government). The Board of Directors should consist of between 3 and 15 members, of which the majority should be UAE nationals, as also should the chairman.

Banks and insurance companies incorporated in the UAE are required to be public joint stock companies, as is any entity in which a UAE ministry or public agency has an interest.

Private joint stock companies

The shares of private joint stock companies cannot be offered to the public for subscription but only to a select group of investors. Otherwise their structure is substantially the same as for public joint stock companies.

Limited liability companies

Limited liability companies may have between two and fifty shareholders and cannot offer their shares generally to the public. These companies are prohibited from engaging in the banking, insurance and financial services/investment areas. Their shares should be of a minimum value of Dhs 1000 each to be fully paid upon incorporation. In Abu Dhabi, the current minimum capitalisation is Dhs 150,000 and in Dubai Dhs 300,000. There is significant flexibility for these companies to be involved in management arrangements. Limited liability companies may be run either by a board of managers or by a duly appointed general manager.

In each case mentioned above, a foreign company can only have an investment of up to 49 per cent of the overall issued capital. By far the bulk of foreign investments in the UAE are made using limited liability companies that, as a practical matter, provide the greatest flexibility. All of the above legal entities are required to maintain detailed accounts that should be audited on an annual basis by a firm of auditors with a recognised presence in the UAE.

Branch offices and representative offices

Branch offices and representative offices are both, in legal terms, similar (both being authorised under the same provision of the Companies Law) except that a branch office may earn profit, whereas the objectives of a representative office are essentially non-profit making. Branch offices have become increasingly difficult to set up and will certainly not be allowed in the areas of general trade (which includes any reference to sales of, or dealing in, products), import/export activity or manufacturing. They may however still be allowed in the areas of general or other contracting, the provision of services or the provision of professional services (e.g. management consultancies). Representative offices generally have as their objective the provision of a promotional, liaison or product support function (e.g. the provision of services and/or maintenance advice) or they may, for example, be the presence in the UAE of an administrative office responsible for the management of private investments outside the UAE. Both operate in the UAE under a commercial registration (or trade licence) which in the case of either a branch or a representative office will prescribe its restricted activities, and both are the effective licensed presence of the foreign company in question in the UAE. Both are required to appoint a national agent (who must be a UAE national or a company entirely owned and controlled by UAE nationals) whose function is to deal with the day to day office requirements for visas and other related administrative matters. The national agent benefits from a written agreement that should stipulate the amounts he is to be paid.

Both branch offices and representative offices are required to maintain detailed accounts. The accounts should be audited by a firm of professional auditors with a recognised presence in the UAE. Those of a representative office should show only expenditure (within its approved objectives) matched by income from the foreign company in question.

Defence companies

Foreign companies in the defence and/or armaments industries with contracts with the UAE Armed Forces can obtain recognition of their status in the UAE by effectively being sponsored by the UAE Armed Forces. These arrangements require a formal invitation by the UAE Armed Forces (possibly on the basis of the urgency or secrecy of the contract in question) – they are not arrangements which a foreign contractor/supplier may request as of right. The foreign company in question is, under letters of authority issued by the UAE Armed Forces, authorised to conduct such business as is necessary to discharge its contractual responsibilities. Thus visas and car registrations can be obtained and the foreign company in question is able to lease its own offices, to obtain its own telephone and facsimile lines and to operate broadly independently of outside interference. Defence companies operating on this basis are not required to appoint a national agent. Technically, a foreign contractor/supplier enjoying these arrangements is restricted to fulfilment of the relevant contract and cannot, for example, engage in marketing/promotional activity. On a strict technical analysis these arrangements do not comply with the requirements of, amongst others, the UAE Companies Law and are therefore of questionable status. As a practical matter, they may well provide a utilitarian solution to an operational problem.

Service companies

Service companies are created under the Civil Transactions Law of 1986 and are effectively professional partnerships for the provision of services. They are suitable for partnerships of dentists, doctors, accountants and other recognised professions. They do not confer limited liability status and, as such, the partners have a continuing exposure for the partnership's liabilities. Service companies may be 100 per cent foreign owned and must appoint a national agent in respect of foreign investment. In practice, the conduct of service professions in the UAE remains substantially unregulated, although regulation of specific areas (e.g. engineers and lawyers) is starting to occur. Potential investors must note that the grant of these licences is discretionary.

Limited liability partnerships

Limited liability partnerships are created under authority of the Companies Law. Non-UAE nationals may only be involved as 'sleeping' partners and, as such, should not involve themselves in management or represent that they are generally authorised to represent the partnership in commercial matters. If these criteria are breached, their limited liability status (as sleeping partners) is likely to be lost. Only UAE nationals may be general partners and consequently only UAE nationals should be involved in their management. As a practical matter, this type of vehicle is not often used because of its inflexibility. Its only conceivable use is as a passive investment vehicle where the non-UAE interests are not involved in management.

Free zones

Many companies wishing to do business find it more advantageous to establish a legal presence within the various free zones in the UAE. The free zones exist outside the area of application of the Companies Law. There are few restrictions in the areas of business which can be effected/transacted in the free zones. This results in the free zone in question issuing the business involved with a free zone licence (which permits the carrying out of commercial transactions in the relevant free zone). Visas can be obtained on the basis of this. In the event that the entity in question conducts trade 'into' the UAE, customs duties and formalities will be applicable. Registration formalities differ between the various free zones. Foreign companies, however, can generally establish a presence in free zones through either:

- *a Special Licence:* this is held in the name of the foreign company: this may be an entity where ownership is 100 per cent foreign; or
- *a Free Zone Enterprise Licence:* these are also known as Free Zone Establishment Licences. Under these a new legal entity is created in the Free Zone in question. On occasion this type of entity may be used in international tax planning;
- *a National Industrial Licence:* this is required for manufacturing operations.

Companies with an existing base or UAE business can establish a presence in the various free zones, invariably through the granting of a general licence by the free zone in question. The licensing procedure in Jebel Ali Free Zone has recently been entirely overhauled and simplified and one can now only be registered there on the basis of trading, industrial or services activity, in respect of which individual licences are issued.

Sponsorships

Sponsorship arrangements preceded the bringing into effect of the Federal UAE Companies Law and were at that time in widespread use. Often these arrangements continue to exist by virtue of administrative or commercial expediency. In practice, it is the legal entity of the sponsor that has a formal presence in the UAE and the foreign company in question trades by virtue of and in the name of the sponsor's commercial registration. If the 'sponsor' is an establishment (i.e. a sole proprietorship) the sponsor may have liabilities for/on behalf of the foreign company – this will not be so where the sponsor is a limited liability partnership (i.e. a private company as it would be known elsewhere). In Abu Dhabi, 'sponsorship' type arrangements, although they commonly still exist and are even now regularly put in place, are highly questionable under regulations going back to 1969 (as amended in 1978) in relation to commercial licensing which state categorically: ... The Licence [Commercial Registration/Trade Licence] shall be personal and for the person licensed [the Sponsor] and shall be restricted to the trade for which it was granted. It may not be relinquished or in any way disposed of, otherwise it shall be deemed cancelled.

Sponsorship arrangements cannot be recommended on a legal basis – they are essentially unlawful. There is case law in Dubai to suggest that these arrangements are both illegal and possibly unenforceable. Whilst a sponsorship agreement may purport to recognise that it is the foreign investor that owns the business in which investment is made, in practice these arrangements are now disadvantageous for both parties: the foreign investor does not necessarily have long-term security (or even own certain assets) and the sponsor has potential legal and personal exposure. More than any other, these arrangements rely on trust and the relationship between the parties rather than on any basis of law. Problems may well arise when the business relationship between the parties breaks down. Sponsorship fees are generally payable calculated as a percentage of the turnover of the business in question.

Commercial agencies and distributorships

Commercial agencies and distributorships are amongst the oldest of the recognised relationships in the Gulf and are both subject to the Trade Agencies Law if registered as commercial agencies into the Ministry of Economy and Commerce. In the event that a foreign company does not wish to effect sales to UAE federal government departments or to local emirate authorities, there may well be an advantage to the foreign principal in not entering with exclusive agreements even for individual emirates. In these circumstances, it is generally considered that the provisions of the Trade Agencies Law are not applicable but that usual

ADVERTISEMENT COPY

Suite 203, Al Riqqa Street,
Al Owais Complex, Suite E 04,
P.O. Box 2268, Dubai
United Arab Emirates
Tel: +971 4 2224548
Fax: +971 4 2224587
Email: hmulla@emirates.ncl.ae
Web address: http://www.hmulla. com
Senior partner: Dr. Habib Al Mulla
Managing partner: Dr. Habib Al Mulla
Total partners in this office: 1
Total lawyers in this office: 1
Total partners worldwide: 3
Total lawyers worldwide: 10
Languages: Arabic, English, Farsi, Hindi
International groupings: Arab law firms association, Macintyre Strater Int. Ltd, International Law Firms, Jurists Association

Nature of Practice: Dr. Habib Al Mulla founded Habib Al Mulla & Co. in 1984. The firm's size has increased notably, especially over the past four years and currently comprises of 10 lawyers and a total staff of 23, making it one of the largest local law firms in the United Arab Emirates. Its office is located in the heart of one of Dubai's most prominent commercial districts. The lawyers of Habib Al Mulla & Co. represent a wide spectrum of legal education and experience, and its attorneys received their degrees and licenses from the U.A.E., Egypt, Jordan and the United States.

The clientele of Habib Al Mulla & Co. is a distinct mixture of Europeans, North and South Americans, East Asians and Arabs.

Furthermore, as a result of its long-standing reputation, numerous international firms seek Habib Al Mulla & Co's advice when dealing with Dubai and the U.A.E., including firms from England, Germany, Belgium, the United States and Brazil.

Habib Al Mulla & Co. is a founding member of the Arab Law Firms Association (ALFA) as well as a member of MacIntyer Strater International's network of professional firms.

The firm is constantly adapting to the growing demands of globalization and deals primarily in a broad range of domestic and international commercial work and advises internationally renowned banks, multinational corporations, airlines, shipping enterprises, privately and publicly held companies, governmental departments and private individuals.

Habib Al Mulla & Co. is perhaps most distinguished for its banking practice. The firm counsels banks with regard to regulations, drafting of agreements, forms and terms and conditions, loan and security agreements and debt collection. It also has a long-standing litigation practice.

The firm's other commercial practice includes the incorporation of local and international companies, joint venture agreements, mergers and acquisitions and takeovers. The firm has represented an extensive array of local and international clients in both litigation and arbitration proceedings. Dr. Habib Al Mulla is one of the U.A.E.'s foremost arbitrators. He is a fellow of the Chartered Institute of Arbitrators (U.K.) and a member of the London Court of International Arbitration (see professional biography) and an ex-chairman of U.A.E. Jurist Association.

Habib Al Mulla & Co. has an extensive airline practice, maritime litigation, intellectual property practice covering the registration of trademarks, patents and copyrights. Other areas of significant work include construction claims and oil and gas agreements.

Client Service: The firm's hallmark is an expeditious, yet thorough, service for its clients. The firm takes great care to develop a working knowledge of a legal matter through close communication and correspondence with a client, and research using codes, statutes, as well as conferring with each other on similar matters.

If matters escalate to the point where litigation is required, upon a thorough analysis of the matter, the litigation attorneys draw up and file the pleadings with the necessary courts. The experienced advocates of Habib Al Mulla & Co. have the right of audience before all of the courts of the U.A.E.

Please feel free to visit our web site at www.hmulla.com.

contractual principles of law in the UAE would be applicable. However, some UAE courts have time and again relied on Article 3 of the Trade Agencies Law and held that UAE courts are barred from entertaining claims related to unregistered commercial agencies. Some foreign principals (e.g. Cassio) adopt a policy of never awarding exclusive agency/distributorship arrangements – this may (or may not be) a viable policy dependent upon the market sector in which one is attempting to capture market share.

Otherwise, a commercial agent or distributor should:

- be a UAE national or a company entirely owned by UAE nationals;
- benefit from an exclusive arrangement either for the whole of the UAE or for a particular emirates(s) within the UAE (in practice, the largest markets are Dubai/Sharjah and Abu Dhabi);
- have these arrangements reflected in a written agreement with the foreign principal.

If the conditions are satisfied, then the UAE commercial agent or distributor can obtain registration of the agency or distributorship in the Trade Agencies Register maintained by the Federal Ministry of Economy and Commerce in Abu Dhabi. This affords protection in the event of 'untimely' termination or termination due to 'circumstances beyond the control' of the commercial agent or distributor. The definition of what constitutes a commercial agency or distributorship is a wide one, being laid down in Article 1 of the Trade Agencies Law: representation of a [foreign] principal by a [local] agent to distribute, sell or offer merchandise [products] or services [in the UAE] against commission or profit.

This is clearly wide enough to cover the activities of commercial agents or distributors and is generally now considered to extend to most franchising activity in the UAE (whether related to products or to services). The Ministry of Economy and Commerce has various powers in relation to disputes arising between foreign principals and local commercial agents or distributors. Should a foreign principal wish to identify the status of its competitors in the UAE market (i.e. whether or not their commercial agent or distributor has obtained registration of its arrangements) it is possible to effect a search to ascertain this.

It is important to note that there are a number of specialist regulations in relation to the conduct of the banking, insurance and investment sectors that invariably involve the Central Bank of the UAE. The UAE Central Bank has the authority to establish requirements and procedures for the licensing of these institutions which are required to comply with the Central Bank credit, reporting and other requirements and to conduct their business according to sound business principles.

2.3

Industrialisation in the UAE

Emirates Industrial Bank

The UAE government, like that of other oil exporting countries of the Middle East, is concerned by the excessive dependence of the local economy on oil revenues. Thus economic diversification has become a key feature of economic policy, albeit in a somewhat different manner from that in other oil exporting gulf states insofar as it lays considerable stress on globalisation. At this time, diversification in the UAE focuses on three key sectors; trading, tourism and hotels and manufacturing. Of these, trading enjoys pre-eminence for historical reasons, having been of prime importance in the economy long before the advent of oil or tourism.

Manufacturing activity in the UAE started after the oil boom of the early 1980s, and became a key sector in the country's diversification programme. As a rcsult, it has progressed from being of virtual insignificance only some 20 years ago to become the third largest contributor to the economy after oil and trading.

The development of manufacturing industries in a country like the UAE faces a number of challenges. The country and its population are small and its raw material resources are overwhelmingly dominated by crude oil. Thus, the domestic market is limited and serious constraints on local labour availability can be implied from the limited size of the population. Despite such obstacles, the UAE manufacturing sector has made significant progress, becoming a vital contributor to the domestic economy.

At this time, manufacturing value added contributes more than 16 billion dirhams (US$4.3 billion) to GDP, which is almost 10 per cent of the total. Today there are 1695 factories registered with the Ministry of Finance and Industry, with almost 300 new units added last year, though this latter figure may be slightly exaggerated due to some long-existing manufacturing units becoming registered for the first time.

The development of manufacturing

The UAE's critical path to industrialisation has been one of 'logistical import substitution'. Commencing from a position of virtually complete reliance on imports, industrialisation was initiated in those sectors where the logistical hardships of import were the strongest.

Thus, the first industries in the country were those that could lead to savings on high transportation costs by manufacturing on-site; for example, heavy and voluminous construction materials. These were soon followed by the development of food and beverage industries, where product 'perishability' made reliance on imports difficult and expensive. Today, the food and beverage industries continue to rely on imported raw materials with their value added being in processing and packaging. This is not to undermine in any way the success of these projects, as many have notably succeeded in edging out international brands – no small achievement for modest domestic industries confronting internationally established brands. In so doing, a highly positive image has evolved of goods 'Made in the UAE'.

Other sectors of importance are:

- chemicals – some 50 per cent of firms are engaged in producing plastic products;
- metals – fabrication workshops are predominant;
- wood – there are 158 furniture manufacturing facilities (some of which are modern factories but with a majority being no more than carpentry workshops engaged in non-assembly production).

Free trade zones

The other significant aspect of the UAE's industrialisation programme has been the role played by free trade zones in attracting manufacturing projects. Once again, logistical considerations have played a role in the success of these, as warehousing for Gulf-wide distribution, the initial attraction for the many companies now operating there, has given way to manufacturing.

Within the free zones, the largest number of establishments is in the fabricated metals sector, followed by the somewhat heterogeneous non-metallic minerals industry. More recently, however, there has been a marked increase in the number of factories producing readymade garments, which development has also had a marked impact on the textile industry, as 33 factories producing textile fabrics have also been initiated.

Location

Dubai and Sharjah maintain a pre-eminent position with respect to manufacturing activity in the UAE. In Abu Dhabi, industry is dominated by a few, large, industrial projects related to the oil and gas industry. In all the other smaller emirates of the north, manufacturing units tend to be small.

Ajman, geographically the smallest emirate, has developed a very large number of small factories for its size, many of which were established in the 1990s and the majority of which are producing garments. Such growth is a prime example of the successful development of export-based industries when the right package of incentives is provided for investors. Ras alKhaimah, the northernmost of the emirates, has emerged as a manufacturer of building materials as well as pharmaceuticals.

Labour

The UAE's manufacturing sector is relatively labour intensive. However, labour is readily available, mainly from the Indian sub-continent. Such labour tends to be inexpensive and thus manufacturing wages in the UAE are still only a fraction of those in the west.

Conclusion

Today the UAE has reached a stage where it has reached self-sufficiency in certain industrial products, on occasion competing successfully against foreign brands. However, manufacturing is unlikely to become the dominant non-oil sector in the UAE whilst nevertheless enjoying excellent growth prospects in view of the UAE's strategic location, excellent infrastructure, free markets, growing population and the rapid development of other, non-oil sectors.

2.4

The United Arab Emirates Offset Programme

Patrick Edworthy, General Manager, BAe Systems Offset (Abu Dhabi)

When foreign companies are considering the possibility of setting up a Joint Venture (JV) in the United Arab Emirates (UAE) to establish a regional presence for either a manufacturing or services enterprise, they might wish to do so under the auspices of the United Arab Emirates Offset Programme (UAEOP).

This option has many advantages. First, there are the benefits of co-investment and associated risk sharing with another foreign company, normally a defence company with an offset obligation to discharge. Second, where the first foreign company is relatively new to the region, it can draw on the experience of the other foreign partner in the selection process for the national company most suited to the business sector for the proposed new enterprise. Third, there is the comfort factor of following a well-trodden path, as over thirty offset JVs have been successfully established in the UAE in recent years. Fourth, the UAE is an excellent base, with well-established infrastructure, from which to address the Gulf and adjacent regional business markets.

The United Arab Emirates Offset Group

The UAEOP is managed by the United Arab Emirates Offset Group (UOG) with the principal office located in Abu Dhabi city. The UOG makes available an excellent guideline publication in both Arabic and English. Included in the booklet are background chapters on the UAE's history, economy, and business sector overview which provide an informative lead-in to the final section on offset. In addition, the UOG provides a frequently updated list of companies with points of contact. The list has five sections comprising international defence contractors, international investors, local investors, banks, and consultants, all interested parties in the UAEOP within their respective roles.

The UOG is also willing to advise foreign companies on the suitability of their business for offset purposes and in more recent years to assist partners setting up offset JV companies in structuring their project to fulfil the local requirement for the Initial Public Offering (IPO). With regard to suitability for the purposes of offset, it is the UOG policy to encourage all business enterprises outside the primary oil and gas industries as per the following:

- activities new to the UAE or to individual UAE firms;
- major enhancements of existing businesses;
- the opening of new markets to UAE products or services;
- non-labour intensive projects.

United Arab Emirates Offset Programme

Unlike other offset programmes within the region, offset credits are earned under the UAEOP by the profits generated by the business enterprise. This is therefore known as an 'output-based offset programme' in contrast to the 'input-based offset programmes' elsewhere, where offset credits are awarded on various criteria including either the registered share capital or equity invested, plus agreed values for technology transfer, employment of local nationals and their training and the use of indigenous products and/or services etc. Failure to earn offset credits in the UAE will make the obligor contractually liable to pay liquidated damages at milestone points across a seven-year period. Being involved in the UAEOP should therefore further assure any would-be foreign companies of the determination of their other partners in the JV to succeed first and foremost as a profitable business enterprise.

By way of background, the UAE government contractually requires offset on all purchases by the UAE Armed Forces or elements thereof which have a duty free imported value of US$10 million and above. Smaller purchase contracts awarded to a foreign company will be aggregated in a given year, including purchases made through a third party, and if the sum is greater than US$10M then offset will apply. More rarely, the UAE government may also require offsets on other purchases on a case by case basis.

The formal mechanism referred to above is implemented by an offsets contract between the UAE government, as represented by the UOG, and the supplier, entered into ahead of the actual procurement contract. The supplier's initial offset proposals are considered and are normally factored into the overall procurement decision. Companies with both existing or potential offset obligations are therefore continuously looking for ideas for profitable JVs in which to co-invest.

As mentioned earlier, credits are awarded on earned profits (PBIT) across a seven-year period. The former is agreed by the UOG following receipt of the annual audit of the offset JV. Offset credit milestones are normally at the end of the third, fifth and seventh years of the company's existence. After the seventh year it would be possible for either the foreign or national company or both to acquire the shares held by the foreign company with the original contractual obligation for offset. These options could be written into the articles of the JV at the time of formation.

Offset obligors

At the time of writing, the list of foreign defence companies currently involved in offset JV comprises the following:

- Aerospatiale
- Boeing / McDonnell Douglas
- British Aerospace
- CASA
- Dassault Aviation
- Deutz AG
- GIAT
- Lockheed Martin
- Marconi Electronic Systems
- Newport News Shipyard
- Tatra a.s.
- Thomson CSF
- Westinghouse.

As previously mentioned, an updated list can be requested from the UOG (details below). This will also include other companies currently bidding or about to bid for new contracts to supply the UAE Armed Forces.

Further details about the UAE Offset Programme

More information concerning the UAEOP and participants can be obtained from the UOG at the following address:

The United Arab Emirates Offset Group
PO Box 908
Abu Dhabi
United Arab Emirates
Tel: 971 2 263 000
Fax: 971 2 263 006
E-mail: offsets@emirates.net.ae

Similarly, information on the UAEOP and British participants can be obtained from the following addresses:

DTI / DESO Joint Offset Investment Office
Department of Trade and Industry
Kingsgate House
66–74 Victoria Street
London SW1E 6SW

Tel: 020 7215 4616
Fax: 020 7215 4669
E-mail: barry.teideman@osov.bti.gov.uk
Website: www.dti.gov.uk/ots/offset

Defence Export Services Organisation
Ministry of Defence
The Offset Advisor
Room 1/55a
Metropole Building
Northumberland Avenue
London WC2N 5BL

Tel: 020 7807 8230
Fax: 020 7807 8175
E-mail: oa@dpa.mod.uk

Table 2.4.1 Establishing a Business in the UAE – Projects Table – The UAE Offset Programme, UAE Offsets Group

List of announced projects implemented under the Offsets Programme

Project Name	*Defence Contractor*	*Local Partner*	*Activity*	*Capital UAE Dirhams*
Abu Dhabi Shipbuilding (ADSB)	Newport News	–Abu Dhabi Government –Local Founders –Public Offering: 23,000 nationals	Construction of shipyard for building, maintaining, repairing, refitting naval and commercial ships operating in the UAE and regional waters.	178,000,000
Laser Re-nu	Boeing/McDonnell Douglas	Emirates Printing Forms Est.	Plant for the production and sale of recycled laser printer cartridges in the UAE and overseas, by using Laser Re-nu's techniques and equipment to improve printing quality and clarity.	

Table 2.4.1 *continued*

Project Name	*Defence Contractor*	*Local Partner*	*Activity*	*Capital UAE Dirhams*
GAM-AERO	Aerospatiale	GAMCO	Technical maintenance services for testing and repairing avionics equipment fitted on the Airbus A320, A340 and Boeing B767 aircraft by using Atec 5000 & Atec 6000 +. More than 80 programmes designed to test 150 types of avionics appliances.	74,000,000
Gulf Energy Systems (Now merged with Tabreed)	Giat	10 N (National Investor)	Design, supply, install, maintain and operate centralised gas-powered chilled water plants to provide air-conditioning in the UAE and other GC countries.	14,680,000
Giralda Emirates	CASA	Al Ain International Group	Manufacturing plant for the production of high quality concrete bricks and tiles for interior and exterior use.	36,700,000

Table 2.4.1 *continued*

Project Name	*Defence Contractor*	*Local Partner*	*Activity*	*Capital UAE Dirhams*
Gulf Solar Company	GEC-Marconi	Awlad Nasser Co.	Manufacture of mobile solar energy generators to produce power with desalination and refrigeration facilities.	11,000,000
Productivity and Leadership Consortium	Westinghouse	CERT	Centre designed to effect information and technology transfer, to provide the region with world class business re-engineering, leadership development and management training resources, linking education with industry to improve productivity and quality.	

Table 2.4.1 *continued*

Project Name	*Defence Contractor*	*Local Partner*	*Activity*	*Capital UAE Dirhams*
Combined Cargo UAE	Giat	ADIC	A shipping company owning and operating vessels and brokering cargo to finance and operate globally a fleet of modern dry bulk vessels and combined carriers in wet and dry bulk traders with a specific focus on transport to and from the Arabian Gulf.	155,000,000
Solex Robotics Services	General Electric	Al Mansouri Specialised Engineering	Inspection services for bulk liquid storage tanks holding refined petroleum and chemical products with a state-of-the-art Robotics system called 'Mavericks', which uses advanced technology and is remotely operated to collect corrosion data from the interior walls and bottom of tanks full with refined product while they remain in service.	7,340,000

Table 2.4.1 *continued*

Project Name	*Defence Contractor*	*Local Partner*	*Activity*	*Capital UAE Dirhams*
CIA. MAR Emirates Marbles, Granite and Stone Industry	Giat	ABS Holding	Plant for manufacturing and processing marble, granite and stones.	55,000,000
Gulf Centre for Remote Sensing	GEC-Marconi	Abu Dhabi Industrial Development Co. (ADIDCO)	A service centre covering satellite and aerial data acquisition and selection and processing of data for specific applications to users in the fields of agriculture, water resources, minerals development, oil and gas production, map making and environmental studies.	5,000,000
National Horticulture Centre (Franserres)	Dassault/Thomson French Fighter Investment & Cooperation Programme	Al Hamed Enterprises	The building of 10 hectares of greenhouses in Al Ain and the establishing of an agricultural management company to provide marketing and technical assistance to farm owners and local groups.	50,000,000

Table 2.4.1 *continued*

Project Name	*Defence Contractor*	*Local Partner*	*Activity*	*Capital UAE Dirhams*
National District Cooling Company (Tabreed)	National District Cooling Company	–Local Founders –Public Offering: 170,000 nationals	Establish, install, own, operate and maintain centralised cooling systems that will serve groups of buildings and complexes.	500,000,000
BSI Bernd Spaeth International LLC	Deutz AG/Tatra a.s.	Emirates Commercial Centre	Specialised in high class advertising and events marketing for government and private sectors.	

Part 3

Ports and Free Zones

3.1

Dubai Ports and Jebel Ali Free Zone

Philip Dew, The Philip Dew Consultancy Limited, Bahrain

For centuries Dubai has been known as the City of Merchants, an allusion to its international trade based on the creek that divides today's city and along which wooden vessels continue to load and unload their cargoes. Importantly, though such trade remains, Dubai has moved on and at the dawn of a new millennium can boast two highly successful ports competing favourably with other entrepots around the world.

The ports

Dubai's two important marine terminals are Port Rashid in down-town Dubai and Jebel Ali Port 35 kilometres to the south of the city. Together they comprise the largest port complex in the Middle East. More than 100 shipping lines serve the ports, which makes the complex one of the great transshipment centres of the world. They have been managed since May 1991 by the Dubai Ports Authority (DPA).

The two terminals have a total of 102 deep water berths and 25 gantry cranes between them. In 1998 2.8 million (TEUs) passed through the ports, propelling them into eleventh place among world container ports. In the first nine months of 1999, total tonnage handled by the two ports rose by seven per cent, when compared with the same period of the previous year, to in excess of 28.7 million metric tons. Over the same period more than 2 million TEUs were handled.

To maintain its position the DPA has constantly sought to invest in state-of-the-art equipment, such that today a unique range of cargo handling equipment is employed including the latest super post-Panamax gantry cranes.

Supporting the substantial container trade are two repair yards, Middle East Container Repair in Port Rashid and Emirates Container Repair in

Jebel Ali. These companies are fully capable of handling the repair of all types of TEU, be they steel or aluminium.

In addition to container traffic, general cargo is also handled and specialised facilities have been developed to meet the specific demands of such trade. Examples of these facilities are the 43,000 cubic metre cold store in Jebel Ali, which is located on the quayside, thereby enabling the immediate transfer of frozen goods from refrigerated vessels, and the area known as Timberland, which is a huge storage and distribution centre for timber and wood-based products.

The Gulf's re-distribution centre

Given Dubai's location at the heart of a vast region which includes the GCC states, Iran, the Indian sub-continent, the CIS and Russia and the eastern and northern littorals of Africa, the twin ports have been developed not only to channel goods to what is a small local market but also, and more importantly, as a hub for distribution throughout those areas. Integral to the development of the ports as transshipment centres by the DPA has been enhanced cargo throughput through the availability of efficient cargo handling, specialised storage facilities, an effective in-house trucking operation and the use of fast, accurate cargo control systems.

A direct result of the growth and efficiency of these ports has been the establishment of operations in Dubai and Jebel Ali by many multinational companies seeking to derive the benefits of being closer to their markets. They have faster turnaround and supply times and reduced investment in stock, all allied to markedly reduced transportation costs to destination countries.

Jebel Ali Free Zone

Jebel Ali Free Zone, alongside the eponymous port, was founded in 1985 and has become today a major warehousing and industrial area where multinationals mingle with a plethora of smaller companies to derive the fullest possible benefits and opportunities of free trade. The whole area is under the management of the Jebel Ali Free Zone Authority (JAFZA) which is inextricably linked with the Dubai Ports Authority.

Built around the world's largest man-made port, Jebel Ali was initially seen as the ideal base for multinationals to warehouse and distribute their products in the Gulf. Over the years, the range of activities has grown from distribution to include the whole spectrum of manufacturing, trading and services, and destination markets have grown to cover all the Middle East, the Asian sub-continent, Africa, the former Soviet Union, Eastern Europe and, for many, the entire world.

By the end of 1999, there were 1600 companies in the Free Zone from some 90 countries, 70 per cent of which are involved in trading and 25 per cent in industry. The remaining 5 per cent are service providers.

As a testimonial to their success, many companies have expanded their operations since setting up in the Free Zone, some of them more than once. Cleveland Bridge, Rank Xerox, Shell, Black & Decker, 3M Corporation and McDermott were among the first companies to establish presences. Sony, Citizen, Reebok, Aiwa, Land Rover, AST, Casio, Daewoo, Honda, Bose, Grundig, Hyundai, Nokia Mobile Phones, TetraPak, H.J. Heinz, Nissan, Murata Machinery, Brother, Mobil Corporation, P&O Containers, Toys 'R' Us, General Motors, IBM, Epson, Western Digital, L'Oreal, Mannes Mann Dematic, Iridium Middle East Gateway Corpn, Osram and Seagram are among the more recent additions.

Whereas in the early days only subsidiaries were permitted in the zone, since the passing of Law 9 of 1992, companies can be incorporated in Jebel Ali as totally independent Free Zone Establishments (FZEs). FZEs have a distinct legal identity and the liability of what can be a single shareholder is limited to the amount of the paid up share capital. FZEs therefore share many of the key characteristics of limited liability companies and may well enjoy significant international tax advantages.

JAFZA is the sole regulatory agency for FZEs that do not need any memorandum or articles of association but are governed solely by the agency's implementing regulations. The minimum share capital is Dhs1million, although this may be varied in special cases.

The advantages and benefits of a Jebel Ali base include:

- 100 per cent foreign ownership: Jebel Ali Free Zone companies do not need a local partner, as is the case with most international companies in the Middle East and developing world. JAFZA itself acts as the nominal sponsor;
- no recruitment/sponsorship problems: the Free Zone Authority also acts as the nominal sponsor of the staff whom companies may wish to hire, but companies are free to recruit for themselves if they so wish. However, employees can be provided by the Free Zone Authority according to client requirements. There are no regulations regarding the employment of nationals, as is the case in many competing incentive zones;
- 100 per cent repatriation of capital and profits: no corporate taxes are imposed and repatriation of both profits and capital is allowed;
- no currency restrictions: Dubai's trading tradition, established over many years, is based on the free flow of capital and profits and the absence of exchange control. The Free Zone derives the same benefits;
- No corporate taxes for 15 years: companies operating in the Jebel Ali Free Zone are exempt from corporate taxes for a minimum of 15 years, renewable for a further 15-year period;

- no personal income taxes: there is no personal taxation within the Free Zone area;.
- Abundant energy: the Jebel Ali Power Station serves both the water and power needs of the Free Zone;
- Ready-made facilities: JAFZA provides ready-made facilities for investors. These facilities include air-conditioned warehouses, the Gulf's largest cold stores and an ultra-modern container freight station. These are backed up by experienced staff, computer monitoring and control systems, computerised inventory control, modern narrow-aisle racking and cargo handling equipment, supported by extensive services which include promotional re-packing, co-packing and shrink wrapping.

Conclusion

Dubai Ports and Jebel Ali Free Zone are major success stories for the emirate of Dubai. From very humble beginnings not much more than 20 years ago, Dubai, in large part because of its excellent port facilities, has grown to become a truly world-class trading centre. The success of Jebel Ali is best expressed in the amazing growth of companies operating there – from nil in 1985 to 1600 at the beginning of the year 2000 – with yet further growth anticipated in the years to come. So confident are the local authorities of such growth that a second large area has been set aside already in case of need.

3.2

Sharjah Ports and Hamriyah Free Trade Zone

Philip Dew, The Philip Dew Consultancy Limited, Bahrain

For many years Sharjah has been an international trading centre with vessels visiting its ports from many parts of the world. Historically cargo was delivered to jetties alongside Sharjah creek, but today modern port facilities are available on both the emirate's coasts – the Arabian Gulf and the Gulf of Oman. The major elements of both parts are their container handling facilities inter-linked by a unique mini-bridge whereby goods can be trucked between the two ports, under bond, in just three hours.

Sharjah container terminal

The Sharjah Container Terminal, on the Arabian Gulf coast, was the first such terminal to be completed in the Middle East. With a 586 metre-long quay and a depth alongside of 11.5 metres, two third generation container ships or two roll-on roll-off vessels can be handled simultaneously.

Overall the terminal covers 150,000 square metres on which there is storage for 8000 TEUs plus a dedicated transit shed and weighbridge.

During the whole of 1998 TEUs handled totalled 80,175 and in the first nine months of 1999 66,303 TEUs had been handled, intimating some 10 per cent growth over the previous year.

Khorfakan container terminal

Located on the UAE's Indian Ocean coast, outside the Arabian Gulf, on the main east–west shipping lanes and avoiding the necessity of transiting the Straits of Hormuz, Khorfakan Container Terminal, sited on the UAE's only natural deep water port, has established itself as the logical container transshipment port of the UAE.

This ultra-modern container terminal now has 1060 metres of berths dreged to 15 metres, allied to more than 300,000 square metres of storage area capable of accommodating 18,000 TEUs.

During 1998 total containers handled amounted to 783,352 TEUs, with only some 7 per cent less at 725,601 TEUs being handled in the first nine months of 1999. Together with its sister port in Sharjah, Khorfakan Container Terminal is served by over 30 shipping lines.

As mentioned earlier, Khorfakan Container Terminal is only some three hours by road from Sharjah, where 40 per cent of all UAE industry is sited, and goods can be trucked under bond by dedicated transporters. Along the route from Khorfakan to the Gulf coast is also Sharjah International Airport and its associated free zone (about which more information is provided below) thus making Sharjah an important sea-land-air bridge for international businesses.

Hamriyah Free Zone

One of the newer free zones in the UAE, Hamriyah Free Zone (HFZ) was established on Sharjah's Gulf coast to the north of the emirate in 1995. The concept behind HFZ is the development of a pre-eminent industrial area with access to world markets through the emirate's sea and airports.

Ten million square metres of land have been set aside as an industrial and commercial area to which has been allied a 14 metre-deep harbour capable of handling petrochemicals and bulk and general cargoes. Whilst HFZ does provide some pre-built buildings it believes investors should have the freedom to develop their own facilities. Importantly, however, an international business centre with 100 executive suites, as well as labour accommodation, is provided.

The incentives offered by HFZ include:

- 100 per cent foreign ownership
- 100 per cent import/export duty exemption
- 100 per cent exemption from all or any commercial levies
- 100 per cent profit and capital repatriation
- 15 year leases, renewable for a further 15 years
- no corporate or personal taxation
- good transportation links
- dedicated electrical paver
- cheap energy
- good infrastructure.

As at the end of 1999, 74 companies were operating in HFZ, out of 77 which had been licensed, of which 27 were industrial ventures, 39 were involved in trading and 11 provided services.

3.3

Airport Free Zones

Philip Dew, The Philip Dew Consultancy Limited, Bahrain

Within the UAE there are six international airports, at Abu Dhabi, Al Ain, Dubai, Fujairah, Ras alKhaimah and Sharjah, but by far the two largest are in Dubai and Sharjah.

Dubai International Airport is already one of the most modern in the world and is currently ranked among the top 50, with over 7.2 million passengers and with 80 international airlines reaching out to more than 120 destinations. Early in 2000, on completion of a US$500 million expansion, Dubai will rise to among the top 20 in the world.

Sharjah International Airport, the recipient of the best international air cargo award in 1998, is one of the oldest in the Middle East and has carved out a niche for itself as a cargo-oriented complex, integral to which is domination of the charter operation sector. Today, Sharjah is the biggest air cargo hub in the Middle East and Africa, with connections to 230 destinations worldwide, of which 75 are within the CIS, and is the site of Lufthansa's second largest hub after Frankfurt, with 300 flights monthly moving over 9000 tonnes of cargo.

With such impeccable credentials, the setting-up of free zones at both airports was perhaps inevitable.

Dubai Airport Free Zone

The Dubai Airport Free Zone (DAFZ) is the UAE's newest free zone, having become operational only on 15 January 1999. The zone has been sited on 1.2 million square metres of land, including apron space of 473,000 square metres, on the north side of Dubai International Airport. Integral to this, which is phase 1 of the free zone, are two four-storey buildings, 24 warehouse units of 353 square metres each and over 200,000 square metres of undeveloped land available for companies to build their own structures.

As DAFZ is situated on the airport perimeter, the activities which are permitted are limited to high value, low volume products, service companies, high technology and IT companies, light industry and assembly operations and activities related to the aviation industry.

By the end of 1999 a total of 65 companies had been licensed to operate in DAFZ, with a number of multinational companies already having established a presence, including Boeing, Chanel, Dell Computers, Estee Lauder, IBM, Johnson & Johnson, Matsushita Avionics, Porsche, Ricoh, Rolls-Royce, Samsonite and Tag Heuer.

The incentives offered by DAFZ include 100 per cent exemption from corporate tax, import and export taxes, personal income taxes and all commercial levies; 100 per cent foreign company ownership and repatriation of capital and profits; abundant and inexpensive energy; and excellent transportation links by air, sea and land to global markets. Licences to set up, which must be obtained in advance, are issued by the DAFZ against the provision of standard documentation from the foreign company including:

- an original or notarised copy of a valid certificate of registration;
- notarised Memorandum and Articles of the company;
- board resolution setting up the branch in the DAFZ;
- power of attorney appointing the manager of the branch;
- notarised specimen signature of the appointed manager;
- passport copy of the appointed manager;
- statement by the principal of the amount of capital set aside for the company's operation in the DAFZ.

Such requirements are substantially the same as those for a number of other free zones around the UAE and wider GCC.

Sharjah Airport International Free Zone (SAIF-Zone)

Sharjah Airport International Free Zone (SAIF-Zone), the first airport free zone in the world to become ISO certified, is sited adjacent to Sharjah International Airport along the road linking Sharjah and Khorfakan Ports – the mini-bridge. Established in September 1995, the SAIF-Zone had become home to nearly 400 companies by late 1999 – of which 47 were involved in industry, 259 in trading and 88 in services.

Integral to the facilities provided by the SAIF-Zone are fully serviced and furnished executive offices, pre-built warehouse units in two sizes with adjacent office space, vacant land for private development, a container parking area and temporary storage areas. Also available are facilities for manufacturing, assembling, packaging and import/export/re-export trading.

The incentives available are much the same as those for other free zones in the region, including freedom from corporate and personal taxation and import/export duties; 100 per cent foreign ownership and repatriation of capital and profits without any foreign exchange restriction; sponsorship and visas for all staff, who may all be expatriates; and 15 year leases renewable for a further similar period.

Within the SAIF-Zone companies will require one of four licences to operate, namely one of industrial, commercial, general trading or service licence, and are allowed to operate in one of four forms – as a Free Zone Enterprise, a Free Zone Company, a branch of a foreign company or as a branch of a UAE company. Whichever route is chosen, the SAIF-Zone undertakes to assist a company to be operational within 24 hours once all the relevant documentation has been presented in order (which documentation is much the same as required at DAFZ) and has been accepted by the management of the zone.

Dubai Internet City

Announced late in 1999, the Dubai Internet City, to be located north of Dubai Airport, will be the world's first Internet free zone. The intention is to incorporate an Internet university specialising in e-business, a science and technology park and a research and development centre.

3.4

Other Free Zones in the UAE

Philip Dew, The Philip Dew Consultancy Limited, Bahrain

As the trading environment in the UAE has grown, so has the role of emirates other than Dubai, Sharjah and Abu Dhabi (see Saadiyat Market in Part 6 below). Thus the four most northern emirates have all developed ports and allied free trade zones.

Such ports and free trade zones have not developed solely as warehousing entrepots but also as industrial centres, centres for information technology or, as in one case, as one of the world's leading bunkering ports. Today's evidence would suggest there to be continued potential for further enhancement of the free trading environment, especially now the UAE is a member of the World Trade Organisation (WTO).

Ajman Port and Free Zone

Established adjacent to Ajman Port in 1998, the Ajman Free Zone (AFZ) is capable of accommodating up to 600 companies. By the end of 1999 there were nearly 500 companies in residence, with AFZ having experienced the highest percentage growth of any free zone in the UAE during the four years from 1995.

Late in 1999 a further 24 warehouse units were built within the AFZ and construction commenced on a purpose-designed IT park with 100 office units. The port alongside which the AFZ has been set up has 12 berths capable of handling 1000 vessels a year. In 1998 the value of Ajman's exports through the free zone exceeded US$153 million.

Many of the benefits of the AFZ are similar to those elsewhere in the UAE, but of particular note are the total elimination of all service charges or hidden fees, 20 year renewable leases guaranteeing a minimum of 40 years tax and duty free and what are claimed to be the lowest tariffs and lease prices in the region.

Companies wishing to operate within the AFZ must first obtain one of five types of licence – trading, industrial, professional/service, national industrial and offshore registration. In the latter case, the types of ownership available are:

- branch of a foreign company;
- branch of a local company;
- free zone entity (FZE) – (minimum capital requirement US$50,000);
- free zone company (FZC) – (minimum capital requirement US$137,000);
- offshore company – (minimum capital requirement US$14,000).

By way of encouragement to set up in the AFZ, all bureaucratic procedures have been kept to an absolute minimum but similar documentary requirements as other free zones in the UAE apply.

Fujairah Port and Free Zone

Fujairah Port and Free Zone are unique within the UAE, being sited on the Indian Ocean coast and therefore avoiding the need for shipping to enter the narrow Straits of Hormuz en route to Arabian Gulf ports. As a result of its location and a relatively calm marine environment, the port has attained a place in the top three bunkering ports in the world.

Given the growth of container traffic, the increasing size of Fujairah Free Zone and the excellent land, sea and air communication links available, the Port of Fujairah has expanded over the years and now has a one kilometre quay, nearly 200,000 square metres of storage yard, facilities exclusively for refrigerated containers and a repair yard capable of handling both steel and aluminium containers.

The allied free trade zone, which was established in 1987, has grown steadily over the years under the name of the 'Zone of Convenience'. The basic incentives offered by, and the applicable legislation of, the Fujairah Free Zone are much the same as elsewhere in the UAE but include the added benefit of being on the east coast, thus offering reduced sailing times to destination markets at tariffs below those applicable within the Gulf. Licences for projects within the free zone, be they trading, general trading, assembling, warehousing and distribution or manufacturing, can be issued in a day and operational overheads and running costs are considered among the lowest, if not the lowest, within the UAE.

The documentary requirements of the FFZ are not onerous, being as follows; an initial document outlining the project, which must be legalised, including:

- status of the company to be formed;
- the capital and mode of investment;
- shareholders and board of directors of the project;
- signing authority of the project.

On presentation of this document and following agreement of the Free Zone Authority, the project may commence.

In late 1999 nearly 90 companies maintained presences here, of which 21 were manufacturers, 35 were trading houses and the balance solely involved in warehousing.

Ras alKhaimah Free Zone

A new free zone is in the process of being established in Ras alKhaimah, but late in 1999 no information on the facilities was available.

Umm AlQuwain – Ahmed bin Rashid Port and Free Zone

Located 45 kilometres north east of Dubai, Ahmed bin Rashid Port, Umm AlQuwain, has four quays capable of receiving vessels up to 210 metres in length and with drafts of no more than 10 metres. During 2000 an expansion of the port is anticipated to accept larger and deeper draught vessels.

Alongside the port 34 light industrial units have been constructed together with labour accommodation and all utilities. This area constitutes the free zone where a number of companies have already established presences.

The incentives to invest here are not dissimilar to those applicable in the neighbouring Hamriyah Free Zone and the procedures for investing and for obtaining the required special licence are kept to an absolute minimum

Conclusion

Every emirate now has, or will have in the near future, at least one free trade zone, with Sharjah and Dubai having extra facilities at their respective airports. There are already over 3000 companies, both large and small, local and multinational, operating successfully in these zones. Their trading or manufacturing activities are by no means confined to the UAE or indeed to the states of the Arabian Gulf, but reach out to global markets and especially those of Iran, the CIS, the Indian sub-continent and east Africa. As these markets grow, so the free trade zones of the UAE are likely to expand.

Part 4

Company Operational Issues

4.1

Forms of Intellectual Property in the UAE

Alastair McNair, (on secondment from Clifford Chance) Hadef Al Dhahiri Associates, Abu Dhabi

Intellectual Property as recognised in the UAE takes three forms – Trademarks, Patents and Copyright. In each of these areas there is Federal Law dealing with registration and protection and enforcement matters.

Additionally to the above, the relevant authorities (in Dubai, the Department of Economic Planning and in Abu Dhabi, the Municipality) have come to take a much more interventionist approach to '*passing off*' cases. These have involved fake or imitation car stereos, watches, garments, tea, software, detergents and other goods, which are regularly seized, often in substantial quantities, and subsequently destroyed. Because of the UAE's World Trade Organisation ambitions, there is a particular focus in this area on software.

Trademarks

The relevant Federal Law is No.37 of 1992, implemented by a subsequent Ministerial Resolution of 1993. Effective from March 1996, the UAE acceded to the Paris Convention on the Protection of Industrial Property – this has however not yet been reflected in trademark legislation. Amendments are, however, known to be under consideration.

The UAE Trademark Registry, located in Abu Dhabi, began accepting applications for the registration of trademarks in April 1993. As of February 2000, there are a substantial number of fully registered (and therefore protected) trademarks.

The period of protection recognised in the UAE is 10 years, subject to renewal. 'Ownership' of a registered mark cannot be disputed where it has been in regular use without challenge for five years. Registration gives the person in whose name registration is made (the owner) the right to use the mark in question and to seek protection/interim remedies or damages to protect it from abuse or infringement.

It is the 'real' owner of a mark who can register its proprietary interest in the mark, thus achieving its protection. As such, foreign principals of a commercial agency, distributorship, franchise or licensing arrangement can register its trademarks in the UAE, thus obtaining their protection. At a practical level, trademarks in the UAE are often registered on a pre-emptive basis – even if not actually in use. Article 22 of the Trademarks Law, however, provides that an interested third party may challenge a trademark for lack of use – they must, however, prove that these have not been 'seriously' in use for five consecutive years – which as a practical matter is a rather difficult burden of proof to satisfy.

The present UAE Trademark Classes do not contain categories for either alcohol or beer – and any trademarks considered offensive to UAE public morality are unlikely to achieve registration.

The owner of a trademark enjoys retroactive protection as soon as the trademark in question is registered – unregistered trademarks are, however, protected under the passing-off provisions in other applicable legislation.

The registration process for a trademark application takes approximately twelve months and involves scrutiny of the application and a Technical Survey. This eventually results in public advertising of the proposal to go for registration and the expiry of a period allowed for objections. Once registered, it is possible to update a trademark registration through an amendment filing. There is also a renewal process and de-registration process.

In the UAE, trademarks may be sold, mortgaged, and their use may be licensed (for example to distributors). Any of these processes require notification and certain publication formalities to take place. Law and practice in the area of trademarks in the UAE is reasonably developed, predictable and logical: providing one uses agents with experience of this area, few problems should be experienced.

Patents

The relevant Law here is Federal Law No.44 of 1992, under which a patent is granted to protect a new invention resulting from an original idea. The law states that both the invention and any improvements for which patents are granted should be based upon scientific research or industrial development. On a practical level, this is given a reasonably broad interpretation. The law requires patent applications based on an industrial development to be 'suitable' for industrial use/utilisable in any form of industry. Where an invention is capable of industrial application but is not considered original enough for a patent to be granted, then a certificate of advantage may be granted. Once granted, a patent or certificate of advantage prevents third parties from manufacturing, importing or selling the protected item.

The registration process involves a technical survey and a public advertisement with the potential for objections to be lodged.

The Patent Law prevents certain inventions from being patented or receiving certificates of advantage:

- biological research in relation to plant and animal production;
- chemical inventions related to foodstuffs or medicines;
- scientific principles and discoveries;
- inventions concerning national defence; and
- inventions whose application would breach public security or morality.

Once granted in the UAE, patents provide protection for 15 years, and certificates of advantage for 10 years. Prior to expiry, patents may be renewed for a further term of five years.

Copyright

Again, the Copyright Law of 1992 is a Federal Law and protects:

> ... *original intellectual works in literature, the arts and sources, whatever may be the value or quality thereof, or the purpose for which they were composed, or the manner in which they are expressed'.*

The important point about copyright in the UAE (as elsewhere) is that registration is not required to achieve protection. Registration is possible through an application to the Ministry of Economy and Culture but it is not a pre-requisite for the material in question to achieve protection. It is this flexibility which has led in particular to the Ministry seeking to stamp out abuse in the form of pirated cassettes, videos and software.

The World Trade Organisation

The UAE is an aspiring member of the World Trade Organisation and in consequence a number of radical changes in various areas will need to take place in the next five years or so. Levels of copyright abuse in the UAE in particular have dropped markedly in the last few years, although the UAE remains on a US watchlist. One can safely expect continued development in the general area of the protection of intellectual property in its various forms during the next few years.

4.2

Mergers and Acquisitions

David Knights, Redwood Partners, Dubai

Overview

This chapter is not intended to be a guide to the steps that a potential buyer or seller of businesses will need to take; it is rather a comment on certain trends and issues in the market. An 'acquisition' is a change in ownership that leads to a change in control. To some extent, however, our observations may apply as much to investors in businesses in the UAE as to buyers and sellers of controlling stakes.

The title of this chapter should not suggest that there is a significant amount of merger and acquisition activity in the UAE. Indeed, although the UAE has perhaps the most dynamic commercial sector in the entire region, in common with many other emerging countries there have, until recently, been few corporate acquisitions of businesses. During the tremendous growth over the past 30 years or so, the typical company has been established as a new venture or start-up. The principals may be local businessmen, local companies or international firms usually working through a local partner.

In the UAE there are basically five types of corporate entity. In all cases these companies must be wholly- or majority-owned by nationals:

- sole proprietorships;
- partnerships;
- limited liability companies;
- private joint stock companies;
- public joint stock companies.

However, in recent years other types of company, not covered under the UAE commercial code itself, have been permitted by individual Emirates. The best examples of these are the free zone companies, which may be 100 per cent foreign owned.

As the commercial structure of the UAE has gradually become more complex, however, a process of acquisition and commercial consolidation has started fitfully to emerge. This is important for the development of the country, as the ability to buy and sell, to reform and reshape businesses is an important constituent of a dynamic corporate sector. There are a number of discernible developments.

Establishment of a stock exchange

The most important development in facilitating a more dynamic commercial structure is the imminent establishment of a stock exchange. There is not, as yet, an official stock exchange in the UAE although an 'over the counter market' exists for certain shares of public joint stock companies. At the time of writing, in late 1999, the draft of the UAE Financial Markets law had just received final approval. The physical structure of the Dubai financial market is already in place and is technically able to commence operations in short order. It is likely that financial markets will be set up in both Abu Dhabi and Dubai, with a third market to be under the authority of the Saadiyat Free Zone. These exchanges will be linked electronically. The precise parameters and regulations for new public issues and for trading shares on the markets have yet to be publicised or defined. It is not as yet known, for example, whether non-nationals will be able to trade on the exchanges from the outset. Nevertheless, the establishment of the market itself is very important. It is likely to have the following implications for the corporate structure of the UAE.

1. Encourage the establishment of more corporate entities with broadly based shareholdings and support a trend away from sole proprietorships or family businesses as the cornerstone of corporate organisation. Such corporates operate in a more transparent way, have a more ready access to capital and are, in many ways, more able to function in a regional or global market. This trend is likely to lead to a greater separation between owners and managers and encourage the further development of a professional managerial corps.
2. Encourage further consolidation through stimulating more acquisition and merger activity. There has already been active public discussion on the need for mergers in the banking sector and a merger between National Bank of Dubai and Emirates Bank International has been under active consideration.
3. Encourage foreign companies or shareholders that currently operate in the UAE through 49 per cent stakes in limited liability companies to set up local joint stock companies whose shares can be traded. Foreign companies can thus establish some liquidity for their shareholdings in the Emirates and can operate in a more transparent way.

Trans-Gulf acquisition activity

Increasingly, a number of companies operating in individual countries in the GCC are looking to extend their activity across their national boundaries. As a result more trans-national acquisitions are starting to be seen. As an illustration of this, in 1998 Renaissance Holdings, an Omani public company that operates a number of service businesses in Oman, acquired Memo Express Services, the largest local express courier company in the UAE. The acquisition was made by Renaissance's subsidiary, United Media Services, which is the market leader in Oman in the field of media, distribution and communications. Memo Express serves the entire UAE with same day document and parcel delivery. Renaissance saw the opportunity for creating synergies between the two businesses by accessing a bigger market for its distribution operations.

Perhaps the most high-profile acquisition recently has been the purchase by the investment company, Cupola, of Inchcape's significant operations in distribution and retailing around the Gulf. A number of these operations have subsequently been broken up and sold to national companies – effectively a demerger of the group.

Another ambitious transaction is the proposed merger between a number of the region's glass bottle manufacturers. Leading companies in Saudi Arabia, Kuwait, Oman and the UAE have been examining what would be probably the most complex merger planned in the region. If this goes ahead it may well stimulate further activity in this area.

Management buy-outs

There are numerous businesses in the UAE which are being actively grown and developed by management teams who are looking for opportunities to participate more directly in the ownership of their companies. The first management buy-out in the region took place in 1993 when management, supported by several regional institutions, acquired the UAE based business, Nico Middle East Limited. In 1998 this business was acquired by an Omani public company, Topaz Energy and Marine, which had been specifically set up for this purpose [see boxed text]. There have been other buy-outs since then.

Privatisation

In some ways, the forces that encourage privatisation in the sense of transferring to private ownership services and businesses that are run by the public sector, are weaker in the UAE than in many other parts of the GCC.

Nico Middle East Limited

Nico Middle East Limited was the subject of the first management buy-out in the region in 1993. At that time, its parent, a major Swedish multinational, operating primarily in real estate and civil contracting, had undertaken a programme to dispose of all its non-core business. Nico was a well-established company operating out of Dubai in the area of ship repair and the operation of supply vessels for the oil and gas industry. A structure was put together whereby management took a 16 per cent shareholding supported by a group of local institutions and other investors. The business was characterised by a strong client base and a reputation for the quality of its work. It had robust cash flows partly resulting from substantial previous capital expenditure. The operations were subsequently expanded and profits increased significantly. In 1998 the company was acquired by a newly formed Omani company, Topaz Energy & Marine, which was specifically set up for the purpose, and which was floated and listed on the Muscat Securities Market. The acquisition provided the original investors with a realisation of their investment and also brought to the developing Omani marine industry a significant company operating in this sector.

This is largely because of the strength of the government financial position in Abu Dhabi and consequently at the Federal level. Unlike Oman, Bahrain and Saudi Arabia, where there are powerful financial incentives for a policy of privatisation, since governments of these countries are constantly facing up to budget deficits, Abu Dhabi is cushioned by substantial surpluses.

Nevertheless the governments of the individual Emirates have begun the process of privatising certain sectors. In the northern Emirates, governments have been attracted by privately financed projects, in particular on a build-operate-transfer (BOT) basis, in the wastewater, power, and desalination sectors. Both Umm Al Quwain and Ajman have initialled agreements for BOT concessions. Sharjah Container Port and Khorfakkan Port are already privately operated.

The most ambitious programme, however, is underway in Abu Dhabi where a privatisation committee for the water and electricity sector has been set up to approve and monitor new projects. The objective is increased efficiency and lower operating costs. The intention is that new power and water projects will be implemented by the private sector, where foreign companies may take up to 49 per cent while government or state owned institutions will take at least 51 per cent. The showcase project is the Al Taweelah A–2 power and water project [see box]. It is likely that the success of the privatisation programme in the electricity and water sector will lead to the introduction of privatisation in other sectors of the economy.

Taweela A–2 Power and Desalination

Taweela A–2 is the first independent water and power project in the UAE. It was awarded in 1998 to CMS Energy Corp. of the USA on a build-own-operate basis. A new company has been formed, with CMS owning 40 per cent and Emirates Power owning 60 per cent. The combined cycle plant is intended to generate 710MW of electricity and 50 million gallons a day of desalinated water and is due to commence production in early 2001. Critical to the success of the project, and to the future of the privatisation programme itself, is the competitive price of electricity and water, which at tariffs of 8.97 fils/kwh for power and Dhs. 11/1000 imperial gallons for water are significantly lower than the current tariffs for the rest of the sector.

Obstacles

A commercial environment which facilitates the process of merger and acquisition is gradually developing. Despite this, however, there remain a number of major obstacles in the way of a well-functioning and flexible commercial sector. Two of the more important of these are as follows.

Cultural attitudes

There remains a traditional reluctance to sell businesses, particularly by individual proprietors. The reverse of this is suspicion of the quality of businesses available for sale – 'if the company is any good, why is it for sale?'

Legal deficiencies

This is the most serious issue. The commercial code and company law in the UAE derives from the old Egyptian commercial code and has a number of serious deficiencies.

It is not the intention in this chapter to describe the various forms of company in detail. The point to be made is that there are many ways in which the commercial code needs to be substantially amended if the UAE's commercial structure is to match its commercial dynamism. For example, the existing law basically envisages companies that are either majority or wholly owned by UAE nationals. Further it envisages only one class of shares, thus excluding preference shares, non-voting shares, warrants and other forms of ownership which facilitate the buying and selling and investing in companies. Both of these have the effect of restricting the ability to buy and sell and to restructure businesses.

A practice has developed whereby many national shareholders in 51/49 per cent joint venture companies are neither involved in the management nor participate fully in the profits of the venture. These national shareholders effectively operate as sponsors even though they are registered as majority owners. These arrangements often work well in practice, but the lack of transparency is frequently a major obstacle when buying or selling the business concerned.

In the meantime, a patchwork of special regulations and exceptions have developed which partly address the needs of international business. Dubai in particular has introduced a flexible code for companies established in the Jebel Ali Free Zone. It has also introduced civil business partnerships which allow companies providing certain professional and consultancy services to be 100 per cent foreign owned. More recently Sheikh Mohammed bin Rashid Al Maktoum has announced the establishment of 'Dubai Internet City', offering e-business companies 100 per cent foreign ownership and 50 year leases on land.

These various arrangements help to alleviate the deficiencies of the commercial code, but do not diminish the need to overhaul the current regulations.

Professional advisers

As merger and acquisition activity increases, it is likely that further modifications to the legal code and to the commercial environment will take place. Nevertheless, it is imperative that any potential purchaser or seller of a business arms himself with experienced and professional advisers who are familiar with the sorts of issues that arise in the UAE. These may include specialist consultants on specific technical or marketing issues. For larger companies, in particular, it is often appropriate to be supported by professional human resources consultants. Most important, perhaps, is proper legal, accounting and corporate finance advice.

Legal advisers

More international firms of lawyers have offices in the UAE than in any other country in the region. Some of these legal practices focus principally on international projects in the region, others also focus on local commercial work. There are also a number of competent local firms. The legal adviser may carry out legal due diligence, advise on pragmatic and appropriate legal structures, and prepare the sale and purchase agreement and other contractual arrangements.

Reporting accountants

Most of the major international firms are represented in the UAE and some of them maintain their principal regional offices in the country. The accounting firm may carry out financial due diligence and investigation, audit and, if appropriate, valuation, together with advice on the accounting implications of a purchase.

Financial advisers

The financial adviser would support the purchaser (or seller) throughout the whole transaction. He may advise on acquisition strategy, on valuation and on negotiation approach, helping to identify the critical issues and pitfalls and proposing ways of dealing with these. The financial adviser will advise on financial structure and, if appropriate, will arrange additional investment capital. Few of the banks in the UAE have specialist corporate finance skills in-house and therefore the potential purchaser (or seller) should give especial consideration to the professional experience of this adviser.

Part 5

The Fiscal and Regulatory Framework

5.1

Accounting Principles, Reporting Requirements and Records in the UAE

John Simpkins, Arthur Andersen, Dubai

The UAE does not have its own accounting standards. However, in practice, most entities that produce financial statements for audit and distribution to shareholders, government agencies and banks prepare such statements in accordance with International Accounting Standards.

Generally, the standard of financial reporting is improving as users of financial statements within the UAE and outside require compliance with international standards and more disclosure. This trend is being encouraged by more rigorous requirements amongst users such as bankers and shareholders. The improvement will need to continue as capital markets in the UAE develop further and the anticipated stock exchange comes into operation.

Accounting guidelines

The commercial companies law states that the accounting principles and practices should be in line with the generally accepted practice and principles of accounting; however, the law does not define these. As a matter of practice, most businesses in the UAE prepare financial statements based on International Accounting Standards.

Reporting requirements

The following legal entities have reporting requirements as per the UAE commercial companies law and practice:

1. branches of foreign companies;
2. limited liability companies;
3. public and private shareholding companies;
4. free zone establishments.*

Reporting requirements entail that all branches of foreign companies, limited liability companies and public and private shareholding companies have to submit annual audited financial statements within 120 days of the financial year end to the Federal Ministry of Economy and Commerce and to the local business licensing authorities in the various Emirates (commonly known in each Emirate as 'the Economic Department' or the 'local municipality') upon renewal of the trade licence. In practice, the requirement to submit financial statements to the Federal Ministry is not always rigorously complied with by smaller entities that are not public shareholding companies. However, the licensing authorities request audited financial statements as part of the licence renewal process

Free zone establishments in the Jebel Ali Free Zone are required to submit their annual audited financial statements to the Jebel Ali Free Zone authority within 90 days from the financial year end.

The law requires that the annual financial statements should include a balance sheet, statement of profit and loss and information on the financial position during the year and the proposed method of distribution of profits.

In addition, and depending on the business activity of the corporation, the financial statements may have to be submitted to other institutions. For example, banks and financial institutions have to submit their financial statements to the UAE Central Bank and courier companies are obliged to submit their financial statements to the Ministry of Finance and Industry.

Accounting records

The requirements for maintaining accounting records in the UAE are prescribed in the following :

1. the UAE federal commercial companies law;
2. the UAE federal commercial transactions law.

According to the federal commercial transactions law, businesses must keep ledgers and books according to their specific business requirements, but in all cases should at least keep the following books:

* A free zone establishment is an entity set up in one of the UAE free zones. As opposed to a branch of a foreign company in the free zone, the distinctive characteristic of the free zone entity (FZE) is that its paid up share capital comprises of a single share, and that the entity is (from a UAE viewpoint) considered an independent corporate person from the owner of that share.

- the daily journal
- the general ledger.

Further details on the information to be included in the above books and the accounting entries required are available in the UAE commercial transactions law. The commercial law obliges businesses to keep an original copy of all correspondence, telex letters and invoices issued or received, but the law also allows certain corporations to retain (instead of these documents) microfilm. All accounting information is required to be kept for a period of five years. The law allows businesses to maintain their accounting records on computer.

5.2

Legal Disputes in the UAE

by Alastair J. McNair, W.S. (on secondment from Clifford Chance), Hadef Al Dhahiri & Associates

Disputes – who needs them? As elsewhere in the world, disputes in the UAE can be expensive and time consuming. They may well require the input of substantial amounts of management time and expertise, particularly where they concern technical aspects. Often they arise as a consequence of the failure by one or both parties to properly evaluate their position and potential exposure, this assessment perhaps being influenced by emotive factors. Either way, think long and hard before going the extra mile into formal dispute. A compromise may well leave both sides content with the outcome but may, where looked at in the overall context, be the most satisfactory outcome, enabling one to proceed in other areas.

The legal environment

Under the UAE constitution each of the seven Emirates has its own court system and the right to promote law (applicable only in that Emirate) in areas permitted by the constitution. The area of commercial law is a matter which, under the constitution, is a largely federal matter with the exception only of Dubai and Ras Al Khaimah (which 'contracted out' at the time of the provisional constitution's ratification in 1971–72), and the court systems operate under the supervision of the Federal Ministry of Justice.

The court structure

For all practical purposes two types of courts exist. The civil courts deal with commercial and civil matters, and also criminal matters. The Sharia courts deal primarily with matters of an Islamic nature, including family law and succession, applying the Sharia in areas where there are no laws of direct relevance.

The lowest courts, with the highest volumes of business, are the Courts of First Instance. The Courts of First Instance deal with most commercial and civil matters, including debt collection. The bench consists of between one and three judges, dependent upon the importance of the case in question.

Appeals from the Courts of First Instance (on either the merits of the case or on points of law) go to the Court of Appeal, where three judges form the bench.

The final appeal court is the Supreme Court (also sometimes called the Court of Cassation). Appeals may only be made to the Supreme Court on points of law. The bench consists of five judges.

Appeals result in the case being referred back to the underlying/junior court with instructions for what is, in effect, 'reconsideration'. As a consequence of this, once an appeal has reached the Supreme Court for the second time its decision in the case in point is absolute and conclusive.

Legislation of direct relevance

Commercial disputes are subject to the Commercial Procedures Law and the Evidence Law of 1992. The former specifically recognises arbitration, whereas the latter is not directly relevant to arbitration. Additionally, the Commercial Transactions Law of 1993 and the UAE Civil Code of 1986 are relevant, together with the remaining concerned laws – for example the Companies Law (as amended) and the Trade Agencies Law.

Procedural and other aspects

Procedurally, matters within the courts system are similar to those elsewhere in the region. It is possible to obtain various 'interim remedies' – for example, the attachment of bank accounts, ships or aircraft, or prohibiting a person from travelling where there is a genuine fear that the person may abscond. The granting of these remedies is a discretionary matter for the judges concerned and may or may not require support by some type of security. A decision issued in this area is not appealable.

The enforcement of foreign judgements

The enforcement of foreign judgements is specifically provided for in the Civil Procedures Law of 1992. A foreign judgement must meet certain criteria:

- the defendant has been properly served with notice of the foreign proceedings (and therefore given the opportunity to be represented in them);
- the foreign decision is absolute (or non-appealable);
- the decision is not contrary to law or public policy in the UAE, such as judgements for gambling debts (as elsewhere in the world) or substantial compound interest elements in Abu Dhabi (at least for these elements).

Judgements for margin calls, etc, as a consequence of the speculative use of derivatives, are probably not enforceable under these arrangements.

The UAE will generally recognise judgements given in Arab League and Gulf Co-operation Council states, under reciprocal arrangements. There is also a reciprocal recognition arrangement with France, which has been enabled under UAE law.

International arbitration

An international arbitral decision is regarded as a foreign judgement and must consequently comply with the criteria stated above. Sufficient to say, it is possible for the parties to agree to international arbitration. However, not in all areas, for example, matters concerning trade agencies, commercial agencies and distributorships where UAE law states that in all cases it has relevance (effectively regardless of what the parties contractually agree), this being binding upon them. To make this cost-effective, the amounts in question must be substantial – but the parties may consider that it is worth it. This may also serve to reassure those involved in projects or other financings. For example, recent privatisation documentation in Abu Dhabi specifically recognises the concept of ICC arbitration in Paris, thus benefiting potentially from the enforcement provisions referred to above.

Problems with the courts

As with elsewhere in the world, the courts in the UAE operate under a substantial burden of work. This is particularly true of the lower courts (those of First Instance) and, partly in consequence of this, there has been a tendency of the courts to refer matters to experts (who report to the court in question). Experts are invariably required to identify the overall factual position and these experts practise in the commercial area in question. The problem with this is simple – in many respects the final decision is made by an arbitrator (or third party) and, as such, one is better off going directly into arbitration. Furthermore, the experts are invariably not well paid under the Ministry of Justice determined rates. As a consequence of this, arbitration is preferable to litigation before the courts.

Arbitration

As an alternative to litigation, arbitration is specifically recognised under the Civil Procedures Law of 1992. Dependent upon the circumstances in question, it may provide a faster and more cost-effective method of dispute settlement – although, as in many disputes elsewhere, the associated legal costs may be substantial. Possibly more importantly in the age of the Internet and increasing press freedom in the area, it is a private forum – whereas proceedings in the courts may be attended by anyone.

Under the provisions of the Civil Procedures Law of 1992:

- References to arbitration must be in writing;
- The number of arbitrators must be uneven (to avoid split decisions) and decisions are by majority;
- Procedural aspects are substantively matters for the arbitrators in question **unless** the parties have previously agreed a specific procedure; and
- The decision should be given in the UAE and requires validation by the UAE Courts.

At a practical level both the Abu Dhabi and Dubai Chambers of Commerce and Industry operate Arbitration Centres. That of Dubai is more proactive, requiring a form of what is effectively mandatory conciliation of disputes brought to it. Each of these schemes has established secretariats, procedures and controls operating on the basis of the criteria set out above. Both operate approved lists of arbitrators with appropriate specialisations. The proceedings in question may take place in English or Arabic, as the parties choose. There is an increasing preference for the use of arbitration in commercial matters, both amongst foreign and local companies and institutions. In at least one case, the parties to a litigation by agreement (this was the only thing they could agree upon) have removed a case from the courts (where it had been for four years or so) and referred it to arbitration, which has now been concluded.

A sample arbitration clause for use in Abu Dhabi follows:

Arbitration

In the event of any dispute, controversy or claim arising from this Agreement or matters related thereto the same shall be referred to arbitration before three arbitrators to be chosen from the approved list/panel of arbitrators maintained by Abu Dhabi Commercial Conciliation and Arbitration Centre ('ADCCAC') at the relevant time. Each of the parties hereto shall appoint one arbitrator with the remaining /third arbitrator to be chosen mutually by the two arbitrators previously chosen. The procedural and other aspects of such arbitration to be governed by the regulations of ADCCAC in force at such time. All arbitration proceedings are to take place in Abu Dhabi, UAE, in the English language except to the extent that compliance with the UAE formalities may so require. The decision of such arbitration [shall be notified to the parties within six months of the reference to arbitration being made and] shall be final and binding upon the parties hereto (and enforceable against them) [save in the case of manifest error or fraud]. The said arbitrators may award legal fees and expenses as they think fit. The said arbitrators shall not award punitive, special or consequential damages nor compensation for loss of opportunity, revenue or profit.

5.3

Taxation in the United Arab Emirates

Bob Peake, Arthur Andersen, Dubai

Although tax decrees exist in the emirates, most businesses are not subject to income tax. The exceptions are oil and gas producing companies, petrochemical companies, branches of foreign banks, and international courier companies. Therefore, the UAE has become an attractive location for foreign companies not only operating in the Emirates but also for the establishment of regional and international activities. Further incentives are provided by free zones established in the various emirates and a large number of multinationals are now located in the country. Despite the limited direct taxation of businesses, the UAE has negotiated more than 12 double taxation treaties. In many cases, these provide exceptional tax efficiencies for multinationals, not only in their home country but also in those countries in which they operate from a UAE base.

There are no personal income taxes. The main taxes likely to affect a foreign business in the UAE are customs duties, sales tax on hotels and municipality tax on property.

Income taxes

There is no federal tax law in the UAE. However, the individual emirates have issued tax decrees. Generally, these potentially tax all companies carrying on a trade or business through a permanent establishment (e.g. a branch, place of management, or a dependent agent) in the emirate. However, in practice, only certain types of companies are subject to taxation. Oil and gas producers and petrochemical companies are taxed in accordance with their concession agreements with the respective governments, and the branches of foreign banks are taxed under the terms of agreements with the rulers of each emirate. There is a turnover-based tax applied to courier companies in respect of income arising from within the UAE.

Double tax treaties

The UAE has concluded, or is in the process of ratifying, tax treaties with the following countries: Belgium, Canada, China, Czech Republic, Egypt, Finland, France, Germany, India, Indonesia, Italy, Malaysia, Pakistan, Poland, Singapore, Sweden, Thailand, Tunisia, and Turkey. It is believed that other tax treaties are at various stages of discussion. The existence of an extensive treaty network gives the UAE a unique position as a tax efficient hub for activities in the key business centres of Europe, the Far East, and the Indian sub-continent. This potential for cost management of international taxation by multinationals is further enhanced by the existence of the free zones, which are generally covered by the tax treaties.

The benefits accorded vary from treaty to treaty. However, the treaty terms are generally favourable, with nil or low withholding taxes on dividends, interest and royalties paid to the UAE. Additionally, the permanent establishment articles normally follow the standard OECD model, demarcating taxation rights and providing for the allowance of costs attributable to business activities.

The free zones

There are free zones throughout the UAE offering an attractive tax and operational environment for a wide range of businesses. The incentives typically include 100 per cent foreign ownership, no personal and capital taxes, a guarantee of no corporate taxes for a set period, no customs duty within the zone, 100 per cent foreign repatriation of capital and profits, and no currency restrictions. Each free zone normally offers a choice of business licences allowing for various types of business to be located there. The main licences are industrial (manufacturing, processing), trading (warehousing, distribution, sales), service (catering, travel agencies, cargo and freight forwarding, legal, accounting, financial etc.). Recent developments have seen the establishment of specially focused free zones including the Abu Dhabi Free Zone Saaiyat Market (international capital and commodities centre) and the proposed Dubai Internet City. The latter will be of particular interest to the growing number of multinationals in e-business. The international taxation of e-business is a complex area and the availability of a tax-free location with an extensive tax treaty network provides a major opportunity for effective tax cost management.

Customs duties and other taxes

Customs duty for imports into the UAE is 4 per cent, the lowest in the region. There is an agreement that the members of the Gulf Cooperation

Council (UAE, Saudi Arabia, Kuwait, Qatar, Oman and Bahrain) will standardise their rates to between 5.5 per cent and 7.5 per cent by the year 2005. Businesses that are at least 51 per cent GCC owned and that add at least 40 per cent value to a finished product within the GCC may export to other GCC member states without customs duty. Free zone businesses may apply for a national industrial licence that, subject to similar conditions outlined above, may also be able to export into GCC member countries without customs duty being paid.

The other taxes that may be encountered by a foreign company doing business in the UAE are a tax on hotel accommodation and a municipality tax on rented residential and commercial property. These taxes range from 5–10 per cent.

Summary

The UAE provides a rare combination of a generally tax free jurisdiction with an advanced economic and commercial infrastructure. The combination of its strategic geographical location, the free zones and a large tax treaty network makes the UAE an attractive regional and international centre for a wide range of multinationals.

Part 6

The Financial Structure and Banking System

Information
Parking
Airport
Bank

6.1

Banking: Introspection Verses Innovation

Paul Hawkins

The growth in assets in the UAE banks over the past ten years reflects the growth in government projects, continued oil revenues, the construction boom, and the continued development of the bread and butter re-export business, in particular in the emirate of Dubai, with particular focus on the markets of the GCC countries, the Indian sub-continent, the Far East and the new economies of the former communist countries. The development of the banking sector is summarised in Table 6.1.1.

The years up to 1998 reflect uninterrupted growth. During 1999, however, the Central Bank has had to take a more cautious approach to the credit issue in the areas of both corporate and consumer banking and, before predicting the future, it is necessary to become introspective and look into the circumstances which have led to the current situation.

A comparison of local banks with international bank results reveals the strength of competition the international banks are facing in terms of local deposits. The future of local banking might well be determined by the amount of investment in technology each bank makes, in particular in the area of Internet and on-line banking, where Citibank and HSBC are among the global leaders. The success of these two banks in the local markets, in particular in the next two years in the areas of customer deposits, could serve as a yardstick to assess the future strategy of banking. Suddenly the inability of the international banks to expand their branch network could be a blessing, as they will have saved considerable costs in an era when the need for branch banking will slowly decline.

1999 – Redressing the balance

To examine the least controversial issue first. Personal lending by UAE banks, which has included loans which are only partially secured, has reached levels which are causing concern to both the banks themselves and the Central Bank. Total lending in such loans by mid-1999 seems to have escalated out of all proportion to other balance sheet components. It

Table 6.1.1 Comparative analysis of results of UAE banks 1996-98

Local banks							
	Year	Assets	Equity	Cust. Dep.	Net. Inc.	RoE	3 Year asset growth
NATIONAL BANK OF ABU DHABI	1998	35,130	2,519	27,727	399	16%	24%
	1997	31,135	2,307	24,600	409	18%	
	1966	28,378	2,085	22,489	313	15%	
NATIONAL BANK OF DUBAI	1998	24,377	3,688	18,812	402	11%	11%
	1997	23,056	3,634	17,884	384	11%	
	1996	22,591	3,598	17,321	363	10%	
ABU DHABI COMMERCIAL BANK	1998	21,631	2,862	14,739	505	18%	46%
	1997	18,580	2,544	13,043	452	18%	
	1996	14,797	2,217	9,101	362	16%	
EMIRATES BANK INTERNATIONAL	1998	19,713	2,822	14,133	473	17%	25%
	1997	17,164	2,453	12,716	442	18%	
	1996	15,786	2,107	11,992	382	18%	
MASHREQ BANK	1998	18,257	2187	12,953	501	23%	18%
	1997	17,300	1,875	12,418	485	26%	
	1996	15,424	1,615	11,521	350	22%	
COMMERCIAL BANK OF DUBAI	1998	6,061	997	4,613	180	18%	55%
	1997	4,757	853	3,597	165	19%	
	1996	3,907	758	2,959	144	19%	

Table 6.1.1 *Continued*

International banks							
	Year	Assets	Equity	Cust. Dep.	Net. Inc.	RoE	3 Year asset Growth
HSBC	1998	12,271	1,371	8,352	369	27%	33%
	1997	11,722	1,182	8,549	321	27%	
	1996	9,168	860	7,072	255	30%	
STANDARD CHARTERED	1998	8,138	580	4,481	128	22%	45%
	1997	5,796	631	4,251	92	15%	
	1996	5,584	539	4,009	84	16%	
CITIBANK	1998	6,162	613	3,331	130	21%	23%
	1997	5,333	484	3,107	114	24%	
	1996	5,015	495	2,698	100	20%	
ARAB BANK	1998	3,660	302	3,096	51	17%	18%
	1997	3,366	271	2,850	56	21%	
	1996	3,109	265	2,613	54	21%	

appears that an unhealthy proportion of this lending is targeted towards either the youth market or borrowers investing in the local stock market, which during 1999 has fallen by 16 per cent, more than any other stock market in the GCC. In contrast, in other similarly-developing economies during 1999 the Egyptian stock market was up by 50 per cent, the Saudi Arabian by 40 per cent and the Turkish by an astonishing 380 per cent.

The more controversial issue is that of Solo Industries and Madhav Patel. Over a period of several years he ran what was considered a reputable scrap metal business with his father and he succeeded in not only developing a top class client base but also in gaining the support of a portfolio of some of the Gulf's major banking institutions, mostly in the area of trade finance facilities. One or two banks withdrew their support two to three years ago but the facilities continued to be offered by all the remaining banks until in April, 1999, his credit-worthiness began to be questioned and, following a hasty departure, bad debts of some US$250 million have been left with a total of 14 banks. Falsified documentary letters of credit and bills of lading were given as the key reason for the fraud. Where it all went wrong with Solo Industries is still open to speculation.

The combination of the Central Bank's stance concerning the risks of unsecured consumer lending and the mid-year credit crisis caused by Solo Industries, has caused a dilemma in the local markets. But it is now time to move on, as the banks have completed their reports, made the necessary year-end provisions, pulled in their reins a little and must now consider the dawning of the new millennium. This new era heralds continued expansion of the UAE economy despite fluctuating oil prices and productivity levels and a continuation of creativity in future government projects which now include Dubai Internet City and the Saadiyat Market. What therefore faces the UAE banking sector?

The future challenge

The following terms are currently ascribed to the future of local banking – globalisation, privatisation, the WTO, mergers and acquisitions, among others. Each of them can be ignored in the context of the current analysis. Each has its own importance but none of them is likely to influence the immediate future. The banking mergers in Saudi Arabia and between Gulf International Bank (GIB) and Saudi International Bank (SIB) have had little effect on the local markets and the merger between the two local Dubai banking giants, although very logical, and being conducted with commendable patience and fortitude, is unlikely to be completed for a couple of years, although as a strategic alliance the two banks are probably already working together. The challenge will be for the two banks to emerge as one at the forefront of technology.

The Internet challenge is the one which is already focusing the attention of the rest of the world. A recent retail banking conference in Florida confirmed what had been suspected. The Internet and e-commerce are beginning to change the face of banking all over the world. This then is the challenge for banks in the UAE and it is not merely a consumer issue. On-line trading of securities is actually taking place and it is now second nature for customers to access their accounts through the Internet, pay their electricity, water and gas bills and make transfers to other accounts. Where one goes from here is anyone's guess, but B2B might have the answer. The most innovative of the UAE banks will find the solution to success in the local markets and begin developing e-commerce alliances with their own customers. Their toughest competitors are likely to be the major foreign banks. It is an exciting prospect.

Dubai Internet City, which is in advanced stages of planning allied to the proposed Internet University, adds some icing to the cake, and with the incredible developments of e-commerce in other parts of the world, this project is not only innovative, it also ensures the Middle East keeps in touch with technological developments elsewhere.

The Saadiyat Market being developed in Abu Dhabi is another project attracting considerable interest amongst local and foreign financial institutions. Tax advantages, commodities trading and the creation of a time zone to take in the Middle East, including the fast growing economies of Egypt and possibly Turkey plus the trading instincts of the Lebanese, and also the Indian sub-continent, are seen to be the keys to success in this project. However, the feasibility of this whole project is still being finalised, which includes the establishment of a legal and regulatory framework which will be acceptable not only to the Central Bank but also to the participating financial institutions themselves.

Conclusions

The hybrid local trading instincts which have been the hallmark of the incredible development of this country over the past 20 years, which has made it unrecognisable to people returning after an absence from this part of the world, will continue to play a prominent role in the future. Indirect taxation, keeping to the forefront of technology, the continued availability of oil revenues for re-investment into the local economy, privatisation and the strengthening of the local stock markets, are the major challenges.The current prognosis is that the UAE will still be in a very prominent position on the map of the world in 20 years' time, due to its political stability and the fact that the advantages of trading here far outweigh the disadvantages.

Paul Hawkins
Writer on banking and technology
Tel: (9714) 3321145
e-mail banktech99@yahoo.com

6.2

Islamic Banking Practices

Dr Bashir O M Fadlalla, Islamic Development Bank

'There are untapped markets, a vast Islamic pool of money out there which hitherto has been rather starved of avenues' *South China Morning Post*, 1 February, 1996

Introduction

This section discusses various Islamic banking products that are currently available to businessmen, both investors and traders. In the context of a perspective of the history of Islamic banking, a working definition of Islamic banking is provided to the reader. It has also been attempted to explain the religious basis of Islamic banking, which has its origin and foundation in the teachings of Islam – a topic which is often not very well comprehended in the West.

Also provided are definitions, features and application of some of the Islamic modes of finance that are currently utilised for resource mobilisation and for the financing of investment and trade. While this review of Islamic banking practices is in no way comprehensive, it does cover the major modes of finance available.

Background to Islamic banking

For a number of years now Islamic banking and finance has grown as a distinctive field of business and of study throughout the Islamic and non-Islamic world.[1] Indeed, its rate of growth has been encouraging, given the

1 The first quasi-Islamic banks were established in Malaysia and Egypt in the early 1960s in the form of the Pilgrims Fund in Malaysia (1968) and in the form of a savings bank in Egypt (1963). But the very first fully-fledged Islamic bank was Dubai Islamic Bank, chartered in the UAE in 1975. The Islamic Development Bank started its operation in the same year, although it was formally set up in 1973. Today there is a confirmed Islamic banking presence in more than 30 countries, notably in Africa, the Middle East, the Far East, Europe and the United States. Three countries, Iran, Pakistan and Sudan, have an Islamic banking system, while Malaysia has a parallel banking system where Islamic financial institutions operate side by side with conventional financial institutions.

short span of time in which it has come into being. Today more than 30 countries throughout the world have Islamic banks operating side by side with conventional banks. These include such countries/regions as the GCC, Africa, Iran, Pakistan, South East Asia, Europe and the United States. The growth of Islamic banks indicates that there is a growing demand for their services and products. In addition, major conventional banks have also opened Islamic banking windows to cater to the financial needs of Muslims.

It is worth noting that after only three decades or so, Islamic banking has come to be accepted as an integral part of the world financial order which, together with other financial systems, is helping through the globalisation process in integrating the world economy. This section seeks to answer the questions:

- what is Islamic banking?
- what are the objectives of Islamic finance and in what way does it differ from conventional finance rendered by conventional banks and other conventional financial institutions?
- what is the underlying philosophy and what are the governing principles of Islamic banking, and what are its operational characteristics?
- what are some of the most important services/products that are currently being utilised as modes of financing for production and trade, and how available are those services to the ordinary investor or consumer?

The answers to these questions as presented in this section are designed in such a way as to indicate the theoretical foundation and the sphere of application in today's business environment. Notwithstanding this, the section seeks to provide a practical guide for those wishing to know more about Islamic banking and finance.

A working definition of Islamic banking

Islamic banking may be defined as the practice of banking business in conformity with Sharia – Islamic law. The main differentiating factor between conventional banking and Islamic Sharia based banking is that in the latter the payment and the receipt of interest (Riba) is not allowed. Islamic banking derives its inspirations and guidance from the religious edicts of Islam and has to conduct its operations strictly in accordance with the directives of Sharia. That is why Islamic banks often need to institute a Sharia Board to be responsible for screening and scrutinising their operations. Over and above this, as may be expected, an Islamic bank also has to comply with the law of the land (jurisdiction). As such it may also find itself in need of the counsel of traditional lawyers.

However, Islamic banking should not be perceived merely in the narrow context of the prohibition of the payment of interest, as is often the case. Rather, it is a financial system which focuses on mobilising and organising resources for the betterment of not only the individual, but also for society as a whole. This is well within the framework of the overall Islamic economic system, which strives to build a society based on social justice, equity, moderation and balanced relationships – a society in which exploitation, deceit and irrationality in the use of resources are very much abhorred. In such a system, the individual Muslim is constantly reminded of the Islamic aspiration that all resources available to human beings 'must always be put to optimum use, and no one has the right to hoard them or to keep them idle, or to squander them, or to use them for conspicuous consumption or wanton display, be it the individual, the community or the state'.[2]

The religious basis of Islamic banking

Islamic banking is primarily based on the Sharia, often referred to in the writings of Western scholars as Islamic jurisprudence. As such, it is part of the overall teachings of Islam which encompasses all aspects of the life and activities of the individual, family, society, state and the *Ummah* – all the Muslim community as a whole.

The Sharia is divided into:

- *Ibadat*, which describes man's relationship with God reflected in worshipping and;
- *Mua'malat*, which describes men's interacting activities among themselves.

A significant part of mua'malat is the daily conduct of economic activities under whose umbrella lie financial and banking activities. Islamic banking, therefore, has its direct origin in Sharia law.

But Sharia itself is derived from two primary sources, namely:

- the *Quran*, which is the ultimate word of God and;
- the *Sunnah*, which is the sayings, teachings and the deeds of the Holy Prophet Mohamed (peace be upon him).

All the laws derived from the above two sources are then categorised into five levels indicating the degree of enforcement of that law. These levels are:

---

[2] Adapted from Muzzam Ali, *Reflections on Islamic Banking* – The Institution of Islamic Banking and Insurance.

- *FARD* or *Wajib* – an obligatory duty, the omission of which is punishable;
- *MANDOUB* or *Mustahab* – an action which is rewarded, but its omission is not punishable;
- *JAIZ* or *Mubah* – an action which is permitted, and the law is indifferent;
- *MAKRUH* – an action which is disliked yet not punishable, but its omission is rewarded;
- *HARAAM* – an action which is absolutely forbidden and is punishable.

Accordingly, banking and financial activities, being part of Sharia law and of mua'malat, are themselves subject to the above categorisation. In conducting his daily business activities, a Muslim would screen his deeds in the light of these guiding principles and would subsequently make decisions. It is, therefore, not only material satisfaction (be it profit maximisation, cost minimisation, attainment of high quality of product or whatever) that guides his decision-making process, but also, and perhaps more so, religious abidance and spiritual satisfaction that are of the essence.

Islamic banking services

Islam allows both equity financing and debt financing. Equity financing is normally effected through profit-sharing contracts, while debt financing is effected through deferred contracts of exchange. The most distinguishing features of Islamic modes include financing of real transactions and rescheduling of financing without interest.

Equity financing

Keeping in mind the five levels of Sharia law discussed earlier, there are no major differences between Islamic finance and conventional finance as far as equity financing is concerned. However, some schools of thought are of the view that equity investment in an enterprise which has even a small portion of conventional debt is not halal. The contract of al-musharakah (joint venture profit-sharing) is, in essence, similar to the conventional concept of the joint-stock company.[3] Therefore, to finance projects through equity participation, float a company on the stock exchange, organise a venture capital company, or form an equity unit trust, would

[3] *BIMB*, 1994, p.22.

generally be the same under Islamic equity financing as under conventional equity financing. However, there is an important qualification in that considering the case of equity alternatives, the given equity stocks must meet some additional criteria to conform to Islamic norms. All business activities of the company issuing the stocks should be 'halal' or permissible. Given this requirement, stocks of companies belonging to breweries, entertainment industries or interest-based (i.e. financed through conventional sources) businesses where the major product is 'haraam', or forbidden, will fall under the forbidden category.

Al-Mudaraba (trustee profit-sharing)

This instrument may be utilised for project financing whereby the Islamic bank becomes the 'provider of capital' and may provide 100 per cent of the capital requirement. The sponsor of the project or the 'entrepreneur' will undertake to manage the project and as such the bank normally does not interfere in the management details, but has the right to conduct follow-up and supervision. The two parties agree a priori through negotiations on the distribution of the realised profits. Should the project incur a loss, the bank bears all the losses. However, it should be made clear that this is true only when no neglect or misconduct on the part of the capital-user is ascertained. It thus becomes clear that the proven viability of the project, the tested managerial capability of the sponsor, and the degree to which the Islamic bank is capable of follow-up and supervision, are key elements in the successful implementation of the project and the avoidance of losses for the bank and its shareholders.

Using this device, the bank may utilise shareholders' funds and customers' deposits to set up wholly-owned subsidiaries, take up equity in (Sharia compatible) quoted or unquoted companies or other types of portfolio investment. The ability of the Islamic bank to identify, appraise, analyse the risk of, and manage that portfolio must therefore be ascertained.

Al-Musharaka (joint-venture profit-sharing)

This instrument may also be utilised to finance acceptable projects whereby the Islamic bank together with the sponsor(s) of the project agree a priori on the proportions of the project's capital each will shoulder. While each party has the right to be involved in the project management, decision to do so or not is voluntary. As in the case of al-mudarabah, the ratio of profit distribution is fixed in advance through negotiations, and this may not necessarily tally with the ratio of participation in capital. However, unlike al-mudarabah, should the project make a loss, all parties bear the loss proportionately.

Islamic (equity) funds

A good example of the musharakah concept is Islamic equity funds which, though a new phenomenon, have already grown into an important source of funds and of investment. As such, they are expected to play a central role in the future of Islamic finance.

Islamic funds have grown substantially over the past 18 years or so, with an estimated annual growth of 10 to 15 per cent. It is widely believed that this market will in ten years' time be responsible for managing at least 40 to 50 per cent of the total savings of Muslims world-wide.

The Gulf region is growing into a centre of financial intermediation with Bahrain being the industry's favourite offshore centre where key players have established themselves. Neighbouring Kuwait and Saudi Arabia command sizeable market shares in terms of managed fund levels. However, the Malaysia experience figures prominently in terms of product blending and financial engineering within the confines of Sharia, particularly to arrange deals which can provide limited or full equity participation for an agreed period of investment on a clearly defined profit-sharing basis.

However, as mentioned earlier, some of the Islamic schools of thought hold the view that investment in equity of an enterprise which has any conventional debt is not in accordance with Sharia. This makes it difficult to find suitable equity investments and much more difficult to set up equity based unit trusts/mutual funds.

The current most popular Islamic funds are open-ended unit trusts or mutual funds with the underlying investments in stocks and shares which are listed on one or more stock markets. This becomes all the more important since there is ample evidence that in the medium and long term, a diversified portfolio of equities in developed markets produces a higher total rate of return than most other types of assets class. Given good diversification across markets and sectors and reliable stock markets, the major risk relating to higher price volatility[4] can be greatly reduced. Even though there are still some differences among Sharia scholars on the eligibility of companies for equity investments, the following general criteria are acceptable by most:

- the company should carry on its business in a manner compatible with Sharia;
- investments should not be made in companies involved in riba-based businesses – thus conventional banking, insurance, finance and securities will not qualify;
- the company should not engage in the manufacture, distribution and trading of any alcoholic beverages, pork or armaments and ammunitions;
- it should not deal in gambling and games of chance;

[4] loosely defined to be the percentage movement of prices from an average price base.

- debts and cash should not constitute more than 50 per cent of the company's overall assets.

Quasi equities
In addition to the above, new modes of financing are evolving such as 'declining participation', which can be classified as quasi-equity.

Debt financing

Debt financing is the area where Islamic financing differs a great deal from conventional financing. In the latter, debt financing is almost entirely interest-based while this contract is totally forbidden in Islam (i.e. haraam).[5] On the other hand, Islamic debt financing instruments of deferred contracts of exchange are not used very frequently in the conventional financial system. An exception will be the contracts of *al-ijara* (leasing) and *al-murabaha* (deferred lump-sum sale) which are often practised in the conventional system.

Al-Bai Bithaman Ajil (instalment sale) for financing the acquisition of assets
It is permissible for the Islamic bank to finance a customer who wishes to acquire a given asset and to pay by instalment or to defer the payment altogether over an agreed period of time. Under this mode of financing, and to comply with the requirements of Sharia, the bank first purchases the asset concerned and then sells it to the customer at the actual cost of purchase plus a mark-up. The mark-up is meant to reflect the cost of administration plus a profit margin.

Al-Ijara (leasing) for financing the use of services of assets
All categories of enterprises (from large-scale to small and medium, i.e. SMEs) require the services of a given asset to help them in conducting their normal business. Here also, the bank purchases the asset desired by the customer and leases it to him for a fixed agreed period of time. Lease rentals and all other terms and conditions are agreed with the customer in advance through business negotiations. Both the rental payment and the lease period are usually determined in light of the projected profitability and cash-flow of the project. Although the asset will need to be insured by the customer, the mark-up will always be designed to reflect various risks.

---

[5] Reference here is to Riba al-Nasia which involves an increment on the principal of a loan to be paid by the borrower. The arrangement is that one party would lend money to another on the understanding that the latter would return the money at the end of an agreed period, the sum of which will comprise the original sum of money borrowed plus an increment in consideration of the former having granted the borrower time to pay.

These risks can be spread between a number of banks/ financial institutions through a syndication arrangement. The bank retains the ownership of the leased assets throughout the entire lease period. After the end of the lease and full payment of the rentals by the lessee, the Bank transfers the ownership of the equipment to the lessee as a 'gift'.

Istisna' financing

Istisna' is a contract for manufacturing/construction and sale or supply of goods (capital goods or other assets).[6] It is a contract where the manufacturer (seller) undertakes to supply the buyer with goods of agreed technical specification, within an agreed time frame and at an agreed price.

Istisna', is an instrument of pre-shipment financing. Unlike in the case of murabahah, *istisna'* is binding on both parties upon signing of the contract. The buyer (beneficiary) is obliged to take delivery of the goods manufactured within the stipulated time and specifications. As is clear, *istisna'* being a medium and long-term financing mode, can effectively enhance the manufacturing capabilities of the economy while availing needed goods and assets for further production. The role of the Islamic bank is to finance the contract thus reached between the beneficiary and the manufacturer through a separate contract with the beneficiary.

Moreover, *istisna'* can be utilised for the financing of infrastructure projects and trade in the private sector and also for intangible assets like gas and electricity. By being suitable for both project and trade finance, *istisna'* helps in creating linkages between various sectors of the economy in the framework of pre-shipment financing which would include financing of working capital which is not otherwise possible under leasing and instalment sale.

Al Murabaha (deferred lump-sum sale) letter of credit for trade financing

While the previous modes of 'project' finance cover both medium and the long terms, the bank may also finance trade mostly on a short-term basis including the financing of working capital. This includes the whole range of import-export (or purchase/sale) of goods and machinery, the acquisition and holding of stock and inventories, raw materials and semi-finished goods.

In the above context, and under an al-murabaha contract, the customer approaches the bank with certain letter of credit requirements. The bank agrees to purchase/import the goods on the understanding that the client will subsequently purchase the goods from the bank on an al-murabaha basis. The Islamic bank establishes the letter of credit and pays from its own funds to the requiring bank. The Islamic bank then sells the goods to

[6] *IDB*, 1996

the client at a sale price covering the cost plus a profit margin. The settlement is deferred to an agreed date.

Concluding remarks

In this review of Islamic banking practices, for the purpose of simplicity, Islamic banking has been defined as 'the practice of banking business in conformity with Sharia – Islamic law'. As such, Islamic banking and finance derives its origins from Islamic jurisprudence whose axioms are the Quran and the Sunnah. Islamic banking is not merely the prohibition of riba, or interest, as it is sometimes mistakenly interpreted. It is rather a financial system which focuses on mobilising and organising resources for the betterment of not only the individual but also of society as a whole.

It has been pointed out that Islam allows both equity financing and debt financing. Equity financing is normally effected through profit-sharing contracts like al-mudarabah (trustee profit-sharing) and al-musharakah (joint-venture profit-sharing) and equity funds, while debt-financing comprises a whole list of products. Examples of such products are deferred instalment sale, leasing, *istisna'*, and deferred lump-sum sale. Therefore there are a number of financial products pioneered by Islamic banking for resource mobilisation, project and trade financing and investment in general. Current efforts in the area of financial engineering are likely to expand Islamic banking products to new frontiers in the foreseeable future.

Islamic banking and finance in the UAE

At the present time there are two Islamic banks in the UAE – Abu Dhabi Islamic Bank and Dubai Islamic Bank. The former of these is a young institution, whereas the latter was established 25 years ago. Late in 1999 these two banks teamed up to form two new Islamic subsidiaries – an insurance company and a finance institution.

In addition, the Islamic Investment Company of the Gulf, a Saudi Arabian-owned Islamic investment company, is registered in Sharjah. Islamic investment funds are also to be found, including the new balanced fund developed by Abu Dhabi Islamic bank and which is to be registered in Saadiyat Market (see Chapter 6.5).

6.3

The Insurance Environment

Iain L Reid, Regional Operations and Development Manager, Norwich Union Middle East

The UAE Ministry of Economy and Commerce statistics for 1996 revealed the total market premium at US$664 million in an insurance industry employing 2619 persons. The 1999 estimate of the figure is US$750 million, which makes it the third largest insurance market in the Arab world, after Morocco and Saudi Arabia and, with a population of only 2.6 million, this reflects the UAE's wealth. Insurance business is polarised between the oil rich Abu Dhabi Emirate and the service-driven Dubai and Sharjah Emirates.

Corporate

Businessmen seeking out government contract business in Abu Dhabi will find they are required to insure through any one of the six national insurers and, whilst insurance rates will be competitive, after sales service is probably some way behind what would be expected from a European insurer. Many international contractors use their broker to analyse, negotiate and place their insurance covers. There are no such restrictions in Dubai or Sharjah that are open and dynamic markets and where competition for business is keen. The UAE offers a highly diverse trading environment from huge petrochemical investments in Abu Dhabi, a world leading aluminium producer in Dubai and a strong re-export trade. While this is currently subdued by normal standards, it has certainly been a key ingredient behind Dubai's success.

With its ports handling over 2 million TEUs per year, Dubai ranks about twelfth in the world. Jebel Ali Free Zone has underpinned its success, having over 900 companies employing some 35,000 people.

Warehousing is a serious risk and a fire in a high concentration of stocks in open configuration will virtually guarantee total losses. Whilst even the

JAFZ has seen serious losses, the frequency is low, which is testimony to its infrastructure and management.

Perhaps it is in marine insurance where underwriters' skills are really tested to the full, whether covering exports/re-exports to Iran – one of Dubai's key re-export markets – Africa, the Caspian region, CIS or further afield. Notwithstanding the journey or hazards, businessmen are able to obtain coverage even now, and at competitive prices. A recent start up of a credit insurance joint venture will undoubtedly help to promote non-oil export from the region.

There are now 50 insurers in the UAE, 27 of which are foreign, and 125 insurance brokers and consultants, providing a plethora of choice. Applications for all new licences have now been closed. All insurance-related entities are regulated by the Ministry of Economy and Commerce in Abu Dhabi, who in 1995 laid down further legislation requiring insurers to increase their paid up capitals to Dh50 million (US$13.6 million) by 2001. Insurance brokers and consultants are required to carry professional indemnity insurance for Dh1.5 million (US$408,500). If mergers were anticipated, none has yet occurred, for in a market which has chronic over-capacity consolidation really is required to bring about a stronger insurance base having fewer but better capitalised players and which in turn will reduce the enormous outflow of reinsurance. For example many local insurers will retain perhaps as little as 10 per cent of their fire, marine or other portfolios.

Players who have not as yet attained a critical mass will find it increasingly difficult to do so in an intensely competitive and innovative marketplace where margins are likely to remain thin. Reinsurance markets can eventually expect to harden and players who have overly relied, unnecessarily so, on the reinsurance markets may find themselves quickly priced out of their own markets by larger players.

Personal

Interestingly, motor insurance is only compulsory by law in Abu Dhabi and Ras alKhaimah. However, in practice it is needed throughout the UAE since the police require evidence of renewal of your annual registration licence. Cars are competitively priced by western standards, though spare parts are expensive and over 70 per cent of cars are insured comprehensively, making it the largest class of insurance business in the UAE.

Whilst the road infrastructure is good and driving standards are better than in many Arab countries, much higher traffic volumes have led to increases in claims' frequencies, which has led to a rapid deterioration in motor results over the last 12 months, exacerbated, of course, by competition between insurers. Where death claims occur, these are settled for a minimum of Dh150,000 (US$40,900), referred to as 'Diya' (blood money).

If there is disablement then a medical committee will report to the court that will then decide the award. Serious injury cases frequently go to the civil court, where awards above the 'Diya' are likely, and there have been numerous claims over US$500,000 if involving permanent disablement.

There is minimum third party policy coverage laid down by the Ministry. Called 'unified cover', this includes unlimited third party bodily injury cover. However, many reputable insurers will provide cover wider than the minimum, virtually along UK lines. Indeed competition has led to novel innovations such as offering a hire car if your car is in an accident, so it pays to search around and also check the claims philosophies; for example, will it be the insurer's appointed garage or the agency garage? Expect to pay between Dh2000 to Dh3000 on a car valued at Dh70,000.

Telesales operations are still a fledgling concept. These are similar to the 'Direct Line' call centre approach in Europe, where the transaction and payment for your insurance can be made over the phone without having to come face to face with the insurer. However, expect the more forward thinking insurers to offer this facility in the year 2000. This will help to keep premiums lower as insurers' overheads will be lower. The use of 'e-commerce' can also be expected to gain momentum, but only when local banks can accept payment of credit cards over the Internet. Always keep evidence of any no-claims discounts, this can be valuable and, if with a European insurer, will hold good when the expatriate returns to his home country.

Most western expatriates insure their household possessions and, whilst crime is not a real issue, it is on the rise. In any case such cover provides protection against virtually any eventuality – with the occasional winter storms probably being the insurer's biggest catastrophe risk. Foggy days in the early part of the year also produce a seasonal spate of motor claims for insurers.

Medical insurance has been the fastest growing segment following the government's decision to charge every expatriate for a health-card costing Dh300 at the time of issue of a work permit unless he or she can show evidence of private medical insurance with a locally registered insurer. Plans range from bronze to platinum type international plans, very comprehensive but expensive. This market is still developing and will become more sophisticated as insurers introduce direct billing facilities enabling entry to a hospital with an insurance card, with the hospital billing the insurance company directly. Currently most schemes are on a reimbursement basis, with the customer paying and then seeking recovery from his insurer, which can often take several weeks.

Life and investment is still a developing market and there are numerous international insurers offering a complete range of plans in the UAE. Bank assurance is a very recent development, with several banks starting to employ their own qualified financial consultants to provide investment products to their customers. This trend is set to continue and, being

Central Bank-approved, is a welcome development as it will marginalise the unregulated and unqualified so-called financial experts who fly in from outside the GCC.

The UAE is a colourful and interesting insurance market and customers can continue to look forward to improvements in innovative practices and service levels, certainly at the top end of the market.

6.4

The Regulation of Banking and Financial Services

Caroline O'Hare, Clifford Chance

The financial markets and their regulation in the UAE are in the process of being redefined and enhanced and this is an exciting time to watch the development of this process. New laws are expected to be enacted shortly and a stock exchange with floors in both Abu Dhabi and Dubai is expected to open in the near future. However, since it is impossible to predict exactly when these changes will take effect, this article sets out the broader regulatory position at the time of writing.

Federal Law No. 10 of 1980 (the *Banking Law*) provides the backbone of the regulatory regime for banking and financial services in the UAE. The principal regulatory authority for the banking and finance industry is the Central Bank by virtue of the powers directly vested in it by the Banking Law. Federal Law No.6 of 1985 (the *Islamic Banks Law*) was subsequently enacted to bring Islamic banks, financial institutions and investment companies largely within the ambit of the Banking Law and under the supervision of both the Central Bank and, additionally, the Ministry of Islamic Affairs and Awqaf.

While both the Banking Law and the Islamic Banks Law contain a broad brush approach to regulation, these laws have been supplemented and fleshed out by secondary legislation. In particular, the Central Bank frequently issues resolutions and circulars through which it sets out specific rules on a wide variety of topics to direct and regulate the institutions under its supervision. Such resolutions and circulars have dealt with issues such as capital adequacy, reporting requirements, large exposures, customer confidentiality and conditions applicable to certificates of deposit.

The Banking Law – Federal Law No. 10 of 1980

The Banking Law states that the Central Bank is established to direct monetary, credit and banking policy and to supervise its implementation in accordance with the general policy of the State. The Central Bank also sets exchange rates and is exclusively responsible for issuing the national currency. Further, the Central Bank acts as the government's bank and safeguards the government's gold reserves and foreign currencies.

The Banking Law also gives the Central Bank powers to organise the banking profession and its development and to control the efficiency of the banking system. Thus the Central Bank is responsible for the licensing and supervision of banking institutions and is also empowered to issue instructions and recommendations to banks to further the attainment of its monetary and credit policies and ensure the sound functioning of the banking business.

The Banking Law does not, however, apply to statutory public credit institutions, governmental investment institutions and development funds, special savings, deposit and pension funds and insurance or re-insurance institutions, all of which are specifically excluded from its ambit. The Banking Law specifies five types of banks and financial institutions to be regulated by the Central Bank and which must all obtain a licence from the Central Bank before they may commence operations. These five categories are as follows:

Commercial banks

Described as establishments that customarily receive funds from the public by way of deposits, or through the sale or placement of bonds, certificates, notes or other securities and which utilise such funds (for their own account and at their own risk) for making loans and advances, the issuance and collection of cheques, placing public or private bonds, trading in foreign exchange and precious metals and carrying out any other operations allowed for commercial banks either by law or by customary banking practice.

Commercial banks are specifically prohibited from engaging in non-banking operations and, in particular, carrying on commercial or industrial activities. They are also prohibited from trading, owning or acquiring goods (unless they are acquired as settlement of a debt due to the bank and the goods are disposed of within a prescribed period), acquiring immovable property (except if it is required for the bank's business or for providing housing or recreational amenities for its staff, or if it is acquired as settlement of a debt due to the bank and is sold within three years of its acquisition).

Commercial banks are also prohibited from holding or dealing in their own shares (unless such shares are acquired in settlement of a debt and are sold within two years of their acquisition) and from purchasing shares of, or bonds issued by, commercial companies which would raise the bank's holding thereof above 25 per cent of the bank's own funds (unless, again, they are acquired in settlement of a debt and sold within two years). Loans to the bank's directors (without prior approval from the Central Bank), granting of credit facilities secured on shares in the bank, and lending money for property construction in excess of 20 per cent of the bank's total deposits (unless Central Bank approval has been obtained or the bank specialises in such investments) are also prohibited. Nor can a commercial bank issue travellers cheques in its own name without the prior consent of the Central Bank.

Failure by a commercial bank to comply with the requirements of the Central Bank and the Banking Law may lead to the Central Bank imposing fines for delay in supplying information, issuing warnings, reducing or suspending facilities for advances, prohibiting or placing restrictions on certain transactions, and in an extreme case, striking the bank from its register (which results in most cases in the mandatory liquidation of the bank concerned).

UAE based Commercial Banks are required to have a minimum paid-up capital of Dhs.40 million (US$10.86 million) and foreign banks registered with the Central Bank to operate as commercial banks are required to allocate an equivalent amount towards their UAE operations. All commercial banks are required to maintain a risk to assets ratio of 10 per cent (this is based on the 1988 recommendations of the Basle Committee on Banking Regulations and Supervisory Practices).

Investment banks

These are described as banks which are usually called business, development or investment banks and which are normally distinguished from commercial banks in that they are prohibited from accepting deposits for a period of less than two years. They are permitted to borrow from their head office, local or foreign banks and the money market generally.

Additionally, the Central Bank has issued a Resolution which lists the activities that investment banks may undertake. These include participation in the equity of companies subject to a maximum of 25 per cent of the capital of the relevant company or 10 per cent of the shareholders' equity in the investment bank (whichever is less), granting medium and long-term loans, providing working capital facilities for periods of not less than two years and opening letters of credit and issuing guarantees in relation to such loans. They may also accept medium or long-term deposits and manage investment portfolios. Investment banks may not borrow or accept deposits for a period of less than three months from their own head office, other banks or the financial markets. An investment bank is prohibited from opening current accounts (other than for clients to whom it has advanced loans or for whom the bank is acting as a financial agent), discounting commercial bills, granting personal loans, financing the purchase of consumable commodities, and trading in the financial or foreign exchange market.

Financial institutions

These are essentially finance companies, and are described as institutions whose principal functions are extending loans or advances to carry out a financial transaction, participating in existing or proposed projects or investing in moveable property. They are prohibited from accepting deposits or loans from individuals and from opening any type of account for an individual. It is also not permitted for a financial institution to undertake exchange activities, the activities of a financial investment company, any activities for which it is not licensed or activities that concern other financial institutions. Financial institutions fund themselves by borrowing from their head office, banks or the money market.

The Central Bank additionally issued Resolution No.58/3/96, concerning financing companies. A licence, which can be obtained from the Central Bank, is valid for two years, is renewable for subsequent years and permits financing companies to carry out one or more of the following activities: granting advances and/or personal loans, financing small businesses, opening credits and issuing guarantees, and subscribing to the capital of projects and/or issuing shares, bonds or certificates of deposit (providing such subscription or issue is within prescribed limits). See also the reference to Resolution 164/8/94 under 'Secondary legislation' below.

As well as the more general limits on the permitted activities of a financial institution, they are prohibited from granting loans or financial advances to members of their board of directors or the companies associated with them, and owning properties save those which are permitted by the Central Bank.

Financial intermediaries and monetary intermediaries

These are described as anyone other than a financial institution who (a) practises the profession of foreign exchange dealer and purchases and sells currencies and travellers cheques or (b) acts as a stockbroker or agent and trades in local and foreign stocks and bonds. See also the references to Resolutions 164/8/94 and 126/5/95 under 'Secondary legislation' below.

Representative offices

These are offices representing foreign banks or financial institutions within the UAE. They may not conduct any banking business, but are permitted to conduct promotional and liaison activities only.

The Central Bank additionally passed Resolution No.57/3/96, relating to representative offices. In order to operate a representative office within the UAE a licence must be obtained from the Central Bank. Having obtained such a licence it is permissible for the representative office to promote the services of the parent in the local market, provide the parent with information regarding the economic developments in the country, provide established clients of the parent with information about the local market and provide clients with banking, investment and financial advisory services.

It is prohibited for a representative office to accept any deposits from investors, open accounts for clients, provide loans or advances, practise or participate in any of the usual banking operations (for example issuing guarantees or opening letters of credit) or deal in foreign currencies, bank notes or metals.

The Islamic Banks Law – Federal Law No. 6 of 1985 concerning Islamic banks

Federal Law No. 6 of 1985 relates to Islamic banks, financial institutions and investment companies whose constitutive documents oblige them to conduct their activities in accordance with Islamic Sharia principles. It states that such institutions are subject to the Banking Law and to other relevant laws, such as the Commercial Companies Law. They must be established as public joint stock companies.

Islamic banks are permitted to engage in banking, trading and financial and investment services and operations. Islamic banks are not permitted to charge or pay interest but instead invest deposits in a variety of ventures and distribute their profits among their depositors. Islamic banks, financial institutions and investment companies are additionally subject to regulation by the Ministry of Islamic Affairs and Awqaf.

Islamic financial institutions and investment companies are permitted to loan money, participate in existing or proposed projects and to invest in moveables or receive and invest cash deposits in accordance with Sharia principles.

Secondary legislation

There are specific references above to some of the Central Bank's resolutions and circulars but, as mentioned at the outset, such resolutions and circulars cover a very wide variety of topics and put meat on the bones of the main legislation. A few further resolutions and circulars which are of particular interest are mentioned below.

Resolution 164/8/94 regarding Financial Investment Companies and Institutions and Companies for Banking, Financial and Investment Consultations, applies to financial institutions, financial intermediaries and monetary intermediaries and relates to the Central Bank licensing requirements for conducting what is referred to generally as 'investment consultations'. This is described as the opening of accounts for the investment and management of portfolios for the account of third parties, preparing economic feasibility studies of projects, marketing of stocks and shares, constituting and/or managing investment trust funds and investment funds, acting as trustee of funds and subscribing in the capital of companies and joint loans.

In order to carry out the above activity within the UAE an additional licence (granted for one year and renewable thereafter) is required from the Central Bank. However, commercial and investment banks, saving funds and private pension funds, professionals (such as lawyers and accountants) who do not usually advise on such matters and whose opinion would be considered extraordinary to the practice of their profession, brokers and dealers where their banking, financial and investment opinions are unremunerated and considered to be unusual in the context of their main activity and publishers of daily news or magazines or financial printed materials, are amongst those specifically exempted from the requirement to obtain such a licence.

Circular No.16/93 on Regulation of Large Exposures, assesses whether a bank's credit policy is deemed prudent and more specifically assesses whether the risk arising from an excessive concentration of credit to a single borrower or to a group of related borrowers is likely to endanger the solvency of a bank.

Large exposures are defined as funded exposures (less provisions, cash collateral and deposits under lien) which a bank grants to a single borrower and his group which in total equal or exceed specified percentages of the bank's capital base. Exposures to UAE federal and local government arms and their non-commercial entities are expressly exempt from the limits and inter-bank exposures are subject to an individual limit of 30 per cent. Exposures to banks operating inside the UAE with a maturity of one year or less are exempt, while those with a maturity of over one year are subject to a 25 per cent limit.

Commercial banks are prohibited from granting credit facilities against collateral consisting of shares in the same bank, and are prohibited from granting loans for the construction of buildings if such loans aggregate to 20 per cent of the bank's total deposits, unless the bank is authorised to specialise in real estate loans or has the prior approval of the Central Bank. A credit risk bureau monitors the borrowings and all commercial banks, investment banks and financial institutions are required to provide to the credit risk bureau the details of every customer who accepts credit facilities of Dhs.250,000 (US$68,000) or more.

Resolution 126/5/95 Regarding Financial and Monetary Brokers sets out licence requirements for these entities. A licence from the Central Bank is valid for one year and renewable thereafter, and permits the holder to carry out brokering activities such as the sale and purchase of local and foreign stocks and bonds, currencies, commodities and stock market transactions. The licensing requirements are intended to impose minimum standards in relation to the professional capabilities and integrity of the licensee by requiring them to be sufficiently experienced; however, they do not provide any objective criteria against which this can be assessed. In order to protect the creditworthiness of the licensee, minimum capital levels, dependent on the activities to be carried out, are imposed. Additionally, a bank guarantee amounting to 50 per cent of the licensee's capital must be placed with the Central Bank.

Only UAE nationals or companies in which UAE nationals own at least 60 per cent of the aggregate paid-up share capital are eligible for a licence.

A licensed entity wishing to undertake marketing of a financial product will need to determine whether or not the approval of the Central Bank is required. For example, the offering of securities by way of public subscription may only be done by licensed entities with the prior approval of the Central Bank. Activities which are likely to be regarded as constituting carrying on business in such a way as to require approval from the Central Bank are:

- cold calling of potential investors or aggressive and high profile marketing of potential customers to whom there is no prior connection or introduction;
- advertising specific securities in the media in the UAE or inviting the public to meet sales representatives at a particular location within the UAE;
- visits to the UAE which may be characterised as constituting a substantial or semi-permanent presence due to duration or frequency of the visits.

As new products and services are developed it will usually be necessary to consult with the Central Bank in order to determine whether prior approval is required. It is established, however, that activities such as the marketing and sale of mutual funds, trading in foreign exchange and metals, and managing investment portfolios may be undertaken by UAE registered Commercial Banks and Investment Banks without the need to obtain the approval of the Central Bank.

The following activities however do not usually require either a licence or the prior consent of the Central Bank and are often adopted by overseas financial institutions to market and sell their products in the UAE:

- discreet offering of securities by telephone and mail from overseas to established clients and contacts within the UAE;
- short visits to established clients in the UAE, at the express invitation of such potential clients;
- low profile marketing activities such as advertisements of a general nature which do not promote any specific investment product;

- offering advisory services in relation to financial products issued by non GCC companies.

Saadiyat Market

The new Saadiyat Market is a free zone that is intended to be a full financial services and commodities market bridging the time zones of Europe and the East. In due course it is anticipated to have a stock exchange, futures and options exchange, commodities exchange and related clearing and settlement systems and also facilities for the physical storage and transport of a number of commodities. Various licensing regulations have been implemented by the Abu Dhabi Free Zone Authority to regulate activities carried on in the Saadiyat Market such as banking, insurance, trading and/or broking in financial and commodities products and operating an investment exchange. These regulations have been drafted in accordance with best international practices and regulation. There is a similar format for each set of licensing regulations insofar as it defines licensable activities, contains exemptions and overseas person exclusions as well as provisions for the ongoing supervision of licensees together with powers of intervention. There is also a comprehensive application procedure: approval will only be granted where applicants meet minimum criteria and there is the involvement of home regulators where the establishment of branches is concerned. There are additional conduct of business rules relating to audited accounts, names, advertising and promotion and financial resources rules. There are also codes of conduct together with other proposed rules, dealing with, for example, the issues of insider trading and money laundering. More details on the Saadiyat Market will be the subject of the succeeding article.

UAE stock markets

The long awaited Law on Stock Market activity was finally gazetted at the beginning of February, 2000. This law anticipates the creation of a Federal Securities and Commodities Commission to ensure the orderly development of domestic stock markets in the UAE and will lead to the present 'over the counter' market being phased out – which of itself should cause a return of confidence to the market.

The new law charges the Federal Securities and Commodities Authority (which it establishes) with responsibility for the development, supervision and regulation of activity in Securities (equity and debt) and Commodities, and lays out an interim timetable for certain of its objectives. It anticipates stock markets being developed in both Dubai and Abu Dhabi, and being electronically linked. It anticipates stock markets being established as local public organisations – that in reality are well on the way to creation in both Dubai and Abu Dhabi.

Interestingly the new law focuses on the areas of disclosure, transparency and insider trading – making transgression in these areas offences – with the clear intention of restoring confidence in the way the market operates.

The new law is clearly a compromise and a development from earlier proposals: regulation of this whole area must be seen as a positive development.

Proposed legislation

Currently under consideration and review is a proposed new banking law (which will presumably take the UAE Central Bank much more deeply into the area of financial services regulation) and a new Companies Law. Both of these will be complex and controversial – as such it is not presently possible to predict when these will come into effect or what their practical effects are likely to be.

Caroline O'Hare
Clifford Chance Limited Liability Partnership
P. O. Box 9380,
Dubai,
United Arab Emirates
Tel: (9714) 3314333
Fax: (9714) 3317951
e-mail: Caroline.O'Hare@cliffordchance.com

For information about Clifford Chance Limited Liability Partnership, Clifford Chance Rogers & Wells LLP and Clifford Chance Puender, including a list of the partners, please see our website at http://www.cliffordchance.com

6.5

Exciting Business Opportunities in the Saadiyat Market

Abu Dhabi Free Zone Authority – Saadiyat

The Saadiyat Market

Saadiyat Island is located just off the business district of Abu Dhabi City and is being developed into an international financial and commodities centre. The Saadiyat Market is positioned to form a pivotal junction for global capital and commodity flows within Saadiyat's hinterland region of the Middle East, South Asia, North and East Africa and the former Soviet Union. Facilities on Saadiyat Island will include an international stock exchange, a futures and options exchange, a commodities trading exchange and a clearing house, which will be able to clear and settle international financial and commodities contracts on Saturdays and Sundays.

The hinterland for the Saadiyat Market has enormous potential. Economic fundamentals are strong, the political environment is stable, there are many ongoing project developments and the region is seeing an increasing trend towards financial liberalisation. Opportunities for companies looking to establish a presence in this market are potentially huge.

The Abu Dhabi Free Zone Authority

The Abu Dhabi Free Zone Authority is the sole regulator of the Saadiyat Market. The Authority was established in 1996 to undertake the administration and organisation of the Saadiyat Market. Its role as regulator includes the establishment of regulations to administer the Saadiyat Market, issuing licences to institutions conducting business in and from the Saadiyat Market, and ongoing supervision of companies and their employees operating within the market. An independent legal and regulatory framework based upon international best practice has been enacted and now governs the Saadiyat Market.

Emirates Global Capital Corporation (EGCC)

EGCC has been granted a 50 year renewable concession by the government of Abu Dhabi to drive the development of the Saadiyat Market. The company will be responsible for creating and administering the appropriate infrastructure and real estate on Saadiyat Island and will also develop the facilities for the market as a whole, ensuring that these meet the appropriate international standards.

The business incentives

The Abu Dhabi Free Zone Authority aims to make Saadiyat the best regulated free market in the world, comprising all the components of an international financial centre. The new legal framework has many liberal features and is designed to encourage business. For example, there are no taxes, no need for a local partner or sponsor and no reserve requirements for banks. There are also no restrictions on foreign ownership of companies or assets. The Saadiyat Market offers opportunities for companies to build profitable market share as it develops into the millennium.

Setting up a branch in the Saadiyat Market

Setting up an office in the Saadiyat Market is a simple and straightforward process. All it requires is a licence from the Abu Dhabi Free Zone Authority. The licensing process is through a single point of contact within the authority that shortens the administrative procedures considerably. The authority will license business activities in the following categories:

- Banking
- Financial and commodities trading
- Financial and commodities broking
- Introducing brokers
- Insurance business
- Insurance broking
- Fiduciary company
- Fiduciary trading company
- Custodian

- Commercial business
- Service providers
- Asset managers
- Collective investment schemes (mutual funds).

Companies must firstly complete a pre-qualification questionnaire stating which business activities are to be undertaken in the Saadiyat Market along with other requested essential information. This is a measure the authority has taken to ensure applicants reach the minimum criteria for the granting of a licence. It also informs the registrar which application forms need to be sent. Providing this stage is reached and the authority is satisfied with the information disclosed, the licence forms will be sent for completion and the licence will be granted.

Cost

The Abu Dhabi Free Zone Authority grants licences for a one year period, which are then renewable after a strategic review of the company. The licence is paid annually and varies depending on which business activities a company wishes to undertake.

Office location

Emirates Global Capital Corporation is responsible for the office developments in the Saadiyat Market. Temporary office space is available until the necessary infrastructure has been completed on the island and will be in a location designated by the EGCC in Abu Dhabi City once a licence has been granted. The rates will be competitive with those found in Abu Dhabi City but will allow companies to operate under Saadiyat Market rules and regulations.

Point of contact

The Abu Dhabi Free Zone Authority has established an information centre that is responsible for storing important user information and making sure queries concerning the Saadiyat Market are answered as quickly as possible. This is the central point of contact for companies wishing to contact the authority.

For more information on business opportunities in the Saadiyat Market contact the Information Centre on Tel: 800 2277 or 02 715156 or Fax: 02 715174. They will provide you with the relevant marketing materials and information you require.

Part 7

Establishing Trading Links with the UAE

ASHARQ AL AWSAT
The Leading Arab International Newspaper
ARRIYADIYAH
The First Daily Sports Newspaper in Saudi Arabia
arab news
ARAB NEWS
Saudi Arabia's First English Daily
URDU NEWS
The First Urdu Daily In the Arab World
AL EQTISADIAH
The National Business Daily in Saudi Arabia
MALAYALAM
First Malayalam Daily Published Outside India
AALAM ALRIADAH
The Sports Magazine for the Young Arabs
AL MAJALLA
The International Magazine of the Arabs
AL - JADEEDA
ASHARQ AL AWSAT Magazine
ARRAJOL
The Monthly Magazine for the Arab Man
SAYIDATY
The Magazine For the Arab Family
AL JAMILA
The Arab Women's Magazine
HIA
The Monthly Magazine for Affluent Arab Women
SAYIDATY FASHION
The Catalogue of the Woman of style
URDU MAGAZINE
The First Urdu Magazine in the Arab World
BASIM
The Weekly Magazine of 8-15 years old
If you have the message, we have the medium.
If you have something to say in the Middle East, say it in the same pages read by more people in more places throughout the Arab world. We're talking about 16 of the biggest titles in the Middle East. From the leading international magazine of the Arabs to the leading Arab international daily. From popular celebrity titles to sports, business, entertainment, children's and women's titles. You're sure to find a title that fits your message perfectly. And brings it home to the right crowd.
Saudi Research and Publishing Co.
The Power to Reach People.
http:/www.srpc.com
Exclusive worldwide advertising representative:
AL-KHALEEJIAH
Advertising & Public Relations Co. Ltd.
http:/www.alkhaleejiahadv.com.sa
Worldwide offices:
Saudi Arabia, Jeddah Tel. 966 2 651 1333 Fax 966 2 651 0533
Saudi Arabia, Riyadh Tel. 966 1 479 3333 Fax 966 1 479 3353
Japan, Tokyo Tel. 813 3261 4591 Fax 813 3261 6126
U.A.E., Dubai Tel. 9714 2628 828 Fax 9714 2665 072
U.S.A., Colorado Tel. 1 303 664 5115 Fax 1 303 664 5116
Egypt, New Egypt Tel. 202 2411 153 Fax 202 2433 322
India, Bombay Tel. 91 22 204 8890 Fax 91 22 287 5718
France, Paris Tel. 33 1 5377 6400 Fax 33 1 4225 1300
Pakistan, Karachi Tel. 92 21 587 4214 Fax 92 21 587 4162
U.K., London Tel. 44 207 404 6950 Fax 44 207 404 6963
China, Hong Kong Tel. 852 2543 2282 Fax 852 2542 0498

7.1

Living and Working in the City of Abu Dhabi

Anthony Trew, Al Sayegh Richards Butler, Abu Dhabi

Introduction

Of all the Gulf states, the United Arab Emirates is, from an expatriate viewpoint, one of the most appealing. The city of Abu Dhabi, with its excellent shopping and recreational facilities, its comfortable accommodation, its state of the art communications, its Garden City environment, and its relative tolerance of cultural differences, makes it an attractive place in which to live and work. Whilst an expatriate will find much that is familiar, be it high rise office and apartment blocks, fast food and shopping chains, cinemas showing the latest films, even his favourite beer (for Abu Dhabi is not 'dry'), this very familiarity can easily lead him to make false assumptions that, because so much is as he knows it, there are no differences. It is important to appreciate that there are differences and to recognise them.

This article will concentrate on providing information which it is hoped will be of interest to those coming for the first time to live in the city of Abu Dhabi, the capital of the UAE, and the centre where most western expatriates working in the Emirate of Abu Dhabi are based.

The people

Probably less than 20 per cent of the local population are UAE nationals. Thus most people in the street – even many in local national dress – will themselves be expatriates. There is a substantial residential population from Gulf Cooperation Council (GCC) countries and other Arab states and from the countries of the Indian sub-continent, as well as from Europe and the US. Indeed, virtually every nation in the world is represented in the local population mix.

Amongst the UAE national workforce itself there is a preference to work in the government, rather than the private, sector but the authorities are now actively promoting 'emiratisation' (i.e. the process of incorporating UAE nationals into the workforce) in the private sector.

Entry and residence requirements

Full British passport holders can still enter the UAE without the need to have first obtained a visa. A visit visa, permitting a stay of up to one month (usually renewable for two further monthly periods) is granted on arrival. Most other nationalities must obtain their visas before leaving home. Multiple entry visit visas are sometimes granted.

A visit visa does not entitle the holder to work in Abu Dhabi – to do so, an employment visa is required which is obtained through the employee's UAE employer.

Residence visas for employment are typically issued for three years. There are no exit visa requirements and the expatriate can enter and exit the UAE freely during that period. However, having left the UAE, the visa holder must return within six months otherwise the visa is automatically cancelled and a fresh application has to be made.

Once an employee has been granted an employment visa and provided minimum salary levels are met, the employee may sponsor his immediate family for residence purposes. Residence visas for dependent relatives are issued broadly on the same basis as employment visas but do not themselves permit the holder to work. The spouse of the holder of a residence visa for employment may however usually obtain a work permit after residence has been established.

The issue of any residence visa to an adult is usually conditional on the need to pass a local medical examination.

Employment

There is a comprehensive labour law, which applies to private sector employment. The law has been written with the aim of guaranteeing the employee certain basic rights and entitlements. It deals with such issues as hours of work, overtime, holiday entitlement, termination of employment and entitlement to end of service gratuity. An employee can negotiate with his employer more generous benefits but if, on the other hand, the employment contract contains terms which are less beneficial than those provided by the labour law, the corresponding provision of the law will be substituted.

Often a contract of employment will stipulate a probationary period of up to six months. If it does so, both the employer and the employee may terminate the contract during the probationary period without notice and without giving a reason.

An expatriate employee may only work for the sponsoring employer. If an employee wishes to remain in the UAE after the initial contract term has come to an end and work for another employer, the consent of the original employer may be required – failing which the employee may have to return to his country of origin and make a fresh application in the name of the new employer. Some categories of expatriate worker in the lower grades may, in any event, be restricted for a period of six months from taking up fresh employment in the UAE and will need to return home in the interim.

The employer is usually responsible for repatriating an employee at the end of his contract term but is not responsible for the repatriation of the employee's family, unless that is a contractual requirement.

Accommodation

There is a wide selection of modern air-conditioned accommodation available – apartment living is common. Villas are available but are relatively expensive and the plots on which they stand are usually not large. There is no obligation under the labour law for an employer to provide accommodation for his staff (although he often does so or provides a housing allowance). A potential employee will need to clarify the accommodation question when initially negotiating the employment contract.

In broad terms it is only UAE nationals who may own property. Expatriate accommodation is usually taken on short term tenancy agreements (typically for periods of one year renewable). There is a standard Abu Dhabi form of tenancy agreement which, more often than not, forms the basis of the contract. Especially in relation to villas, the owner does not always take out insurance. Since the occupier may be held liable for damage to the property during the occupancy, the insurance position needs to be carefully checked and appropriate cover separately obtained if it is lacking.

Education

There is a broad choice of schools (from Kindergarten to Secondary) catering for the requirements of many expatriate communities, but they are all fee paying. Whilst some employers pay for or contribute to school fees, this is by no means universal.

Travel around the city

Although there is an Abu Dhabi city municipality bus service, it is not particularly comprehensive and is not widely used by western expatriates. The universal mode of travel within the city, other than by private car, is the ubiquitous local taxi (painted white and gold). At present they can be hailed anywhere in the street but the authorities are in the process of installing taxi lay-bys and it is anticipated that when this programme is complete, taxis will only be permitted to pick up and drop passengers at those points. Taxi fares, when compared with those in most European capitals, are cheap and all main areas of town are within a quarter of an hour's ride or so of each other. It is as well to have some idea of the geographical location of your destination before setting out, as there is no equivalent to the London cabbies' 'knowledge'. Taxi drivers also have an endearing, but confusing, habit of referring to roads by names which they have not held for twenty years!

In addition to the white and gold town taxis, more expensive (but still reasonably priced) radio taxis are available – especially useful for late night or longer distance travelling.

All taxis are metered but there are fixed rates for travelling to, for example, Abu Dhabi International Airport and Dubai.

Driving and licences

To drive, a resident must hold a valid UAE driving licence. Nationals of some countries (the UK and US are examples) who hold full licences in their home countries can obtain a UAE driving licence on the strength of their home licence – otherwise a UAE driver's test must be taken, which can be a protracted process requiring many attempts. An eye test is a requirement for obtaining and renewing a driving licence.

Visitors to the UAE on a visit visa and holding an international driving licence may be able to obtain a temporary permit to drive. The position should be checked carefully with the car hire company, however, as there are quite severe penalties for driving without a valid licence.

It is mandatory to stop if an accident (however trivial) occurs and to call the traffic police. Accident repairs cannot be carried out without clearance from the traffic department. Where there is a dispute as to the cause, it is common for the traffic police to confiscate the driving licences of all those involved and to require them immediately to go to the traffic police station to make statements. If an accident results in an injury, the drivers of the involved vehicles may be detained whilst the seriousness of the injuries are ascertained and the likely blame established. In cases of serious injury this may mean a protracted stay.

On no account should a car be driven if alcohol has been consumed, however moderately. Penalties for 'drunk' driving (which means having consumed alcohol rather than 'being drunk' in the western sense) are extremely severe. If any accident, other than the most trivial of bumps, occurs it is prudent immediately to inform the employer so that any necessary support can be provided.

However indignant or aggrieved one may feel at the actions of another driver, it pays to keep one's temper and remain calm and polite at all times.

Only a holder of a valid UAE driving licence may own and register a private motor car and the number is usually limited to one per licence holder. Motor car registrations are renewed annually. As part of the registration process, a brief mechanical inspection is carried out.

Recreation and pastimes

Not surprisingly, in view of Abu Dhabi's coastal location, all forms of water sport are popular, as is desert driving, camping and picnicking. Health clubs and fitness centres abound and squash and tennis are popular. There are also thriving football and rugby clubs, and golf, on immaculate grass courses, is popular too. Less well known is that Abu Dhabi has a first class ice skating rink. There are numerous beach clubs as well as wide expanses of public beach which are freely accessible. The authorities maintain a ladies, beach with refreshment facilities which is open, for a small fee, only to women and young children. Many clubs and societies cater for a wide range of pursuits and interests. Camel and horse races take place regularly and are popular with spectators. Sailing dhow races and local rowing races, with as many as eighty oarsmen to a boat, take place from time to time and are a fine spectacle.

Culturally, art exhibitions are frequent and visiting theatrical productions, concerts and operatic performances are regular features, often organised in conjunction with one of the Capital's many hotels. On a lighter note, well known pop artists and groups regularly pass through in concert. Again, these events are usually organised by hotels.

Whilst Dubai is still perhaps the shopping capital of the region, Abu Dhabi is fast gaining ground, with many of the US and European chain stores and specialist boutiques being represented. Cinema going too is popular and there is a choice of cinema complexes showing a broad spectrum of up-to-the-minute films – others are planned.

The UAE is tolerant of other faiths and many religious denominations meet together and have places of worship.

Etiquette and dress code

Suffice it to say, polite and courteous behaviour is appreciated; rowdy, aggressive and rude behaviour, especially in public, is not, and will lead to swift intervention by the authorities. Penalties for infringers can, in western terms, be severe. Any form of street altercation is frowned upon. If an incident does arise, it is seldom productive to be aggressive or over excited, whatever the apparent provocation. It is always better to remain calm and polite.

Whilst in Middle Eastern terms the UAE is very tolerant of western dress styles, nevertheless it is polite for men and women to dress conservatively in a public place. It is, for example, inappropriate (and offensive to many) for women to wear shorts or short skirts or go about with uncovered shoulders in the downtown areas – although acceptable for jogging and cycling on the Corniche, where many now take regular exercise. Similarly, shorts for men (except when taking exercise) and bare torsos are not appropriate. Swimwear should be strictly confined to the beach. It is also polite, when visiting senior officials or important nationals, for men to wear a suit or at least smart slacks and a shirt and tie, and women should dress correspondingly.

As air-conditioning in shops, residences, offices and cars is now universal, the high climatic temperature and humidity are of less concern to the Abu Dhabi city dwellers than heretofore. Ordinary western lightweight clothing (rather than specialist tropical gear) is fine for the average city resident. Nevertheless, for much of the year Abu Dhabi is very hot indeed and adequate precautions to protect against sun and heat should be taken for even comparatively short trips in the open. Cars heat up quickly too and children and animals should never be left unattended in a closed car.

Photography

Care should be exercised when taking photographs. In general, do not take photographs of government buildings, military and industrial installations, docks, airports and telecommunications equipment or centres. Normal tourist photography is permissible, but remember to ask permission before taking a stranger's photograph.

Alcohol

Alcohol is tolerated in Abu Dhabi (although not in every emirate of the UAE) but there are strict regulations regarding its consumption, of the details of which, experience shows, many expatriates may not always be fully aware. It is very important that an expatriate acquaints himself with the detailed rules at an early stage. Briefly, resident non-Muslims may apply for a licence to purchase alcohol from one of the outlets licensed for the purpose. Licence holders can then purchase alcohol to a maximum of a given amount per month for their own personal use at home. Many hotels are licensed to supply alcohol to their residents. The consumption of alcohol in public is strictly prohibited. Remember too that it is an offence to be drunk in public, even if licensed. As mentioned earlier, on no account should one drink and drive. Even as a pedestrian, extra care should be taken to behave with decorum in public if alcohol has been consumed, since any incident is likely to become more serious if the presence of alcohol is detected. All alcohol related offences are serious.

Health

Abu Dhabi has a number of modern government hospitals and clinics where treatment costs are subsidised. Access to the subsidised service is through a government health card, which it is wise to obtain. The Capital's maternity hospital is one of the busiest in the world. There are many doctors and specialists practising in the private sector and most western expatriates consult private sector GPs for day to day ailments. Medical insurance is advisable.

Conclusion

One cannot cover all aspects of expatriate life in a short article. Many embassies publish more detailed guides for their nationals, which are well worth obtaining. In addition, there are a number of more comprehensive commercial publications, which are readily available in local bookshops and can also be obtained through Internet bookstores. A visit to the appropriate website or a browse through the local bookstores on an early visit can be rewarding.

7.2

Dubai – City of the Millennium or just a Miracle in the desert?

Paul Hawkins

The UAE was the last GCC State to discover oil. The reason for this rather bold initial statement is to highlight the fact that living here in the 60s and even 70s was not easy and certainly merited much praise and admiration for the initial 'settlers' as well as the indigenous population. It also merited large doses of hardship allowances for expatriates arriving from overseas.

You might ask, 'But what about those beautiful beaches and palm trees – they were surely there even 30 years ago?' Well, 'settlers' were frankly in the same situation as Captain Bligh's mutinous crew of *The Bounty* when they settled on Pitcairn Island. Lying on the beach, looking out on to that beautiful deep blue sea and picking luscious fruit off those beautifully sculptured trees was OK for a couple of weeks. *Treasure Island* must have been equally glamorous for a short period, but the treasure hidden there added a new perspective to the island and so it is with modern-day Dubai, a city truly of the millennium. In recent years it has developed its own brand of treasures: pursuits; sports; social, leisure, aesthetic, artistic and scientific interests. In fact you can do anything in Dubai. The amazing vision of the government has created a country which has become in the space of ten years one which is attracting not only workers keen to put their skills to use in a buoyant economy, businessmen using Dubai as the platform for their Gulf operation, but also tourists in increasing numbers from other parts of the Gulf, the USA, South America, Africa, eastern and western Europe, Russia and the CIS, Japan, the Far East and the Antipodes.

A major point arises here. When considering the potential for retail business in Dubai, one must immediately discount Dubai's small population of approximately three quarters of a million, many of whom send all their earnings home at the end of each month. What is significant in retail terms is the 'floating' population of business visitors and tourists, which is substantial in number for most of the year and also, of course, Dubai's 'bread and butter' re-exports to other parts of the Middle East.

Anyone who lives here every day of the year feels there is something quite unique about it. The Emirates Golf Course, apart from creating one of the biggest triumphs in golfing history in building a championship golf course on foundations of little more than shale and sand, was voted the number one course in 'Europe' by players on the Volvo PGA Circuit. The Jumairah Beach Hotel, a spectacular example of modern day sculpturing comparable to the influence of Oscar Niemeyer in Brazil in the 1960s, was voted the best hotel in the world by a prominent magazine, but has this amazing structure now been eclipsed by the latest tourist offering – Le Royal Mirage? Al Bustan is the third new five-star hotel to open in the last two years and this is also quite spectacular, with a Thai restaurant fit for gourmets. If you live here you can witness all of these works of art for yourself. In fact you dare not go away for long – you will miss the construction of yet another landmark.

The World Cup, the icing on the cake for the amazing horse racing triumphs of the ruling Al Maktoum family, is now the richest race in the world, and one of its winners, Cigar, is one of the greatest racehorses of all time. The annual ATP Tour Tennis tournament has attracted Boris Becker, Tim Henman, Ivan Ivanisnovich, Carlos Moya, Pat Rafter (for the Millennium) and a host of other top names. Power boat racing; the annual Rugby Sevens, now on grass, is slowly becoming the premier rugby sevens competition in the world. Snooker, squash, cricket in Sharjah all figure highly in the calendar of sporting events, but what impresses everyone who attends these events year after year is the incredibly high level of organisation that has been achieved.

So what do you do when you get here? Reasonably priced villas, some of them on 5–50 villa compounds with swimming pool, tennis, health club activities, and luxurious apartment blocks are found all over town from Jumairah and Umm Sequeim at the Abu Dhabi end of Dubai to Bur Dubai, the emerging business centre with its shopping malls and computer souks, to the more ancient but equally attractive commercial centre of Deira, alongside the Creek, where Dubai's well-heralded trading instincts took root several centuries ago.

Estate agents abound, and word of mouth can help you get a 'good deal'. Prices may be on the turn after years of price escalation. A three-bedroom villa on a small compound with swimming pool is likely to cost Dhs100,000–120,000 per annum (£17,000–£20,000) in Jumairah and two to three-bedroom apartments vary in price from Dhs60,000–Dhs90,000 depending on which area of town you are targeting. Schools for expatriates are numerous, but nevertheless many have waiting lists.

However, although the tax structure is inviting, it is very easy to spend money in Dubai, so if you are coming to save money, be warned. There is so much to do and so many pursuits that will add value to your own life and your family's, you will soon forget about saving money.

The Dubai Shopping Festival is in its third year and goes from success to success. The dates now cleverly coincide with the Dubai Desert Classic Golf Tournament and the Volvo PGA Tennis event, so tourism during this period is maximised to its fullest extent. This is also an opportunity to visit Dubai's shopping malls, from the original ones at the Ghurair Centre, Bur Jurman and Hamriya to the latest at the Wafi, Palm Court and the magnificent City Centre with adjacent hotel. Spinneys and Choitrams compete in a friendly way for the grocery business.

The gold souk offers the least expensive gold in the world and has created a huge re-export business for Dubai. The spice souk with its heavy blend of aromas is typical of the traditional Arab bazaar. There are many precious metals on offer, from the inexpensive gold to silver from Italy, as well as precious stones and natural pearls.

The free zone which was created in 1990 at Jebel Ali, 15 miles from the centre of Dubai, has since attracted a total of 1400 companies, amongst them some of the world's leading industrial companies. At the heart of the free zone is the 65-berth Jebel Ali port built in 1979, when it was the largest man-made harbour in the world.

Dubai Internet City, the half a billion dollar Government project which is already beyond the planning stage, will provide opportunities for 100 per cent ownership to high-tech companies specialising in the latest technology, in particular the Internet and e-commerce, and will also offer 50 year leases. It is expected to include a research institute and an 'Internet University' offering training programmes on e-commerce and business over the web. Internet City has received an enthusiastic response from local businessmen, particularly in view of the recessionary lull which has followed the 'Solo' embezzlement, which left debts with several local and international banks in excess of $US250 million.

Dubai has a healthy non-oil based economy, with a population of approximately 800,000 people of which 20 per cent are UAE nationals and 60 per cent of Asian origin. The remainder are mostly European, South African, American or Arabs from Egypt and the Levant countries. The consumer market depends heavily on the floating population of tourists and business visitors and also re-exports. The climate ranges from warm winters (70–80°F) to hot, humid summers (90–110°F). The humidity can be unpleasant for some, but air-conditioning provides welcome relief. Any rainfall will probably occur in the winter, but it is not unusual to go the whole year without rain. The sun shines literally every day of the year, with a very occasional bleak, cloudy day.

'City of the millennium? Miracle in the desert?' Who are we poor mortals to judge?

Paul Hawkins
Writer on banking and technology
Tel: (9714) 3321145
e-mail banktech99@yahoo.com

7.3

Setting Up Agency and Distributorship Agreements in the UAE

Bryan Cave LLP*, Dubai and Abu Dhabi*

Under UAE law, entities located outside of the UAE may make private sector product sales directly to customers in the UAE without using an intermediary such as an agent. However, by law only UAE nationals or wholly UAE-owned entities may conduct certain 'commercial agency activities' within the UAE. While there is no precise definition of 'commercial agency', the practical effect of such restriction precludes foreigners from trading in other parties' products in the UAE pursuant to a duly registered agency or distribution arrangement. Further, UAE law requires all parties to obtain a trade licence to sell products or provide services within the UAE and branch offices operating in the UAE generally are precluded from obtaining trade licences which would enable them to import goods in commercial quantities for resale.

As a result of the foregoing restrictions, foreign service providers and manufacturers of products typically marketed and sold from inventory or through means of an on-site sales force often find it necessary to (i) engage a UAE commercial agent or other UAE representative to penetrate the UAE market or (ii) establish a licensed presence in the UAE, usually in the form of a registered branch office or limited liability company (in which the foreign ownership is limited to 49 per cent), to undertake the desired activity. Since establishment of a licensed presence requires a more significant investment of time and money and may be subject to limitations with respect to the licensed activities (bearing in mind that 'commercial agency' activities are reserved for UAE citizens or companies wholly owned by UAE citizens), foreign parties often opt to appoint a UAE agent or representative to act on their behalf.

It should be noted that while 'commercial agencies' represent a broad variety of relationships, there are relationships between foreign entities and UAE parties that do not constitute commercial agencies. In particular, foreign branch offices generally are required to engage a UAE national agent or 'service agent' and the relationship is not governed by the commercial agencies regulations described in this article. Local service agents perform mainly administrative functions for the foreign party, and should not be confused with commercial agents.

All foreign entities engaging an agent or other representative for the UAE should be aware of the application and impact of UAE law on such relationship. This article focuses on the legal requirements and practical aspects of setting up commercial agency and distributorship agreements in the UAE. Following this, a brief discussion of issues related to local service agents used to sponsor branch or representative offices of foreign companies is provided.

Commercial Agency Law

The UAE Commercial Agency Law (Federal Law No. 18 of 1981, as amended by Federal Law No. 14 of 1988) regulates and governs the appointment of commercial agents, sales representatives and distributors in the UAE. The coverage of the Commercial Agency Law is quite broad as it encompasses any arrangement in which a foreign company is represented by a local agent for the distribution, offer, sale or marketing of a product or service within the UAE against payment of a fixed commission or profit. The Commercial Agency Law is supplemented by the Commercial Transactions Law (Federal Law No. 18 of 1993). Together, the Commercial Agency Law and the Commercial Transactions Law provide the main regulatory framework for relationships pursuant to which foreign manufacturers sell and distribute products and services in the UAE through a UAE agent, distributor or other representative.

In practice, the Commercial Agency Law makes no distinction between commissioned agents, distributors who purchase for their own account, franchisees and sales representatives. While the Commercial Transactions Law does recognise different types of commercial agencies, such distinctions are beyond the scope of this article and all such arrangements are here referred to generally as 'commercial agencies'.

Requirements for the commercial agent

Commercial agent status can only be obtained by UAE citizens or companies wholly owned by UAE citizens. Further, the commercial agent's name must be recorded in the Register of Commercial Agents maintained by the Ministry of Economy and Commerce.

Requirements for the commercial agency agreement

Authentication and notarisation requirements

In order to be registered, the commercial agency agreement must be an executed written document that has been notarised by a UAE notary public. If both parties sign the agreement in the UAE, it can be prepared in Arabic only, or in side-by-side Arabic and English. The representative of the foreign principal will be required to produce proof of his authority to sign the agreement to the UAE notary public. This will generally take the form of a fully authenticated and officially pop popd power of attorney issued by the foreign principal to its representative. In some cases the UAE notary public may also request to see the board resolution or other similar document that authorises the issuance of the power of attorney, so it is advisable to have that document fully authenticated and officially pop popd as well.

If the foreign principal will not travel to the UAE, the agency agreement can be prepared in English (or other native language assuming it can be officially pop popd to Arabic), signed by the foreign principal, notarised, legalised and sent to the UAE for authentication before the UAE Ministry of Foreign Affairs, and then officially pop popd. The commercial agent can then take this document to the UAE notary public and have his signature notarised.

Required or implied provisions

The commercial agency agreement can grant a single commercial agent exclusivity over the entire UAE, or over only one or more of the seven emirates. In practice, it is not uncommon for foreign companies to appoint a separate commercial agent in different emirates as the emirates are distinct markets in many respects. One common approach is to appoint one agent for Abu Dhabi and another for Dubai and the Northern Emirates due in part to the fact that, in practice, commerce often is separated by such geographic distinction and commercial agents often have a strong reputation in one region but not the other.

The commercial agency agreement can cover an entire range of products or services for a territory, or only a limited number of specific products or services offered by the foreign principal. The commercial agent must also supply the necessary and adequate spare parts, equipment, materials and accessories for maintenance of any durable goods they import. While this requirement is found in the Commercial Agency Law, it is advisable to have more detailed provisions included in the agreement.

All commercial agency agreements registered in the UAE will be subject to UAE law, specifically the Commercial Agency Law and the Commercial Transactions Law, even if the agreement states otherwise. Additionally, all such agreements will be subject to the jurisdiction of the UAE courts, and generally any decisions regarding enforcement issued by a foreign court will not be enforceable in the UAE.

Statutory rights of the commercial agent

Commercial agents are granted formidable statutory rights under the Commercial Agency Law that are designed to protect an agent who may expend considerable efforts, including monetary expenses, to build a profitable market for the products or services. These statutory rights include:

- Commercial agents are entitled to receive commissions on sales of the specified products or services in their designated territory irrespective of whether such sales are made by or through the agent.
- Since all registered commercial agency agreements are treated as exclusive (even if the agreement is silent on this, or indicates that the agency is non-exclusive), registered agents are entitled to prevent products subject to their agency from being imported into their designated territory if the agent is not the consignee.
- Without proof of substantial justification by the foreign principal, commercial agents are entitled to receive compensation from the principal if (i) the agency is terminated or (ii) if the agent's agreement is not renewed in circumstances where the agent shows that its activities led to the apparent or obvious success in the distribution of the principal's products or services and that non-renewal will cause damage to the agent. The agent also may be able to preclude the foreign party from registering a replacement agent in such circumstances, unless the replacement agent pays the original agent what it is due under the original agreement.
- No registration of a new commercial agent in the territory of an existing commercial agent for the same products or services will be allowed until the existing arrangement is terminated (i) with the agreement of the existing agent, or (ii) with substantial justification as determined by the Commercial Agency Committee (with an appeal procedure to the UAE courts being available).

Due to these protections, foreign companies must carefully consider the person or entity they choose as their commercial agent. While the protections are designed to protect hard-working local agents, they also benefit those who choose not to perform as expected and can work to prevent a foreign principal from replacing an under-performing agent unless the foreign principal pays considerable compensation to the agent.

Enforcement of the commercial agency agreement

The Commercial Agency Law establishes a Commercial Agency Committee that considers disputes regarding registered commercial agency agreements. The Committee, chaired by the Under-Secretary of the Ministry of

Economy and Commerce, is authorised to appoint experts as it deems necessary to assist in the review of disputes. However, decisions of the Commercial Agency Committee do not necessarily constitute final judgements and either party may file an action with the UAE courts where the matter may be subject to *de novo* review under the normal judicial process of each emirate, unless the court chooses to rely on the Committee's decision which was properly substantiated and based on the facts and evidence of the matter.

General observations regarding commercial agents

The statutory protections of commercial agents under the Commercial Agency Law create an obvious disincentive to foreign entities to do business through registered commercial agency agreements if alternative means are available. In this regard, foreign parties may find it possible to conduct direct sales into the UAE without the assistance of a UAE commercial agent. In the alternative, for foreign parties whose products or services are sold primarily in the private sector, the foreign entity may be able to locate a UAE party willing to act as sales representative or distributor other than pursuant to a registered commercial agency agreement, assuming the party's trade licence authorises it to undertake such activities. While this type of arrangement is possible, it may make it more difficult for the foreign party to make public sector sales, including sales to the various entities within the Abu Dhabi National Oil Company group.[1] In addition, many commercial agents will insist on a registered agreement in order to avail themselves of the protection of the Commercial Agency Law. The foreign principal may be forced into this position if it desires to appoint a UAE party with considerable influence within the territory.

If the decision is made to pursue business through a registered commercial agency agreement, the foreign principal must undertake a thorough due diligence investigation of the proposed agent in order to ensure the long-term relationship will be formed with a reputable agent. Additionally, the foreign principal is well advised to spell out precisely what it expects of the commercial agent in the way of performance. This is often a carefully drafted section of the agreement that will include such items as minimum sales and financial quotas, stock requirements, support requirements, and financial reporting requirements. The agreement should also restrict the agent from representing competitive products or services.

[1] Another area that is worth noting is that foreign suppliers of certain strategic military weaponry are prohibited from having a local agent involved in a sale pursuant to a current policy issued by the General Headquarters of the UAE Armed Forces ('GHQ'). An in-depth discussion of this area is beyond the scope of this article.

Such objective criteria may prove useful if the foreign principal finds itself needing to show substantial justification to terminate a registered commercial agency agreement.

In recent years there has been much discussion regarding modification of the Commercial Agency Law to be less protective of the local UAE agents or distributors. This stems in part from the general liberalisation of the UAE economy, and as part of the UAE's efforts and desire to further satisfy the requirements of the World Trade Organisation. A similar movement towards liberalisation has also occurred in other GCC countries and is expected to continue throughout the region.

Local service agency discussion

Pursuant to Article 314 of the UAE Commercial Companies Law (Federal Law No. 8 of 1984, as amended by Federal Law No. 13 of 1988) a foreign company may establish a wholly-owned branch or representative office in the UAE. In order to obtain a licence from the Ministry of Economy and Commerce, the foreign company must engage a UAE citizen, or a company wholly-owned by UAE citizens, to act as its service agent.[2] The service agent's obligations to the branch office, the foreign company and third parties generally are restricted to its contractual obligations under the service agency agreement. By law, the service agent may not own equity in the branch office, contractually bind the branch office or the foreign company, participate in the management of the branch office, or have any right, duty or authority except as set forth in the service agency agreement.

In practice, the service agent's obligations and expectations vary widely. For foreign companies that are familiar with conducting business in the UAE, the service agent may be required to simply sponsor the company in its licence registration and renewal procedures. Such companies will generally rely on a knowledgeable public relations officer to handle all other administrative functions required by the branch office and its employees, and will generally rely on its own employees familiar with the local customs and culture to promote its business in the UAE.

On the other hand, foreign companies with little experience in the Gulf region or who will have only a minimal level of employees present, who may not be intimately familiar with the local business climate, will often require more extensive services from the service agent. These services can include representation before, and liaison with, local authorities, handling

[2] A UAE government entity may act as the service agent in certain instances. Foreign suppliers of strategic military weaponry may be required to use GHQ as their service agent. The UAE Central Bank often acts as the *de facto* service agent or sponsor for foreign banks/financial institutions that have branch or representative offices in the UAE. Establishing these types of offices requires special procedures not within the scope of this article.

of all visa and permit requirements for the branch office and its employees, registration of vehicles, assistance with customs and port authorities, leasing of residential and office space, and other detailed requirements. Of course, service agents performing such services will expect a greater level of compensation, which is a matter of contract between the parties.

Some foreign companies are also looking for a service agent that can act as local 'partner' for the branch office. These companies will look for local agents who are intimately familiar with their area of expertise (i.e., oil and gas, information technology, telecommunications, engineering, etc.). In addition to other administrative services, the service agent will be expected to provide the proper introductions necessary for success in the field of expertise, keep the branch office apprised of potential business opportunities, and otherwise assist in promoting and developing the business of the branch office.

Whatever the level of service required by the foreign company may be, it is a matter of contract between the parties. Service agents for foreign branch offices are not protected by the Commercial Agency Law or similar statutory requirements. However, a foreign company interested in obtaining a licence for a branch or representative office should recognise that its choice of a local service agent will affect its experience in the UAE. As with choosing a commercial agent, the foreign company is well advised to conduct thorough due diligence on the agent and to carefully draft the service agency agreement to ensure that the requirements and understanding of each party are clearly set forth.

The foregoing overview of the agency and distributorship agreements in the UAE is not intended to substitute for legal advice on specific matters.

7.4

Some Business Structures Available to Foreign Companies in the UAE

Anthony Trew, Al Sayegh Richards Butler, Abu Dhabi

The aim of this article is to provide background information on some of the usual business structures found to be of interest to international companies wishing to establish or be represented in the United Arab Emirates, with particular reference to the Emirate of Abu Dhabi. It cannot hope to be comprehensive and it is no substitute for taking appropriate professional advice – which a company contemplating a UAE business relationship should always do at the earliest opportunity. Also, many business activities in the UAE are subject to special regulations that must be taken into account. By way of example, an Armed Forces Directive prohibits defence contractors from utilising the services of agents, intermediaries and the like.

While the position is broadly similar throughout the UAE, there are regional variations, especially as to licensing. If a foreign company plans to have an office or do business in more than one emirate, it will need to take account of the specialist requirements of each of them.

Most emirates also operate (or are actively contemplating operating) free zones. These are commercial areas aimed at providing favourable regulatory and tax climates to companies established in the zones. However, the exemptions and benefits available to a free zone established company do not apply once it sets up or begins to trade elsewhere in the UAE outside the free zone. Like any other company, it must then comply with all applicable UAE and Emiri regulations.

The three structures discussed

Broadly speaking, there are three types of relationship usually of most interest to foreign companies wishing to be represented or to set up a place of business in the UAE, each of which normally requires an association with a UAE national or wholly owned entity. Irrespective of which structure is chosen, the UAE associate's relationship is likely to be officially regarded as an exclusive one and he will be afforded, both by legislation and practice, a high degree of security of tenure. In practical terms, it is difficult to change a local associate if he does not agree.

While it is common for a potential local associate to offer his services for the UAE as a whole, many foreign companies prefer, in view of the diversity of markets within the UAE, to establish relationships on an emirate by emirate basis – which is permissible.

It is as well to bear in mind that the concept of intent is of greater force in the UAE than in some other western jurisdictions, and care needs to be taken at initial discussion stages to avoid unintentionally establishing a binding commitment.

Of the three options as to structure discussed here, two (the branch presence and the local limited liability company) involve the foreign company, either itself or with its partner, having an official local presence. The UAE Companies Law provides the framework for these. The other option (that of trade agency), which is governed largely by the UAE Trade Agency Law, does not involve the foreign company having an official local presence of its own. In outline, the three options are as follows.

Limited liability company

This involves the establishment of a locally incorporated limited liability company (LLC) with at least 51 per cent national participation.

In Abu Dhabi, the principal advantage of this method of operation is that, because LLCs are regarded as 'local' companies, certain preferences may operate in their favour and, indeed, some contracts are open only to local companies. These preferences operate primarily in the government and oil and gas field purchasing sectors and it is often commercially necessary for companies with active local operations in those areas to be in a position to take advantage of the preferences – either because of the benefits *per se* or because their competitors are in a position to do so.

The principal features of an LLC are:

- There must be not less than two, but not more than 50, shareholders (in the companies law, called 'partners') and at least 51 per cent of the shares must be held by UAE nationals or entities so wholly owned. The shares may not be publicly traded and existing partners are given a 'first option' to purchase shares offered by another partner to third parties.

- The initial share capital, which must be paid up in full on incorporation, is at least Dh.150,000 and individual shares should have an equal value of not less than Dh.1000. (In practice the registration authorities may require a higher initial share capital.)

- Generally the liability of a partner is limited to the extent of his holding, but in certain circumstances, e.g. where he is party to the passing of a resolution which contravenes the companies law, additional liability may accrue. Further, a partner who is also concerned with management may accrue liability as a consequence of his acts of management e.g. for maladministration.
- An LLC is not permitted to be engaged in the businesses of banking, insurance or investment for third parties.
- The LLC's constitution is contained in a 'memorandum of association'.
- There is no absolute requirement to appoint a board of directors. Instead the partners may appoint a single manager or a board of managers (not exceeding five). Where there are seven or more partners, a supervisory board must be established.
- The manager (or board of managers if one is established) has certain statutory filing responsibilities with the registration authorities.
- To be valid, corporate resolutions must be adopted by a number of votes representing at least one-half of the LLC's capital. A higher majority may be stipulated, permitting the 'deadlock' concept to be introduced.
- Ten per cent of the LLC's net profits must be retained annually until the retention fund has reached a sum equivalent to one-half of its paid-up capital.
- Auditors must be appointed and local annual accounts prepared.
- The life of an LLC is usually for a specified term, which can be extended.

Independent licensed branch

This option involves the foreign company establishing its own independently licensed branch office. Regulations regarding this structure are largely Emiri based and differ from emirate to emirate

Once established and duly licensed by the Emiri authority concerned, however, the branch is permitted to carry on its business, autonomously and in its own name. It may, for example, within the scope of its licence, sponsor its own personnel for employment purposes, rent its own office and sign contracts in its own name. It may, however, need the assistance of its own sponsor to import.

Branches are licensed to conduct business in particular categories. It is important that the correct category is chosen. The various emirates have different ways of categorising. In Abu Dhabi, for example, foreign branch operations are usually categorised for licensing purposes into trading, contracting and services companies. Professional consultants form a further and somewhat distinct category. Again, in Abu Dhabi it is not possible to hold more than one licence nor may the licence extend to more than one category.

Regulations require that to obtain a licence, foreign companies must have a local (i.e. a UAE national) sponsor. This should not be confused with a trade agent appointed under the Trade Agency Law, of which more below. Although it is not unknown for a sponsor to be 'active' – providing, for example, promotional services – it is not a requirement that he does so. A sponsor may do little more than 'lend his name' to assist the company to initially register its branch and thereafter annually re-register with the licensing authorities, yet he is entitled to a fee. In Abu Dhabi particularly, a sponsorship fee tariff has been established which, if the branch operation itself is commercially successful, can result in substantial fees being paid. Because foreign companies do not always realise that promotional activity on the part of the sponsor is not necessarily a pre-requisite to the payment of a sponsorship fee, unnecessary misunderstandings can arise.

The terms of an agreement with the sponsor are formalised in an agreement which is registered with the authorities in the course of the licensing process. Although there is no standard form for that agreement, it should nevertheless be prepared locally since it will always be construed under local law and there are particular provisions which the registration authorities require to be incorporated.

Despite the local sponsorship requirement, branches of foreign companies are not regarded as 'local' and, for example, the preferences available in Abu Dhabi to local companies, mentioned above, do not apply. This factor may be commercially decisive for some companies. In other emirates, the scope of a branch's activities may be curtailed.

Agency/representation

It is important to understand that this option does not involve the foreign company having its own presence in the UAE. Primarily it is intended for those wishing simply to sell their products or services through an agent or representative without themselves establishing a separate local presence. Some foreign companies do, however, use agency arrangements as a means of conducting business locally. The foreign company does not have its own separately licensed presence but, in effect, operates under the 'umbrella' of the agent's licence – officially not a separate entity but a division of the agent's own organisation.

Since the foreign company is not a separate entity, it must accept a considerable loss of autonomy. For example, goods or products can only be imported and warehoused in the agent's name and it may only bid for and take contracts and orders by reference to the local agent. Customers may well insist that payment is therefore made to the agent rather than the principal. Further, it is the agent who sponsors the foreign company's personnel for the purposes of visas, work permits and the like. In short, official matters can only be effected in conjunction with, and through, the local agent, and thus by implication only with his consent and assistance. These restrictions substantially limit the viability of this option.

Since trade agency legislation can heavily impact on a foreign company's local business activities, a brief outline follows:

- All commercial arrangements between a principal and an agent to 'distribute, sell or offer for sale a commodity or service in the UAE in return for a commission or profit' come within the ambit of the UAE trade agency legislation.
- No real distinction is made between a commercial representative and a distributor, so the expression 'agent' is interpreted to apply equally to both a main distributor and to a representative as well as to a commercial 'agent'. The expression 'agent' is therefore used throughout in this broader sense.
- Official agents must be nationals of the UAE or of wholly owned companies.
- In the UAE, local trade agency legislation prevails over conflicting foreign laws and over express provisions to the contrary which may be contained in any trade agency agreement.
- A foreign principal may appoint an official agent for the UAE as a whole or may appoint agents on an emirate by emirate (or group of emirates) basis. In either case, under local law, the agent's appointment is an exclusive one, generally relating to all the principal's business in the territory. Exceptionally (although the legislation is not specific on the point) it is usually accepted that the principal may appoint different agents in the same territory for entirely separate and distinct classes of products. Different official agents cannot, however, be appointed in the same territory to 'target' different groups of customers (e.g. governmental bodies as opposed to the private sector) or to act in competition with each other in respect of the same class of products. The official agent has the right to appoint sub-agents or distributors in its territory.
- The official agent is entitled to commission on all transactions in its territory, even if those transactions were not concluded as a result of his efforts or involvement.
- Trade agency agreements should be presented in Arabic and duly legalised, notarised and authenticated for use in the UAE. Despite the fact that the legislation provides that agencies not registered are not effective and that claims regarding them should not be heard, in practice, non-registration is not conclusive, especially if the failure to provide documents in registerable form arises from an act or omission on the part of the principal.

- In the event of any inconsistency between the Arabic text of an agency agreement and another language, the Arabic will prevail.
- The legislation does not permit a principal to validly terminate, nor to abstain from renewing, an agency agreement unless there exists a reason for justifying the termination or non-renewal.
- Re-registration in the Commercial Agents' Register in the name of another agent is not permitted even if the lifetime of the previous agreement has expired, unless dissolved through mutual consent or if there exist fundamental causes justifying the termination or non-renewal which satisfy the Committee of Commercial Agencies established pursuant to the legislation.
- If an agency is withdrawn at an 'improper' time or without due reason (even if the period has expired), compensation is payable to the UAE national agent. Since a principal's goods can only be cleared into the territory with the consent of an official agent and, in the event of a dispute, a new agent cannot be appointed until the committee has determined the issue – which can take a not inconsiderable time to resolve – an official agent often has a formidable lever to encourage an amicable compensatory settlement.

Conclusion

As mentioned earlier, this article outlines three of the more common business structures of interest to foreign companies – there are others. There are, too, regional differences and it is always as well to take professional advice in the emirate in which the company's business operations are likely to be centred.

Part 8

Marketing in the UAE

8.1

Marketing Information for Business Planning – Look Before you Leap

Julius Fernandes, Stafford Associates

As a tourist to the UAE, it is not uncommon to stop, stare and marvel, as tourists are wont to do, and come away astonished and amazed. Golf courses, a Manhattan-like skyline, the comfort of five-star hotels, a high standard of living, simplicity and sophistication, all blend together to give rise to a vibrant country that has all the trappings and excitement of a modern day western city. And all this built on what were, not so long ago, desert sands.

But as a businessman and entrepreneur, one is not merely interested in the city-built-from-sand romance. There is a need to dig deeper and look behind the elegance of the skyscrapers, above the buzz of a fast-paced city, beyond its gloss and glamour, to unearth the information that is vital not only to create business plans more accurately, but also to enable the implementation of those plans more efficiently. The need to sift through the sand and find the underlying rock upon which the foundation of any business can be built is absolutely essential.

Assimilating relevant information is never going to be easy, especially in a market like the UAE that is rendered more complex because of its diversity and paradoxes. The UAE is primarily an expatriate community with more than 75 per cent of its population composed of people from as far east as the Philippines and as far west as the USA, each bringing to the country his or her own brand of culture, language and business style. And despite this disparity, there is a definite, harmonious co-existence.

There is a diversity of the economy as well. No longer can the UAE be considered as just an oil exporting country; it is a country that has quickly industrialised and decreased its dependence on oil by diversification into other sectors such as trade, tourism, manufacturing, logistics and services, and with remarkable success. It is a country that has a population of about 2.5 million, but serves a market of about one billion, as it performs the role of a centre for trade and finance, not only within the Gulf region, but also

Trend Setter

Dubai is already living in the 21st century as many of us would agree. But what today is a bustling, modern hi-tech city, a show-piece, and the Hong Kong of the Middle East, was a drab and dull outpost in the Arabian desert, as recently as in the 1970.

In those days, the only source of news for residents of Dubai was a cyclostyled sheet of paper brought out by the Reuters. Until the morning of April 16, 1978. On that day Khaleej Times rolled off the press and newsboys across the country slipped the world under the doorsteps of readers.

With Khaleej Times debut in 1978 the flow of information not just in Dubai or the UAE, but the entire gulf underwent a dramatic transformation.

Khaleej Times pioneered journalism in the Gulf and enhanced the quality of expatriate life besides satisfying the hunger for news from home. The paper spoke to its readers language, provided them with information, education and entertainment, and all this in a reader-friendly manner.

Fast Facts

Khaleej Times is an English language newspaper and an independent business entity within the Galadari Holdings Group. It was the first to come on stream in Dubai on April 16, 1978. In 1999 it posted a turnover of over Dhs 150 million and expects a growth rate of 16% in the forthcoming years.

Unrivalled Readership

Khaleej Times is only ABC (Audit Bureau of Circulation) certified newspaper in the United Arab Emirates. The customer base represents its readers on the one hand and its advertisers on the other. The Khaleej Times addresses over 70,000 homes in the Gulf States. The ABC of London, ranks it as the highest circulating English language newspaper in the Middle East.

Unrivalled market share of advertising spend

Ninety per cent of the UAE advertisers using the English Press advertise in the Khaleej Times, while 45% advertise in it on exclusive basis.

As a single media entity, Khaleej Times retains 35% share of the total advertising appropriation expanded in the UAE.

Profile

Khaleej Times since has grown by leaps and bounds and crossed some frontiers.

Correspondents are stationed in key capitals including Bombay, Colombo, Dhaka, Delhi, Doha, Islamabad, Karachi, Lahore, London, Manama, Manila, Muscat, Peshawar and Trivandrum.

Our branch offices operate in Bahrain, Pakistan and the United Kingdom but there are also representative offices in India, Oman and Qatar.

Wire agency arrangements and other tie-ups

Khaleej Times is a subscriber to almost all relevant international wire agencies including AFP, Associated Press, Reuters, Press Trust of India (PTI), United News of India (UNI) and Wam. It also has exclusive tie-ups with Los Angeles Times, Newsweek, London Observer and the Daily Mail.

Memberships

It is a member of IFRA (International Association for Newspaper and Media Technology), Germany, and has retained the Thomsun Foundation, UK, as consultants. Key personnel are also members of the International Advertising Association (1AA) UAE Chapter.

The Khaleej Times head office, Dubai, U.A.E.

WE DIDNOT FILL THE OCEAN
...but we fathomed the depth of it.
YOUR INSPIRATION will lead US TO THE MILLENNIUM
Khaleej Times
No.1 by far
P.O. Box 11243, Dubai, U.A.E. Tel: +971-4-3384545, Fax: +971-4-3383345,
E-mail: ktimes@emirates.net.ae Website: www.khaleejtimes.com

for other markets such as the CIS, Africa, and Indian sub-continent. The existence of nine free trade zones in the country underlines this role of the UAE, and of Dubai in particular. The emirates have a fast-growing indigenous population, yet their dependence on foreigners will continue for a considerable time, and they are important members of the Islamic community, but at the same time perhaps some of the most tolerant and liberal in the Arab world.

So just how does one go about obtaining meaningful information about a market like the UAE, that will not only equip one with facts and figures, but will provide also a better insight of the market? How does one start acquiring information that not merely informs but which provides a basis for decision?

The gathering of accurate market intelligence needs to be high on any company's agenda as it starts to look at the UAE as a potential market. This article attempts to provide assistance in this regard.

The first need is to accumulate the maximum possible information on the general circumstance and conditions of the UAE, to have a broad feel for the country's economy, its people and characteristics, and the laws and regulations governing its society and businesses. Clearly, the need is to have sufficient information to help paint an overall picture of the UAE, within which a specific company's market is contained. Knowledge of the wider background will be essential to enable the placing of any proposed business activity in context and so gain a better understanding of the more precise information that will be required later. Such general information will no doubt be very broad and will not have the depth ultimately needed, but it certainly will be an ideal start to gain a sense of this country as well as highlight areas which will need to be investigated more thoroughly and in more detail, depending on one's specific industry, products or distinctive business.

This sort of information is available from a variety of sources, with differing levels of accuracy and reliability. Perhaps the easiest starting point will be the UAE Embassy in London or other major city, which can provide information on the laws and regulatory framework surrounding setting-up businesses in the country. The current UAE laws afford considerable choice in how legally to set-up operations, depending on the type and nature of the business, as will have been seen from Part 2 of this book.

From within the country here, information can be obtained from the various chambers of commerce and industry and each local government's economic department. These bodies publish trade statistics, economic indicators and industry related magazines that provide some idea of the business climate prevalent in the UAE, although the validity and accuracy of such published data need to be carefully considered. Nevertheless, as a starting point and by way of initial information, these can be quite useful. Included amongst such publications are:

- *Import and Export Trade Statistics*
  — published by Dubai Chamber of Commerce
- *Dubai Development Statistics*
  — published by the Department of Economic Development
- *Trade & Industry*
  — monthly magazine of The Dubai Chamber of Commerce and Industry
- *The 1999 UAE Yearbook*
  — Ministry of Information and Culture in Abu Dhabi.

In addition to these publications, the Dubai Department of Tourism and Commerce Marketing (DTCM) can be helpful in providing information about the UAE and about the prevalent business environment in the emirates, especially Dubai, through their various publications. In pursuing an aggressive policy of encouraging investment as well as tourism to the UAE, organisations like the DTCM have set up offices in several world capitals for the purpose of providing information to those interested in the UAE as a possible location for their business.

Apart from government publications, there are several trade magazines and journals that cover the country reasonably well and which tend to provide a higher quality of information. Some of the more popular magazines available include *Middle East Economic Digest*, *Gulf Marketing Review*, *Gulf Business* and *Gulf Construction*.

Additionally, local banks are a prime source of information, especially in helping one to gain a better appreciation of the economic environment of the UAE market. HSBC (formerly the British Bank of the Middle East) is one such bank able to help foreign companies wanting to gain information about the UAE market. Regular publications by this bank can be useful sources of information on the financial and economic performances and trends in the UAE as a whole.

The British Embassy is assiduous in compiling data on new projects and developments and would also be a source for obtaining general information about the local conditions, business climate, economic conditions, and estimates of future trends. Likewise, the British Business Groups (BBGs) in Abu Dhabi, Dubai and the Northern Emirates are active and offer practical advice and information. Their primary activity is encouragement of the development of British business in the UAE. They have a membership of several hundred British companies and provide vehicles for British individuals and organisations to meet regularly for the purpose of exchanging information and views. The BBGs are a storehouse of information on current and anticipated trends in the UAE. Other countries' embassies, consulates and trade offices also provide a wealth of information and a number of other international businessmen have also formed national interest groups within the UAE.

Such sources are quite effective in building the larger picture of what the UAE is all about and an image of whether it is a place in which one's specific company can do business. No doubt this will be a blurred image, but it will be clear enough to help one in recognising those areas which need more detailed study.

Subsequently, one will need to become more focused and more selective in seeking that information which will enable the decision to be taken about doing business, or not, in the UAE. To assist in this quest, the commissioning of a locally-based consultant might well be an ideal starting point. Having someone on the ground working expressly on one's behalf can be of immense value. If the answer proves negative, the time and expense of travelling to the UAE will have been saved. Over the years too many companies have been identified who have joined trade missions to the UAE, making a fruitless investment, when a small outlay in advance will likely have indicated whether such a visit was appropriate. Naturally, if such enquiry does prove positive, then a visit to the UAE becomes essential.

Once research has been completed and the indications are positive, a fact-finding visit must be planned to make detailed investigations of this market. It will be found that the UAE is exceedingly visitor-friendly and welcoming and being in the country, even on a short visit, will give one insights to a market which no published data can possibly match.

By being in the emirates, one can add to one's knowledge and data through meeting with and talking to people and organisations which have been operating in the UAE for a sufficiently long time to be able to offer advice and opinion that contribute to gaining a higher awareness of the market. The BBGs, for instance, are most willing to offer such counsel and advice. They have several Special Interest Groups (SIGs) – a forum for BBG members with common interests – which centre around specific sectors such as manufacturing, trading and services, shipping and transport, banking and finance to name but a few. The SIGs can provide significant information specific to a particular interest or industry and a high degree of validity can be placed on the information so obtained.

Managers and senior partners of organisations in the UAE are also reservoirs of information that one can tap into. Meeting with a range of organisations in terms of size, operations and industries will certainly give one an improved insight of the workings and mechanisms of this market. Once again, someone on the spot can set up an itinerary in advance, thereby saving substantial time and cost.

Experienced consultants in the UAE have the capability and qualifications to understand an individual company's information needs and deliver its specific requirements. No amount of desk research from London and no amount of publications can even come close to replicating the value to be gained from the 'people factor'. Choose the right people on the ground, who have rich experience locally, to share their expertise of local conditions and to assist in executing a detailed analysis of one's business needs, in terms that are relevant to a specific business or product. In addition, it is important to ensure the selected consultant has the capability to offer long term support, not only in providing market information but also in being able to offer assistance during the move from market investigation to product testing and planning.

The importance of selecting the right local partner at the very first stage cannot be overstated. It goes back to the 'people factor', and one needs to ensure the right people are working with you and for you. It is essential to get this absolutely right. After all, the UAE market does promise a multitude of investment and business possibilities but, at the same time, the market is equally complex and intricate so that attaining the rewards may not be as straightforward or matter of fact as originally perceived.

Working in the UAE is a rich international experience as well as a rewarding market. The assistance available is generous and wide-ranging and will make sure that initial periods of hesitancy, culture-shock and uncertainty about who to trust do not discourage doing business in this most cosmopolitan of markets.

Landor

creating and building brand power worldwide

Landor Associates
Creating and Building Brand Power Worldwide

Tim Ellett
Executive Director – Middle East
Landor Associates
1st Floor, Century Plaza
Jumeirah Beach Road
PO Box 62615
Dubai, UAE
Telephone (+971 4) 344 0340
Fax (+971 4) 342 0405
E-mail tim_ellett@ae.landor.com
uae_info@ae.landor.com
Web site www.landor.com

Brand consulting & design for the leaders of today . . . and tomorrow.

Landor Associates

Established in 1939, Landor was, and continues to be, a true pioneer in brand consulting and design. With over 700 professional staff worldwide and twenty one offices we provide a range of branding and design solutions to world class companies from pure consulting through packaging, literature, corporate identity, e-branding and retail environments, across all industrial sectors.

Our philosophy, echoed throughout the Young & Rubicam Group of whom we are a part, is to establish a partnership with our clients, helping them build their business through the power of their brands.

We have been working in the Middle East for close to a decade and are proud of our long term relationship with Sabic in Saudi Arabia, and our work for Eppco, Philip Morris and National Bank of Dubai in the UAE.

The Young & Rubicam network

Young & Rubicam is one of the major global communications groups in the world with more than a decade of experience in creating integrated marketing programs that deliver marketplace results for our clients.

Whilst each operation can be considered an industry leader in its own right, we have a philosophy which makes us even stronger through collaboration for the benefit of our clients.

Thus we can be considered the best alone, but even better together.

The Young & Rubicam Network is well represented in the Middle East with not only Landor but Team Young & Rubicam headquartered in Dubai.

Team Y&R are the largest advertising agency network in the Middle East/Gulf covering 24 capital cities and are a highly creative agency with a glittering array of awards to their credit – indeed they hold the title of Middle East Agency of the Year for 1999.

8.2

The Media in the UAE

Jack Pearce, Managing Director of Jack Pearce Associates, the Middle East PR affiliate of Saatchi & Saatchi

The virtually simultaneous announcements in November 1999 of the launch of Dubai TV's *The Business Channel*, the creation of an Internet City free zone and the establishment of the Dubai Press Club are indicative of the emirate's desire to establish itself as a, if not the, media centre of the Middle East.

Although Abu Dhabi is the capital of the UAE, it is nowhere near as aggressive as Dubai in cultivating new industries and the media are seen as an important component in helping to put the city on the world business map. Nearly all the leading advertising agencies have their regional head offices in Dubai, as do a growing number of international wire services and satellite channels such as *Showtime*, *Orbit*, *The Disney Channel* and *Star*.

The Press

The UAE daily press is generally of a high standard and has a considerable readership in neighbouring countries. While not overtly censored, when reporting on sensitive local issues it exercises a restraint that can best be described as 'self censorship'. Overseas visitors are often surprised at the amount of international news covered, which reflects the origins of the expatriate labour force that makes up over 80 per cent of the population.

There are three main Arabic dailies: the Abu Dhabi government-owned *Al Ittihad* (The Union), having the largest circulation, followed by Sharjah's independent *Al Khaleej* (The Gulf) and the Dubai government *Al Bayan* (The Announcement).

The *Khaleej Times* and *Gulf News*, both independent and virtually facing each other across Dubai's busy Shaikh Zayed Road, grapple to have the largest slice of the English language readership, while the recent newcomer *The Gulf Today*, published by *Al Khaleej*, finds it hard to gain even a sliver of the pie.

International dailies such as the *International Herald Tribune* are readily available from newsagents and at hotels the day after publication.

Many of the locally published magazines on the news-stands are also from the same publishing houses, but are generally very light reading as they steer away from anything remotely controversial.

Up until recently there were very few trade publications, but in the last few years the sector has started to gather pace. Information technology (IT) titles in particular have proliferated, with three Dubai-based publishing houses, AF-ITP, CPI and DIT, accounting for all but one of the Arab world's 14 main IT monthlies.

Broadcast

In retrospect, the invasion of Kuwait in August 1990 was a turning point for the Middle Eastern broadcasting industry. Suddenly everyone wanted access to *CNN* and *BBC World* for up to the minute news that the government-run terrestrial TV and radio services were both reluctant and ill-equipped to provide. Satellite dishes mushroomed and an industry was born.

For Arabic viewers the most popular channels from abroad include *ART, MBC, Al Jazeera (Qatar), Egyptian Satellite Channel* and the locally broadcast *Abu Dhabi TV* and *Dubai TV*, all of which are free to air with the exception of *ART*.

In English the only significant free to air channel is *BBC World* and viewers wanting variety must subscribe to one of the three regional satellite providers. First on the scene was Rupert Murdoch's *Star*, followed by Saudi-owned *Orbit* and then *Showtime*, a joint venture between the US's Viacom and Kuwait's KIPCO. Since then, however, the order has reversed, with *Showtime* having the largest subscriber base and fastest growth figures.

Viewers in Dubai can also subscribe to a bouquet of ten satellite channels on *Dubai Cable Network*, which is somewhat of a misnomer as it is rebroadcast on a terrestrial system with some of the saucier scenes pixilated. The market will soon become even more competitive as Etisalat, the UAE telecommunications provider, has plans to launch an actual cable TV service in the near future, although with what programming remains a mystery.

As for radio, the launch of Ajman-based *Channel 4 FM* in 1998 upset the somewhat complacent western popular music *Dubai FM92*, which had to fight back to regain its share of listeners and advertisers in the northern emirates. This skirmish of the air waves appeared to inspire the equally sleepy Abu Dhabi *Capital Radio* which in November 1999 split into two channels, *Emirates FM1* for the latest popular music and *Emirates FM2* for greater variety.

Arabic commercial radio stations in Abu Dhabi, Dubai, Ajman and recently Umm AlQuwain broadcast 24 hour music channels. Abu Dhabi also hosts the UAE's 24 hour religious station *Holy Koran* that offers Islamic teachings, lectures and phone-in programmes in addition to recitations from the Koran.

Hum FM based in Sharjah caters for the UAE's large expatriate Indian population with a musical variety channel, and Ras alKhaimah Radio Asia provides a popular Hindu/Urdu service from 11am to 1pm followed by a Malayalam service to 4pm. Ajman's *Channel 4 FM* plans to launch its own Hindi station in the near future.

Cinema

The cinema scene has also developed rapidly since intellectual copyright laws passed in the early nineties killed the flourishing pirated video industry. Currently there are 14 screens in Abu Dhabi, 20 in Dubai and 13 in Sharjah and the northern emirates, showing approximately 60 per cent western, 30 per cent Asian and 10 per cent Arabic movies. A number of new multi-screen Cineplexes are also in the pipeline, including one of six screens in Ajman and several in Dubai.

Internet

Although not quite qualifying yet as mass media because not everyone has access to it, the Internet is perhaps the first true 'medium' as it does not dictate the content or messages being conveyed but simply provides a neutral conduit for it. However some of this content is patently undesirable for a Muslim nation and Etisalat, the monopoly Internet Service Provider (ISP) in the UAE, has taken it upon itself to block access to several good sites and topics along with the many bad.

Connectivity to the World Wide Web has grown rapidly since the service was launched in August 1995. At the time of writing Etisalat claims a subscriber base of 160,000 which, assuming a multiplier of four users per subscription, suggests over 20 per cent of the country's population now has access to the Net.

However, there are many who feel that Etisalat's monopoly status enables it to get away with a sub-standard service and hope that the plans for a world-class Internet City free zone will force it to upgrade its offering. It may even herald competition, though a more likely scenario is that a fibre-optic 'backbone' will be provided exclusively for those within the zone.

Advertising

Healthy sceptics take newspaper and magazine circulation figures in the Middle East with a pinch of salt and put more trust in advertising revenues as a reflection of the media's relative reach and influence.

Advertising expenditure in the UAE also needs to be seen in the light of the country's position in the Gulf Co-operation Council (GCC) and pan-Arab market, where there is a growing shift towards regional rather than country specific advertising. According to Pan Arab Research Co (PARC), from 1995 to 1998 the share of pan-Arab media spend grew from 20 per cent to 25 per cent, with satellite television garnering a dominant 75 per cent and magazines 20 per cent.

The UAE has the second highest advertising expenditure in the GCC after Saudi Arabia, but by far the highest in per capita terms, standing at about US$80 per person as opposed to US$17 per person in Saudi.

Part of the answer to this discrepancy is the overspill from the UAE media into neighbouring gulf states, which makes them more attractive to advertisers than strictly domestic media. This not only applies to Abu Dhabi and Dubai's satellite TV channels but also to its strong daily papers, particularly the *Gulf News*, *Khaleej Times* and *Al Khaleej*.

Overall, newspapers are still by far the most dominant medium, attracting some 55 per cent of ad spend with a projected value in 1999 of $106 million (based on PARC year to date figures to the end of September.) Almost equal in second place come television and magazines, worth $34 million and $32 million respectively, though while television has grown by 9 per cent over 1998 figures, magazines have suffered a 7 per cent decline.

Radio advertising was the biggest gainer in 1999, rising by 14 per cent to total $10 million. This also elevated it to fourth place in the advertising league tables at the expense of outdoor advertising, which slipped 14 per cent into fifth place at $9.5 million.

By sector, service industries accounted for almost a third of advertising expenditure, worth US$61.7 million, followed by clothing, jewellery and personal accessories valued at US$47.3 million, a further 25 per cent of the total. Toiletries and motoring were worth 13 and 12 per cent respectively.

Etisalat was once again the number one advertiser in the UAE in 1999 with a projected ad spend of $2.9 million, almost all in newspapers. This contrasts with the second and third placed Dubai Summer Surprises and Al Massa cineplex, which favoured TV for getting their more immediate messages across. Fourth-placed Emirates Airline also favoured the daily press while Toyota, in fifth place, was the strongest purchaser of magazines space by a large margin.

8.3

Market Research in the UAE

Stuart Campbell-Morris, Regional Managing Director, Middle East and Africa, NFO MERAC, Dubai

'Collect knowledge from the cradle to the grave'
Prophet Mohamed (PBUH)

Technological advancement in many product categories has progressed these days – and the UAE and other Arab Gulf markets are no exception – to a stage where manufacturers and suppliers have little scope left to differentiate their products on the basis of purely rational benefits. In fact, even emotional benefits attached to products when they are presented to the consumer as brands tend to be very similar nowadays. Hence the scope for ultimate success lies more and more in information, ie one's knowledge of the market, and using that knowledge to commercial advantage. This is the role of market research, providing an understanding of underlying conditions in the market, how the trade operates, how the consumer sees your brand, etc; such knowledge is real power and can make all the difference between success and failure.

It is still occasionally said that for one reason or another – usually due to culture limitations, such as access to housewives – market research in this region is not able to provide this insight. After more than 20 years' experience carrying out market research throughout the region I believe I can confidently say that this is simply not so. However, this preconception is probably one of the reasons why the level of expenditure researching the habits, wants, likes and dislikes of Gulf consumers remains so low. For example, the total population of the six GCC states is equivalent to Canada – at approximately 30 million – yet the per capita expenditure on market research in Canada is currently around four times that in the GCC.

Another restriction on the size of the region's market research industry is that suppliers have not effectively developed the market, or even worked together to remove the ambivalance of some local authorities towards consumer market research as an activity advantageous to the business community. Market research as an industry in the Gulf still needs an agreed set of rules and practices, rules which are sensitive to the cultural requirements of these markets. As well as a general acceptance by the authorities that the profession is a worthwhile and legitimate business activity. Perhaps because of a strong heritage of trading and merchandising, the UAE authorities are amongst the most understanding.

The original market research agencies in the Middle East originated in Beirut, followed by Nicosia after the outbreak of civil war in the Lebanon. Nowadays there are market research agencies in all of the main markets in the Gulf. In the UAE, the focus is more on Dubai and Sharjah. All of these are still generalist, ie offering all types of market research. Given the size of the industry, it is not so surprising that the Gulf market has not yet evolved sufficiently whereby agencies specialise in one type of research or another as in the more developed markets in the West.

There are essentially two basic techniques in market research. The first and possibly the more familiar is referred to as 'quantitative' – the kind in which interviewers approach a sample of consumers and ask a series of questions from a highly structured questionnaire. This data is then processed by computer and presented in a series of analytical tables.

The other approach, called 'qualitative', is based on methods using clinical psychology. Small groups of consumers are convened and largely allowed to talk for themselves, albeit under the guidance of a professionally trained moderator. Qualitative research is often used as preliminary exploratory research, but its main strength is to explain consumer motivations, attitudes and provide answers to the question 'why?'.

Both techniques are possible in all markets in the Gulf, but always providing local cultural and other conditions are recognised right from the design stage of the project.

There are only two sources of data in market research – data already published and in the public domain, or, alternatively, going out and collecting your own. The first type of data is called secondary and the latter is called primary, as it comes direct from the source.

Quantitative: secondary data – desk research

Collecting secondary data involves desk research only, tracking down copies of published data sources and then extracting the information of interest. This sounds easy but like all other kinds of market research in the Gulf markets, it can present its own challenges.

As few social surveys or even official population censuses or national income and expenditure surveys are published in the region, let alone conducted, the most obvious type of secondary data on offer in these markets is macro-economic. The most useful to a market researcher is usually trade statistics, imports and exports by volume and value. This is an opportunity for the researcher to size the market. Some care is needed, however, especially if trying to aggregate across different Gulf markets.

Although the Harmonised System (HS) of classifying goods and commodities – a recent development of the UN SITC (Standard International Trade Classification) codes – is now being adopted in many of the Gulf states it is still by no means uniformly applied, and so the foreign trade statistics of the Gulf states still suffer from disparities across markets.

Some care is therefore needed when comparing or aggregating figures across markets. It can also pay to collect the same information from the other end (having identified the supplying countries) to also obtain trade statistics and therefore verify figures published by both exporter and importer.

Trade statistics in many of these markets also suffer from lengthy delays in publication, although the Dubai statistics tend to be the most up to date in the region.

Quantitative: primary data – consumer surveys

Already in the USA Internet penetration in certain segments of the population is approaching one-third, and so conducting surveys on the net is becoming increasingly common – it is fast and inexpensive. Internet penetration is possibly more advanced in the UAE than elsewhere in the Gulf. However, sometimes the telephone offers an alternative to the basic approach of a personal, face-to-face interview when surveying consumers of mass market products or services.

And the emphasis should be on 'sometimes', as telephone penetration is by no means universal across all segments of the population in many of these markets. Stipulating the telephone as the survey technique can therefore introduce a bias into the sample and its representativeness.

Therefore the great majority of respondents in consumer surveys conducted in the region are interviewed face-to-face; amongst men often in their place of work and amongst women in the privacy of their own homes. Random intercepts in streets or shopping malls, or knocking on the doors of a random selection of homes, are techniques generally not acceptable in the UAE or elsewhere in the Gulf for obvious cultural reasons – they are considered as an unacceptable intrusion of privacy.

Instead, a market research agency will look to build up its required sample of consumers by setting quotas or targets of different types of people, specifying by, amongst other things, such criteria as nationality, sex, age, income level, product usage, etc. Scaling the data from such a sample back to the population as a whole often represents a further challenge, as few Gulf states publish such statistical detail about their resident populations, even if they collect it in a national population census.

In fact, marketers in the region are even left debating the size of the total population in many cases, never mind its structure. Recent estimates of the population of Saudi Arabia have placed it at anything between 12 million and 20 million, so even a task as basic as sizing the market opportunity can obviously be difficult.

Inside these quotas respondents are picked up by what has become known as 'snowballing' – perhaps a rather inappropriate choice of word, given the Gulf climate. However, the concept behind the term validates its use as the idea is to find an original contact who fits the eligibility criteria and then try to 'roll out' from that primary contact by asking for referrals to acquaintances who may also be the kind of people we wish to include in our sample.

Whilst accommodating most of the cultural considerations necessary in these markets, the snowballing technique is fraught with danger when it comes to the eventual representativeness of the sample. Many rules need to be laid down, eg no more than two other respondents from an original contact, many layers to the sample to ensure adequate spread, and many controls and much supervision. Callback rates in the Gulf in a snowball sample of 30 per cent are not uncommon to check that the interview took place and to check some key answers, much higher than for a quota sample in a survey in the West. All of this adds to the cost of research in these markets, but it is absolutely necessary to protect the representativeness of the sample and hence the usefulness of the data.

A further danger to the quality of fieldwork in many of the Gulf markets is the lack of security felt by part-time interviewers. Their status under the various Labour Laws – sponsorship and work permits – is often poorly defined, or even actually prohibited, and so they may be inclined to limit the risk to themselves by cheating, filling in the questionnaires themselves. Agencies must be ever vigilant to this possibility, but the real solution wherever possible is to clarify their legal position before the survey begins. This is easier said than done in many of the Gulf markets.

Qualitative: primary data – consumer surveys

In qualitative research small groups of between six and eight consumers of a similar type or classification are brought together in a suitable hotel venue, office or home to explore the subject under research in a more relaxed environment. Such sessions typically take two to two and a half hours in a Gulf environment.

Depending upon the market in the region, female consumer groups of this type may or may not be able to convene in a hotel or an office. And even if a private home is used a Gulf Arab housewife may be uncomfortable being invited to visit a stranger's home on her own. Understandably she may wish to bring a friend along for companionship and security. However, these friends may not fit the eligibility criteria for the sample, and so the integrity of the research can be jeopardised.

It is always easiest for the person charged with recruiting such groups to simply resort to a close circle of friends and again the integrity of the sample is lost. So once again ground rules must be laid out in advance and then monitored.

However, properly organised qualitative research can be especially effective as Gulf consumers are still by-and-large more gregarious, more sociable than their counterparts in the West and so feel more relaxed in the environment of a group discussion.

A few words of caution

Finally, when considering results from research amongst Gulf consumers it is worth noting one other aspect of Gulf society. It is still very much an other-directed conformist type of society, with everyone watching everyone else and looking for what is accepted as the norm – at least in public. Hence a kind of courtesy or conformist bias can develop which can be misleading, as public norms and private preferences are not always the same obviously.

Nevertheless with the right type of controls and a culturally sensitive approach to both the research design and the eventual data interpretation, successful consumer market research is possible in all the Gulf markets. It should, however, be obvious by now that it is rarely a market in which to buy on price alone. If as a research buyer you receive widely different quotes from research suppliers ask yourself and your potential suppliers why. Do you know exactly what you are getting for your money? Especially in qualitative research in the region there are many grades of product, and rarely can the cheapest deliver the quality of information needed, a real insight into your Gulf consumer, his or her behaviour and beliefs. But always remember, in today's highly competitive markets in the Gulf, more than ever before, a final Arab proverb is very apt, 'noor al mariffa', which freely pop pops as 'knowledge is power'.

MERAC (Middle East Research and Consultancy)
P. O. Box 60992, Dubai
Tel: (9714) 282 2688
Fax: (9714) 282 2711

8.4

Exhibitions and Trade Fairs

Philip Dew, The Philip Dew Consultancy Limited

Exhibitions have become a major feature of the commercial environment in the UAE and contribute significantly to the country's economy. Exhibition centres have been set up in a number of emirates, drawing the interest of both exhibitors and attendees from all over the world.

Given the country's high level international trading activities, it is self-evident international exhibition and fair organisers should seek to arrange events in the UAE, and especially in Dubai, Abu Dhabi and Sharjah – but not to the exclusion of Fujairah on the other coast. Today, as a result, the UAE can boast some of the best exhibition facilities in the world.

Exhibition facilities

The major exhibition facilities in the UAE are:

- Dubai World Trade Centre
- Abu Dhabi International Exhibitions Centre
- Sharjah Expo
- Fujairah Exhibition Centre.

Dubai World Trade Centre (DWTC)

Inaugurated in 1979, the DWTC has become the leading venue in the UAE, possibly within the GCC, for a wide array of high quality exhibitions. Today the DWTC has seven exhibition halls comprising a total area of 33,000 square metres in which it holds in excess of 50 exhibitions a year – many of which, such as GITEX (The Gulf Information Technology Exhibition), are major events in the Middle East business calendar.

Table 8.4.1 Exhibitions in Dubai – second half of 2000

Start–end	*Activity name*
4–6 September 2000	Chemtex-Processtech incorporating Corrosion Middle East
17–20 September 2000	Packtech-Printech-Plastech 2000
17–20 September 2000	Tekno 7
18–21 September 2000	Premium 2000
25–27 September 2000	Gulf Beauty
26–29 September 2000	Motexha Autumn incorporating Motexha Shopper, Men's Lifestyle and Fashion Shows
26–29 September 2000	Ambiente Arabia
26–29 September 2000	The Leather Show
26–29 September 2000	Arab Hunting
4–8 October 2000	Index
4–8 October 2000	Arabshop
15–19 October 2000	Big 5
16–19 October 2000	Middle East Elevators and Escalators Technology Exhibition
28–1 October/November 2000	Gitex
26–1 October/November 2000	Computer Shopper
15–19 November 2000	Woman
19–22 November 2000	Autostop
19–23 November 2000	International Autumn Trade Fair
21–23 November 2000	Glass and Ceramics Manufacturing Equipment Exhibition

Abu Dhabi International Exhibitions Centre (ADIEC)

ADIEC is an integral element of the Abu Dhabi Chamber of Commerce and Industry and presents a comprehensive array of international exhibitions every year. In recent years the centre has been increasing in importance and today hosts some of the region's most prominent international exhibitions including IDEX (The International Defence Exhibition), ADIPEC (Abu Dhabi International Petroleum Exhibition) and MIDCOM (International Communications Exhibition). The main organiser of exhibitions in Abu Dhabi is The General Exhibition Corporation (GEXCO).

Table 8.4.2 Exhibitions in Abu Dhabi – second half of 2000 and first half of 2001

Start–end	*Activity name*
2–12 September 2000	Back to School
1–6 October 2000	Arab Industry
4–14 October 2000	Cars and Motor Cycles
7–11 October 2000	Safety 2000
15–18 October 2000	The 9th Abu Dhabi International Petroleum Exhibition and Conference (ADIPEC 2000)
1–6 November 2000	Food Stuff and Processing Equipment
5–6 November 2000	Arab Real Estate
6–10 November 2000	Arab Jewellery and Watch Show 2000
10–20 November 2000	Abu Dhabi International Motor Show 2000
6–15 January 2001	Gifts and Toys
4–8 February 2001	Environment 2001
7–16 February 2001	Décor, Furniture and Carpets
7–16 March 2001	Computer and Electronics
18–22 March 2001	IDEX
16–26 April 2001	ADIF 2001 – Abu Dhabi International Fair

The Expo Centre, Sharjah (Sharjah Expo)

The Expo Centre in Sharjah was set up in 1977 under the auspices of the Sharjah Chamber of Commerce and Industry and thus enjoys the accolade of having been the pioneer in its field. Today Expo Centre presents some 20 events annually at its 88,000 square metre, part open, part covered facility. A new centre is now under construction for completion in 2001.

Table 8.4.3 Exhibitions in Sharjah – 2000

Start–end	*Activity name*
22–25 March 2000	National Career Exhibition
3–7 April 2000	Watch and Jewellery Millennium Show
12–16 April 2000	Gulf Interiors Fair
22–28 April 2000	Sharjah International Fair
2–8 September 2000	Kid Expo
12–15 September 2000	Texpo
19–22 September 2000	Thailand Exhibition
27–30 September 2000	Leather Expo
27–30 September 2000	Al Hida'a
8–13 October 2000	International Food Fair
14–16 October 2000	German Technology Showcase – Baden Wurttemberg
24–28 October 2000	MidEast Watch and Jewellery Show
3–14 November 2000	Sharjah World Book Fair
20–24 November 2000	Automobile Show
18–31 December 2000	Eid Al Fitr Fair

Fujairah Exhibition Centre

Inaugurated late in 1996, the Fujairah Exhibition Centre, as part of the Fujairah Chamber of Commerce, Industry and Agriculture, has begun to establish its presence on the region's exhibition map. However, no details of exhibitions to be held in late 2000 are available.

Part 9

Labour Issues in the UAE

9.1

Compensation and Benefits

Martin Mankowski, Hay Management Consultants

Why is the Middle East different – and what makes the UAE special?

When one talks about pay systems, the UAE is different. If one is setting compensation levels in the West these days, it is often in the wider context of meeting a broad package of employee needs. Pay is one aspect of a range of employee requirements which include the ability to provide a preferred life style. The new generation are less likely to be prepared to give up leisure time activities for a premium in pay. Leading human resource (HR) managers provide the following reasons:

- In the West, the tax system limits the impact of any major pay increase – as income tax systems are progressive, added payments provide diminishing levels of benefit to the employee. Why give up leisure time if the tax system is likely to minimise any cash benefit?
- Benefits in the West usually include a reasonable pension system, so employees do not have to save for their retirement. While nationals are able to participate in state pension schemes in the GCC, most expatriates receive a once-only end of service payment – again cash becomes more important.
- Finally, expatriates employed in the Middle East tend to feel more vulnerable to dismissal; they are therefore more focused on building up a cash balance to cushion such an event.

In the GCC and particularly the UAE, cash remains a powerful motivator. However, there are other factors to consider. Those involved in HR see a range of needs from hard cash to a complex mix including benefits and provision for a relaxing life style. This matches the requirements of two main categories of employee: expatriates and nationals.

Expatriates represent the majority of the workforce in the GCC and a very large majority of those employed in the UAE. They occupy a wide range of positions from unskilled to chief executive officers (CEOs) of major organisations – in other markets, notably Saudi, Kuwait, Oman and Bahrain, it is less usual to see expatriates in top positions. For this reason, some of the highest paid expatriates are located in the UAE. In addition, the UAE is perhaps the most attractive market for unskilled labour and some of the lowest paid workers are also located in this market. In between the lowest and highest paid employees one sees a number of categories seeking different types of remuneration:

- The lower paid need food and shelter in addition to cash – which is normally remitted to families in home countries.
- Skilled, professional and middle to senior managers are more focused on cash to promote their image and save for a somewhat uncertain future. While benefits are on offer, these are increasingly preferred as cash alternatives.
- The same applies at the top of the tree to CEOs, although base pay may represent a smaller portion of the total cash paid out because not only are a range of benefits on offer, but also a fairly substantial bonus (both short and long term), often closely linked to corporate performance, is provided.

Nationals have different requirements of which life style plays an important role. There are examples of nationals who have rejected very tempting offers because the location is outside the main city area. Graduates are in very high demand, with average starting salaries around Dhs7000 per month (US$1900) – although the right graduate can negotiate a much larger package. The preferred candidate is often a person with a range of skills – both academic, technical and behavioural.

Given the complexity of the market, sophisticated techniques are required to survey the range of factors which contribute to the total pay package. Hay has invested heavily in research and analysis of this market, which is carried out by sector, by nationality and by the different elements which make up total pay in order to understand the main forces at work. Demand for a rapid response to pay questions has resulted in Hay's worldwide compensation database being accessible to HR managers instantly on the Internet.

The UAE is perhaps the most progressive market in the Middle East for payment systems. One is seeing the development of precisely focused methods of payment designed to attract high performing individuals. While not all these systems are state of the art in western terms, many are highly effective in recruiting targeted staff from competing and often more vulnerable organisations. Reasons for this include the presence of regional offices for many multi-national companies, with established systems supported by professional HR staff who know how to structure a deal and develop the career of a preferred candidate. In addition, business in the UAE is competitive – recruiting the wrong person because he is prepared to accept a low cost package or losing the right person because he feels under-paid can represent a very expensive mistake.

Market specifics

While Hay surveys are confidential and tend to be tailored for specific client needs, there are some non-proprietary facts that can be shared. First, average pay has increased by around 5 per cent in the past year – this level varies according to a number of factors including industrial sector, emirate and nationality. Next, the difference in compensation for similar jobs between the higher paying and the lower paying sectors is around one third. Finally, securing a job which pays above average rates can be an elusive goal. There are some guidelines but there is no magic formula:

- Jobs which closely link the level of remuneration to the individual's contribution are likely to pay more. For example:
  - a good salesman on commission can earn more than his boss
  - positions where the variable bonus is relatively large in relation to fixed pay tend to pay more.
- Employers who have well developed HR systems and good professional HR staff tend to be better able to recognise the value of an employee's contribution. However, that does not always mean that employers in this category pay the highest salaries – there are examples of well run companies that are not the best payers even though they are usually fair payers. One HR manager reported that, 'We know how to select the best people and get the most out of them – that knowledge is of benefit not just to the employer but also to the employee both in terms of job satisfaction and remuneration.'
- Making general statements about higher paying industrial sectors can easily be challenged. It is generally accepted that the banking sector pays well – however, there are many exceptions. These exceptions can be reduced if consideration is given only to international banks with a comparatively large presence in the area, but anomalies remain. Similarly there is an established view that competitive rates have fallen in the construction sector. This is difficult to confirm, although there is a considerable spread of rates in this area for similar sized jobs.
- Hay was once asked to confirm that pay rates in the Northern Emirates were lower than in other areas of the UAE and that Dubai now pays the highest rates. Once again it is difficult to generalise – and there are certainly many exceptions.

- Rather than using the industrial classification code or the company's geographical location as an indicator of pay potential, it is often more accurate to examine the so-called 'reward strategy' that an employer adopts. Hay has worked with companies which have the stated objective of paying rates that are relatively high in comparison with the market so that they can attract and retain the best. Similarly, some companies will deliberately pay below the market average in order to be more cost competitive. While neither example can always be a winning strategy, either strategy can be effective under certain conditions. Interestingly, a number of companies favour paying below average rates for smaller (more junior) jobs and above average rates for more senior jobs, the rationale being that there will always be a surplus of applicants for smaller jobs and the discretion to make a difference at that level is relatively low – so why pay a premium? However, for larger jobs, getting the right person is far more important and therefore the company is willing to pay a premium. This can be a cost effective and efficient approach. This strategy steepens the pay gradient and can sometimes be contrasted with the policy adopted by government offices, which may favour a flatter pay gradient.

Future trends

Increasing competition for high performing individuals combined with the continued drive for improved efficiency and the need to meet increasingly demanding localisation targets will have a major impact on the manner in which compensation is structured in the UAE. Trends that are likely to continue and perhaps accelerate will include:

- The development of a closer relationship between contribution and reward, leading to a higher proportion of performance-based variable payments – particularly for larger-sized jobs.
- Consolidation of allowances (social, service, etc.) into base pay because they do not provide a clear link between contribution and reward.
- Increased use of long-term incentives particularly to attract and retain high performing nationals.
- Traditional benefits like housing, transportation and education being replaced by cash payments tailored to individual needs.
- A steepening of the pay gradient (paying more for larger jobs and less for smaller jobs) as a declared policy of some companies and because labour is shifting from the government to the private sector.
- A narrowing of the differential between payment lines for different countries of origin, particularly for larger sized jobs.

Historically, employees in Saudi Arabia and Kuwait were, on average, paid better than employees in the UAE who were working on similar sized jobs. Now the picture is less clear. Average pay increases have been higher than those in Saudi Arabia recently and pay for top jobs in the UAE is seen to be competitive in comparison with that in Saudi Arabia. Interestingly, pay for nationals in smaller sized jobs has actually fallen in Saudi Arabia while this trend has not occurred in the UAE. In the words of one enlightened HR manager, 'We know some of the trends in reward and how these correlate with market forces – but we are always faced with surprises, there is no room for complacency.'

One can conclude that the UAE is a dynamic and volatile market which will continue to draw a wide range of job seekers, from unskilled to highly experienced, successful professionals. Right now, the market is particularly attractive to entrepreneurs who know the contribution that they can make to a business and who are able to identify employers that have structured their pay systems accordingly.

9.2

UAE Labour Law and Employment Law*

Bryan Cave LLP, *Dubai and Abu Dhabi*

Federal Law No. 8 of 1980 concerning Labour in the Private Sector (the 'Labour Law') governs the employment of workers by most private enterprises in the UAE. The Labour Law is a Federal UAE law and, therefore, applies in each of the emirates. However, the Labour Law does not apply to government workers, members of the armed forces, police and security forces, domestic servants (e.g., housemaids) and workers employed in certain agricultural fields and grazing. There is civil service legislation applicable to most public sector employees not subject to the Labour Law. In particular, the primary federal civil service legislation applicable to employees of the Federal UAE government and its instrumentalities is Federal Law No. 8 of 1973 (the 'Federal Civil Service Law'). Generally there are also separate emirate civil service rules or regulations applicable to employees of the individual emirate governments and their instrumentalities. Of course, the same varies on an emirate-by-emirate basis and thus is beyond the scope of this article. Moreover, it should be noted that there are special labour related regulations applicable in some of the free zones in the UAE (e.g., the Jebel Ali Free Zone). This article focuses on employment in the private sector and the UAE Labour Law.

Employment rights and 'emiratisation'

As a preliminary matter, it is important to note that employment is the right of UAE nationals under the Labour Law. Non-UAE nationals may be employed only after the approval of the Ministry of Labour and Social Affairs (the 'Ministry of Labour') is obtained (generally in the form of a work permit or 'labour card' issued by the Ministry of Labour; see page 198 below for further details). In particular, the Labour Law prescribes that

*This overview of the UAE Labour Law is not intended to substitute for legal advice on specific matters.

Ministry of Labour approval of the employment of non-UAE national employees generally is conditioned on the unavailability of qualified UAE nationals (and where there is a shortage of UAE nationals, preference is stated to be granted to nationals of other Arab states).

These preferential rights provisions are an extension of the UAE Constitution, which states that the Federal Union must endeavour to ensure that employment, and vocational training related thereto, is available for all UAE citizens. An outgrowth of such legislation is the current emiratisation policies of the Ministry of Labour, which encourage or often require the employment of UAE nationals in certain job sectors. These initiatives to employ UAE nationals, which are also being encountered in Saudi Arabia and other Gulf Cooperation Council (GCC) countries, are expected to increase in the future, especially in the context of foreign branch offices registered in the UAE which frequently operate only or primarily with expatriate (i.e., non-UAE national) employees.

The critical components of the UAE Labour Law

Employment contract and duration

The Labour Law requires that all employees be employed pursuant to employment contracts reflecting the wage, term (i.e., fixed v. indefinite) and nature of the employment. In the absence of a written contract, adequate proof of the terms of employment relationships may be established by any means of evidence (e.g., wages can be evidenced by cheques or other transfers of funds).

The Labour Law permits a 'probation period' with respect to all employment relationships, but only if expressly set forth in the written employment contract, which cannot exceed six months. An employer can dismiss an employee during such probation period without any notice and without paying any end of service benefits.

Working hours

The Labour Law prescribes maximum working hours in the UAE of:

- eight hours per day (arranged so that no more than five consecutive hours are required without intervals of at least one hour for rest, prayers and meals);
- six days a week (and therefore a maximum of forty-eight hours of work is permitted per week);
- with one day of rest (ordinarily Friday in accordance with Islamic customs), subject to certain exceptions in business sectors where different work hours may be required (hotels and restaurants).

The maximum permitted daily hours of work are further reduced by two hours during the Islamic holy month of Ramadan (which is based on the lunar calendar and therefore changes from year-to-year). However, these working hours limitations do not apply to persons in certain categories of administrative or supervisory type positions (i.e., certain senior management), and crews of naval ships and certain other marine employees. Work beyond eight hours on a given day, or on the day of rest, requires the payment of overtime wages to employees as described in the Labour Law.

Holidays, annual leave, sick leave and maternity leave

The Labour Law also grants employees the following official paid holidays:

1. Hijri New Year's Day;
2. Gregorian New Year's Day;
3. Eid Al-Fitr (two days);
4. Eid Al-Adha (three days);
5. the Prophet's Birthday;
6. Isra' and Mi'raj (1 day);
7. National Day.

Additional official paid holidays are often declared by the government (e.g., Sheikh Zayed's accession as the Ruler of Abu Dhabi) on a case-by-case basis. Furthermore, employees are entitled under the Labour Law to thirty days of paid vacation each year (after completing one year of service), and two days a month if the employee's period of service is more than six months but less than one year. Pro-rata leave is earned for employees who complete at least one year of service.

Also note that all Muslim employees are entitled, once, to a leave for pilgrimage to Mekkah not exceeding 30 days. Such pilgrimage leave shall not be deducted from the other vacation and holiday entitlements described above.

The Labour Law also permits annual sick leave for employees, except during the probation period (if applicable), as follows:

1. fifteen days of sick leave at full wage;
2. additional thirty days of sick leave at half wage; and
3. additional days of sick leave thereafter without pay.

In instances where an employee takes leave from work due to sickness or injury, he or she is required within two days to report such illness to the employer. The employer is permitted to take the necessary steps to have the employee examined to verify his illness.

The Labour Law also has specific provisions applicable to juvenile and female employees. For example, female employees are permitted 45 days of paid maternity leave, inclusive of days taken prior to the birth of the child. After expiration of the 45 day period, a female employee is entitled to 100 consecutive or non-consecutive days of unpaid leave in the event of any sickness resulting from the birth, provided the sickness is verified by a medical certificate. However, a woman who takes maternity leave is not entitled to the paid vacation for the same period.

Termination issues

The Labour Law addresses termination issues, which are fact specific and will vary depending on the term of the employment relationship. As a preliminary matter, it is important to characterise whether a labour relationship is for a fixed or indefinite term.

If an employer terminates a fixed term labour contract for any reason other than the 'for cause' justifications provided in Article 120 of the Labour Law (see below), the employer is required to compensate the employee for his loss. This amount shall not exceed the wages due to the employee for a period of three months, or the remaining duration of the labour contract, whichever is least. Likewise, if the employee terminates a fixed term labour contract for any reason other than as provided in Article 121 of the Labour Law (i.e., (i) if the employer has not fulfilled his obligation towards the employee as provided in the relevant labour contract or in the Labour Law; or (ii) if the employee was assaulted by the employer or its representative), the employee shall compensate the employer for his loss. This amount shall not exceed one-half a month's wages for a period of three months or the remaining duration of the labour contract, whichever is least.

For an indefinite term contract, either party can cancel the labour contract at any time for a legitimate reason upon at least thirty days notice to the other (unless longer notice is expressly agreed in the relevant labour contract). Also, of particular importance, Article 120 of the Labour Law permits an employer to dismiss an employee without notice and without paying the severance award only in the following cases:

1. if the employee adopts a false identity or nationality or submits forged certificates or documents;
2. if the employee is engaged on probation and is dismissed during the probation period (as described above) or on its expiry;
3. if the employee makes a mistake resulting in substantial material loss for the employer, on condition that the employer notifies the Ministry of Labour of the incident within forty-eight hours of its becoming aware of its occurrence;
4. if the employee disobeys instructions respecting industrial safety or the safety of the work place, on condition that such instructions are in writing and have been posted in a conspicuous place;
5. if the employee does not perform his basic duties under the contract of employment and persists in violating them despite the fact that he has been the subject of a written investigation for this reason and that he has been warned that he will be dismissed if such behaviour continues;

6. if the employee reveals any secret of the establishment in which he is employed;
7. if the employee is finally sentenced by a competent court for an offence involving honour, honesty or public morals;
8. if the employee is found in a state of drunkenness or under the influence of a drug, during working hours;
9. if, while working, the employee assaults the employer, the responsible manager or any of his colleagues; or
10. if the employee is absent from work without a valid reason for more than 20 non-consecutive days, or more than seven consecutive days in a one year period.

If an employer terminates an employee's contract for reasons other than those specified in Article 120 of the Labour law, the employee generally is entitled to a severance award, as specified in the Labour Law, provided that the employee has been employed for more than one year. Moreover, if an employer terminates an employee's contract for reasons that are deemed 'arbitrary', commonly referred to as an 'abuse of right', the employee may claim and be awarded compensation according to the nature of the job, the damage caused to the employee and the length of service. However, such compensation awarded for arbitrary dismissal, if any, shall not exceed the employee's wages for three months.

In the event of unjustified termination (i.e., resignation) by the employee, such severance award usually is reduced, or altogether forfeited, as provided in the Labour Law.

Workplace injuries and occupational diseases

The Labour Law also addresses, *inter alia*, workplace injuries that involve an occupational disease or a disability in accordance with schedules implemented by the Ministry of Labour, and the benefits afforded to employees with respect thereto. However, a complete analysis of the same is beyond the scope of this article.

The overlap between labour and immigration issues for expatriates working in the UAE

Immigration matters in the UAE are governed primarily by Federal Law No. 6 of 1973 Regarding the Entry and Residence of Foreigners, as amended by Federal Law No. 13 of 1996 (the 'Immigration Law'). The vast majority (i.e., in the range of 75 and 80 per cent) of residents in the UAE are expatriates (i.e., non-UAE nationals). As such, the Immigration Law directly impacts the majority of residents in the UAE.

Pursuant to the Immigration Law, foreigners may not work in the UAE without an employment visa (or labour card with respect to dependants sponsored by their spouse or parent) secured by their employer sponsor. Notwithstanding the foregoing, in most cases GCC nationals may work in the UAE without an employment visa. In addition, expatriate employees generally are not permitted to work for persons other than their employment visa and/or labour card sponsor. Transfer of employment (i.e, sponsorship) also is constrained by the policies of the Immigration Department of the Ministry of Interior and the Ministry of Labour, the primary relevant authorities with jurisdiction over immigration and employment matters in the UAE, as well as the permission (i.e, no-objection) of the current employer sponsor. These requirements that tie an expatriate's immigration/residency status to his/her employment status are fundamental to the control of the expatriate-dominated labour force in the UAE. The particular procedures by which 'sponsorship' is granted or transferred are the subject of detailed internal and public regulations which frequently change, often without notice.

Recent Labour Law Amendment

The Labour Law was recently amended pursuant to Federal Law No. 14 of 1999 Amending Certain Provisions of Federal Law No. 8 of 1980 Concerning Labour in the Private Sector (the '1999 Amendment'). The primary impact of the 1999 Amendment was to supplement Article 131 of the Labour Law. The 1999 Amendment requires certain employers to submit to the Ministry of Labour a bank guarantee as security for end of services benefits and repatriation costs related to their employees. Unfortunately, the implementing regulations related to the 1999 Amendment, which will supplement Article 131 (as amended by the 1999 Amendment) with the critical detail related thereto (e.g. which types of employers are required to post a bank guarantee, the type of guarantee, the amount and submission procedures related thereto, etc.), were not yet published prior to the time this article was submitted for publication. However, in any event it would appear that certain employers will be required to establish a bank guarantee as security for end of service benefits and repatriation costs for its employees, a procedure already applicable to employers in most of the free zones in the UAE.

9.3

Human Resource Related Issues

Martin Mankowski, Hay Management Consultants

The role of the human resources professional is in the ascendancy in the UAE, where there is perhaps greater recognition of the value of this function in this area than in other Middle Eastern countries. Why is HR regarded as a relatively important function and why is the UAE different? HR managers provide a number of explanations:

1. The UAE is often the first choice for expatriate labour seeking a market which offers stability and growth. It is politically stable, the diversification of the economy has provided some resistance to the volatile swings in oil prices and the level of inflation is relatively low, being considered to be less than Qatar, Kuwait and Saudi Arabia. The attraction to this area has created a dynamic and volatile market. To harvest this rich market requires greater HR expertise.
2. Many multi-nationals have located their regional head offices in Dubai. They have brought in world class HR professionals who know how to apply state of the art HR processes to ensure that the value added from their staff is optimised.
3. The pace of change is greater and the demand for quality is higher as the drive to develop new lines of business which are independent of oil and gas revenue increases.
4. The UAE is less protected and more exposed to competitive forces than some other markets. There is therefore greater pressure to increase business performance and recruit staff with the right capabilities and competencies.

In comparison with other markets, a greater variety of HR tools and techniques are being applied in the UAE and these are often supported by more creative initiatives.

Demographics

While the population of the UAE is low, there is a need to think about the consequences of the demographic profile. The total population is around 2.9 million with a high growth rate (estimated to be currently running at about 4 per cent) and a low proportion of nationals (being about 23 per cent of the total population). The majority of the population is made up of Indians and Asians. Estimates of the population break down are as follows:

Nationality	*% of Total*
Nationals	23
Other Arabs	13
Indian Sub-Continent & Asians	62

Other

The total workforce is around 1.4 million, but a relatively small proportion (around one-fifth) of nationals are currently employed and they are estimated to make up only 10 per cent of the total UAE work force and a minuscule 1 per cent of the private sector work force. The low level of employment is not too surprising given that nearly half the national population is below working age, the vast majority of the female population do not work and retirement can take place at a relatively early age. The proportion of nationals employed in sectors like the government and the military is high – in some areas above 50 per cent. The proportion of nationals employed in sectors like construction and manufacturing is relatively low and in some areas is below 1 per cent.

Demographic trends which have an impact on HR initiatives in the UAE include the following:

- a reducing number of foreigners;
- as the number of foreigners falls, the average age of the population also falls as nationals with large families become more predominant and the proportion of foreign workers with bachelor status falls;
- within the foreign population there are an increasing number of Asians and a reducing number of Westerners;
- the level of urbanisation is increasing, now around 70 per cent. There are fewer opportunities for employment in rural areas.

HR considerations by emirate and principal project

How HR solutions are developed varies. There are geographical, project, management, cultural and many other differences which contribute to the manner in which a solution is structured. It is difficult to generalise, but some of the factors for consideration are set out below, first regionally and then by considering some of the major programmes or projects.

Abu Dhabi is the largest emirate in terms of landmass, population, oil & gas reserves and off-shore investments. It is the land of the mega-projects – this is the emirate with the economic muscle to make things happen. However, it sometimes is seen to proceed in a rather ponderous manner and can appear a little cumbersome in comparison with its dynamic neighbour, Dubai.

Dubai is viewed as the emirate of opportunity. Small businesses grow and flourish, deals are made and executed rapidly. It is now the most diversified of the GCC economies and has perhaps the most far-sighted policy in terms of the manner in which it develops and enriches its economy. Many of the economic diversification programmes are initiated by the economic department, which has demonstrated an enlightened approach to changing the economic profile of the emirate. Plans proceed for Dubai to further develop, aiming to become a hub for:

- tourism;
- distribution;
- information;
- health care.

There have been set-backs to the diversification strategy, not least of which has been the economic downturn in Asia and in particular the fall in visitors from the CIS. The consequence of this in late 1998 until the present time is that many of the huge shopping malls built in Dubai have not reached their projected revenue targets. An import statistic for many retailers has been the fall in gold imports, down by 43 per cent in 1998. Mobility in the labour market is therefore high, with a strong focus on self improvement and the need to identify where the best opportunities are emerging and how to structure the deal to gain a competitive advantage.

Sharjah and the other Northern Emirates have a less significant impact on the economy. Sharjah has the image of being the cheaper alternative in comparison with its richer neighbours. Rents for accommodation are lower, many factory-produced goods from the sprawling industrial estate are also lower in cost and the retail outlets tend to focus on providing low cost products and services. While this alternative is attractive to some segments of the market, Dubai's focus on quality seems to be the winning formula. The other emirates are relatively small and tend to provide nationals for the other more developed emirates but offer few local employment opportunities.

Key projects which are having an impact on the manner in which the HR function has developed include the following: The Jebel Ali Free Zone (JAFZ) remains the bench-mark in the region for how a free zone should operate. While it has attracted criticism because it does not offer a cost-effective solution to certain investors and it favours industries that increase port activity, its success is unrivalled. It continues to grow and expand and has attracted an international pool of professional expertise that will continue to expand the business base. When it first became a contender for international investment in the mid-1980s, the huge industrial cities in Saudi Arabia seemed far more attractive. This has all changed; JAFZ offers minimum bureaucracy and enables entrepreneurs who rely on excellent infrastructure to become rapidly established.

The UAE has fallen behind other GCC countries in the race to become world class suppliers of petro-chemicals. The new ADNOC-Borealis joint venture, Borouge, which has been set up to produce polyethylene, represents the first cautious step by Abu Dhabi to join the race. The plant will be located at Ruwais, where the expansion project for ADNOC's second refinery is also located. The full potential of these developments at Ruwais has still to be realised.

An area where substantial capital investment has taken place is the aluminium smelter Dubal, which has successfully completed the first expansion phase ahead of schedule and below budget and is embarking on a further phase

Abu Dhabi's ambitious Saadiyat Market is proceeding. The development of the zone, under a 50 year concession from the Abu Dhabi Free Zone Authority – Saadiyat will be carried out by the public company Emirates Global Capital Corp, capitalised at US$3.3 billion. The zone will concentrate on the transshipment and trading of commodities and raw materials in international markets. An ambitious programme is being developed to attract world class professionals to work in this area.

Following the rather gloomy banking sector appraisals from a number of credit agencies early in 1999 (including S&P and Moody's), which primarily focused on regulations, policies and issues around transparency, there has been more encouraging news from this sector. Merger activity may be about to overcome the rather independent and conservative nature of many of the banks in a market which is often described as 'over-banked'. This is being catalysed by the proposed merger between Emirates Bank International and the National Bank of Dubai.

Investor confidence is slowly returning to the stock market after the speculative and volatile trading which characterised much of 1998. The government has approved a law to set up an official securities market and discussions are in progress to consider whether foreign companies can be listed on the exchange and if expatriates will be allowed to trade in local shares. A tightening of standards, with which listed companies will need to comply, is also under review and some would say overdue. The long awaited law setting up a formal stock exchange may at last be issued in draft form in 1999. The Bourse will be operated by a securities exchange markets board regulated by an independent securities and commodities authority. By permitting multiple trading floors, one of the main obstacles to the inauguration of the exchange, the location of the Bourse, has been by-passed. There are 88 joint stock companies and 44 companies are traded informally. It is estimated that there are around 220,000 UAE national shareholders currently served by 37 licensed brokers.

Defence contracts worth US$175 million were announced at IDEX 99 in Abu Dhabi, less than at some previous exhibitions, but nevertheless confirming that Abu Dhabi retains a major strategic role in the region's defence.

The UAE Offset Group announced at IDEX that an outline agreement had been signed with Qatar General Petroleum Corporation to develop and supply 3 billion cu ft per day of gas to the UAE and Oman. Once again the UAE is positioning itself as an area which is able to add value to imported feed stock.

Emiratisation

In addition to the diverse needs of the market, there is a further dimension which underlines the need to develop the HR process – the increasing importance of meeting emiratisation targets. While the pressure to meet localisation targets is not as high as in Saudi Arabia and the dependence on cheap foreign labour remains as a barrier, the localisation process is becoming an increasingly important issue. For some organisations, the recruitment and retention of nationals who can deliver substantial value to the organisation has become the top priority. There are good national candidates in the market. However, the traditional approach of selection based on academic scores is proving to be a blunt instrument. Some of the more enlightened organisations, particularly in the finance sector, are using a variety of tools and techniques to improve their selection and development processes, leading to better career planning for nationals, supported by more focused training programmes. The processes applied fall into a number of categories including highly targeted and selective recruitment, demanding induction and initial learning programmes, use of structured assessment centres, performance management, manpower development, career planning and the application of effective reward strategies

HR managers agree that meeting emiratisation targets in a positive and responsive manner requires much higher standards of recruitment and

career planning. The pressure for localisation will also lead to an improvement in training facilities. Learning English and becoming computer literate tend to be the top priority. Another successful training approach has been for companies to sponsor nationals on distance learning programmes with quality business schools, the MBA being a popular programme. Gaining additional business knowledge on these programmes has proved very useful both to the jobholder and the organisation. It also improves retention levels amongst the more ambitious nationals. There is no evidence that nationals automatically leave for better jobs once the training is complete. If HRD is allowed to create the right organisational climate and nationals have clear career paths, then they tend to be loyal employees.

A key question over the next ten years and a very important issue for HR managers will be how to increase the level of nationals in employment and reduce the level of dependence on foreign workers. This problem will become more acute as an increasing proportion of young nationals enter the labour market seeking interesting and rewarding careers.

The strategic role of HR

The development of the strategic role of the HR function has brought about significant changes in the way business is conducted. HR managers are spending more time with the executive team to determine how best to add value to the business. Manpower plans are now more professionally prepared and more closely integrated with business plans. At the same time, targets set in business plans are more frequently being adopted as part of the performance management process. The need for good HR processes has never been stronger. Many organisations agree that the manner in which the HR function is performed has changed substantially in the past few years and it is no accident that Hay Consultants are repeatedly asked to recommend good HR managers.

In particular, the drive to be more competitive has required that the reward strategy is very carefully developed. Good managers and executives can deliver significant value to the organisation – the manner in which their package is structured should reflect this contribution. Accordingly, packages are becoming more flexible and the variable proportion linked to the achievement of realistic targets is increasing. The finetuning of top executive packages requires substantially more competitive information and HR consultants are under pressure to provide more detailed surveys with each successive year.

The conclusion from a review of the above issues is that there is increasing recognition of the value that a professionally managed HR function can provide in developing an efficient and effective organisation.

9.4

Nationals and Expatriates – the Labour Force in the Emirates

Philip Marsh, Managing Director, Stafford Associates

The hot topic in the emirates and all other Arab states is the burgeoning indigenous population, the explosive growth in school and college leavers and the consequences for job creation and economic growth. There is another agenda in the GCC states, which is the disproportionate percentage of foreigners in the labour force at all levels, and especially in the private sector. One obvious way of finding jobs for new entrants to the pool of employable nationals, apart from economic growth, is to replace the foreigners. Policy and public statements in some GCC states can muddle up the issues and these are posing an increasing threat to the already strong feelings of insecurity amongst expatriates. If this feeling grows too strongly then expatriates will become increasingly unlikely to train nationals to succeed them.

As is well known, the oil price jumps in the early 1970s led to the truly remarkable economic growth in the Gulf region to the point where modern cities abound which are the equal to the best in the world and where the material abundance and quality of life are superb. Modern homes, unsurpassed infrastructure, hot and sunny weather all year, goods available from all over the world, virtually no crime, an exotic international community, all hosted by a people who are warm, peaceable and hospitable and who have welcomed foreigners of all origins to help them build their countries.

The UAE is the epitome of this process. The seeds of this growth were laid many centuries earlier. Gulf Arabs have always been international in outlook, trading along the coasts from southern Arabia and Iran to the tip of the subcontinent and beyond, meeting and inter-marrying with little class or status consciousness. Europeans, especially the British, tried and succeeded in controlling trade routes and keeping a level of orderliness at times among competing tribes and territories. And between them for a very long time were tradespeople and intermediaries and functionaries from India.

The basis of this rapid growth was therefore already in place. The unprecedented oil revenue flows funded the creation of the current labour market structure.

The indigenous population has taken its share of national wealth through an ingenious and effective system of land grants, soft loans, the restriction of foreigners to rented accommodation and in the requirements of 51 per cent local ownership of virtually all commercial organisations. Within the labour market, real and sinecure jobs in government and the public sector have had the triple effect of (a) providing regular and virtually guaranteed income, (b) ensuring nationals are in control of an economy where they are a minority, and (c) concentrating UAE employees into the government sector almost exclusively, thus skewing any normal distribution across industries and occupations.

In the private sector it has been estimated that national employees may be as little as 1 per cent of the total workforce. Some figures indicate the unusual balance of the labour force as well as its astounding growth over so few years.

Table 9.4.1

	Total Population	*Nationals*	%	*Expats*	%
1968	180,425	114,607	63.5	65,818	36.5
1975	655,940	200,000	30.5	455,940	69.5
In Employment	296,720	45,000	15.2	251,720	84.8

There was a further growth in employment in the private sector of 41.5 per cent in 1977 compared to 1975.

Table 9.4.2

The distribution of nationalities in the expat population in 1975 was:

Expat Arab	62,000	24.5%
Sub-Continent	163,000	65.0%
Iranian	21,000	8.3%
Western Expat	5,000	2.0%

Now there are about 2.3 million people in the UAE, overwhelmingly concentrated in Abu Dhabi, Dubai and Sharjah, as has been the case since the 1960s. The population balance is about the same, with the notable addition of people from the Far East, who began to appear in the late 1970s and, in the 1990s, a noticeable presence from the former Soviet Union republics.

The UAE is perhaps better placed than all other Gulf states to continue to grow and is also better able to absorb the 20,000 or so national additions to the labour market. Saudi Arabia, for instance, needs to find about 250,000 new jobs a year whilst nearby Iran needs a massive 650,000 annually.

The structure of the labour force remains one where nationals hold government jobs, with expat advisors and subordinates from Arab, western and sub-continent countries. The private sector is majority sub-continent managed and staffed but with a very strong presence of western multinationals giving a strong appearance of western management.

There is a presence of some sort from every country, making the UAE probably the most cosmopolitan and complex labour market in the world.

Perhaps the strongest influence on the structure of the labour force in future is the likely membership of the WTO. In the UAE as well as other GCC states, membership brings in its wake more foreign investment free of majority local ownership, employment of foreign labour without a requirement for local sponsorship, the possibility of land and/or property ownership (already announced in Bahrain) or long leases (announced in Sharjah, January 2000) and even rights of permanent residence to proven and worthy expatriates (as has been suggested in Bahrain).

Thereafter, the way in which nationals will be employed will be a function of the rate of growth. Whilst government jobs are full and sinecures reducing in volume, nationals are being encouraged to join the private sector at lower salaries and uncertain tenure. High economic growth rates will make this easier whilst low growth rates are more likely to lead to expatriates being replaced. There are also sectoral pressures, with the government requiring banks and insurance companies, for instance, to accelerate employment of nationals.

It must be strongly emphasised that the government of the UAE and its individual emirates are very realistic with regard to the continuing employment of more expatriates over time as well as realistic about indigenous talent. Everything points to more growth, more expatriate employees and a growing number of nationals in the private sector.

Emiratisation of jobs – illusions, fallacies and threats

Unbelievable growth in population, the economy, the number of foreigners as well as changes besetting the rest of the world could be fertile ground for conflict and dissension. Yet in the UAE all nationalities live and work together in harmony and there is a peacefulness and mutual tolerance which is unknown anywhere else in the world in the writer's substantial international experience. It is true that many talk in the language of national stereotypes, but those same people work calmly together and with great cultural sensitivity.

Nevertheless, there is a natural level of deference towards Emiratis and an understandable fear by expats of non-renewal of contracts. Short-term employment contracts, shorter-term housing contracts and the need to perform do engender an exaggerated short-termism in people's feelings. Even those resident for 20 years or more are known ritually to announce that they may not be here next year.

Therefore, the big family size of nationals whose children are coming to the market are seen as a threat. For nationals it is only proper that they do not expect to be unemployed when there are tens of thousands of jobs held by foreigners. It is hardly possible to be otherwise.

The UAE government has invested heavily in further education designed to prepare nationals for useful and productive employment. More than a decade old is a network of Higher Colleges of Technology, staffed largely by western faculty and delivering graduates of about Higher National Diploma standard. All complete computer and English courses before being allowed to join the courses and the flows of qualified nationals to the private sector will come largely from this source. As in most Arab countries, female graduates are more than half of the total.

There has been a veritable rash of new universities in the last two years. In addition to the older and well-established University of Al Ain, Sharjah has a 'University City' of very grand, monumental buildings plus high hopes of high standard graduates. Sheikh Zayed University will graduate highly computer-literate women, and each emirate, where there are nearly 50 private institutes, is offering a variety of higher education courses for local and expatriate managers and professionals. For instance Stafford Associates has nearly 400 managers and professionals of 57 nationalities, studying for master and doctoral programmes in management, marketing and education, with the Universities of Leicester, Sheffield and Exeter in the United Kingdom. Thus the UAE labour market is well poised to offer well-trained, good quality staff at all levels, with lots of in-country provision for continuing professional development.

As one of the most complicated markets in the world, there are other characteristics potential investors and employees might wish to know. Perhaps as much as 50 per cent of the expatriate labour is unskilled, or paid at unskilled wage rates. Many tasks are labour intensive with little attempt at automated processes or use of machinery equipment or tools, which would be routinely available in any advanced country. Conversely the UAE is also a very advanced country in many ways and it takes a little while to get used to the bewildering array of work standards and efficiencies, from the most sophisticated all the way down to crude, low-level, very third world work practices, and everything in between. Companies here need to adapt to the mix. Some of the drawbacks are obvious, yet there are also great benefits. Vehicles and labour can be hired and working in minutes if you have a sudden removal or transport job. People will work very long hours and be very keen to meet your standards. There are networks of friendly associates and fellow countrymen who help each other all the time in the interests of work, trade and income and therefore deliver at speeds unimaginable in the West. This is sometimes accompanied by unaccountable delays in gaining Government approvals; yet sometimes such approval is immediate.

Any employer needs to acquire understanding of this mix of nationalities and cultures and work out his own way of getting benefits and value.

Over time, the UAE government is committed to reducing the high numbers of lower grade labour and promoting high value and high tech employment. At the lower end, the creation of a more mobile labour market will be combined with controls over petty trade and sundry services.

At the higher end are the continuation of the great visionary projects of the nation's leadership – most notably the creation of a world financial centre in Abu Dhabi and an Internet City in Dubai. And for all expatriate staff there will be compulsory health insurance.

In short, the UAE is embarked on an upgrading of its entire labour force, with major emphasis being on the English and computer literacy of the whole education sector for nationals, plus a controlled phasing out of lesser skilled expatriates and a continuing welcome to high quality, well educated foreigners.

Part 10

The Real Estate Market in the UAE

10.1

The UAE Residential Property Market

Ian Albert, Cluttons, Dubai

Essentially, the UAE property market is available to foreigners through rental only. Freehold ownership is restricted to AGCC (The Gulf States) nationals only. When considering locating to the UAE, rent allowances for employees must be considered as this can contribute considerably to annual overhead expenditure. Housing allowances vary according to the grade of the employee, from full rental payment including furniture allowances and utility payment to a simple all-encompassing housing allowance included within the salary.

The correct identification of staff grades and subsequent expectations should be clearly identified prior to entry into the market. Once established, a discussion with a real estate agent can assist in the likely budget for each grade of employee. Set the budgets and instruct a real estate agent to locate suitable property. Due to the fluid nature of the residential market, quick decisions (and payment of rents) are a must, as property availability changes day by day. Delays in the availability of funds or in the decision making process can mean losing the property.

Due to the number of expatriate workers in the UAE, consideration should also be given to the location of the proposed 'home'. People of the same nationality prefer to live in close proximity to each other and, as such, certain areas are associated with, say, the European or Asian communities. Newcomers to the region can feel uncomfortable in communities that have separate cultures with which they are unfamiliar.

In general, the residential market can be viewed as stagnant or falling in terms of rental levels. Whilst not as technically complex as the commercial market, companies should pay close attention to the extent of both the landlords' and tenants' responsibilities as set out in the following financial and leasing information.

Residential – villas

Financial/lease information

1. The lease agreement Residential leases are normally for a period of one year, renewable thereafter on an annual basis. Leases are the standard approved municipality lease issued by the landlord and conforming to the requirements of the rent committee of a particular emirate, the terms of which are not usually negotiable. The rent committee allows an increase over a two-year period of between 15 per cent and 25 per cent biannually.

Two copies of the lease agreement are issued. When these have been signed by the tenant and returned to the landlord with all payments due, both copies of the lease agreement are signed by the landlord, a receipt issued and one copy of the agreement is returned to the tenant.

2. Payment terms Ascertain the number of cheque(s) the landlord will accept in payment. Some landlords will offer a discount off the annual rental if payment is made in full at lease commencement. If payment is made by more than one cheque, the first cheque must be of current date and the others post dated.

3. Security deposit Ascertain the amount of the security deposit, which usually varies between Dhs2000 and Dhs5000. This is normally fully refundable at the time of vacating the premises at the end of the lease term. However, check on any stipulations by the landlord relating to the condition of the premises on handing over. Some landlords request outgoing tenants to repaint the property internally and will withhold this cost from any refund due, although this is not common practice.

4. Agency fee This is 5 per cent of the annual rent, payable by the ingoing tenant/company to the real estate agent.

5. Municipality tax A tax of 5 per cent of the annual rent is payable annually and this amount may vary from emirate to emirate. This is paid by the tenant/company.

6. Utilities deposit There is a Dhs2000 refundable security deposit payable for the supply of electricity, water and sewerage services to the property. This is refundable on vacating the property once the final bill has been paid.

Property Information

1. Maintenance This is normally the responsibility of the landlord but confirmation of this should be obtained and specified on the lease agreement. It is also useful to know that the landlord or his appointed agent can be easily contacted in the event of an emergency.

2. Schooling When looking for a villa, it may be useful to take into account the proximity of schools and travel time involved.

3. Sewerage Some areas of the UAE are still not connected to mains sewerage. It is useful to ascertain the position. If the property is not yet connected to the mains sewerage system, then at some point in the future this work will be undertaken and may cause inconvenience and difficulty in access to the property when the roads are dug up.

4. Surrounding vacant land If the property is surrounded by vacant land, if possible it is prudent to try and ascertain the use to which this land may be put in the future e.g. construction of a mosque or school etc.

5. Pool If a communal swimming pool is provided on a compound, the maintenance of the pool is normally the responsibility of the landlord. If a private pool is provided, sometimes the landlord will pay for the maintenance, but usually it is the responsibility of the tenant. The monthly cost of maintaining a small pool is approximately Dhs500.

6. Internal/external repainting Normally the landlord will pay for the internal repainting of a villa every three years, and the exterior every five years.

7. Cleaning of water tanks This is normally the responsibility of the landlord. As per UAE regulations, water tanks should be cleaned once per year.

8. Location of power points/venting for dryer Some properties are very poorly serviced in this regard and it is advisable to check the number of points provided, especially in the kitchen, and venting for dryer either in kitchen or laundry room if provided.

9. Satellite TV This is sometimes provided by the landlord; otherwise it will be a tenant's cost for the dish installation, de-coder and programme subscription.

Residential – apartments

Financial/lease information

1. The lease agreement Residential leases are normally for a period of one year, renewable thereafter on an annual basis. Leases are the standard approved municipality lease issued by the landlord and conforming to the requirements of the rent committee of a particular emirate, the terms of which are not usually negotiable. The rent committee allows an increase over a two-year period of between 15 per cent and 25 per cent biannually.

Two copies of the lease agreement are issued. When these have been signed by the tenant and returned to the landlord with all payments due, both copies of the lease agreement are signed by the landlord, a receipt issued and one copy of the agreement is returned to the tenant.

2. Payment terms Ascertain the number of cheque(s) the landlord will accept in payment. Some landlords will offer a discount off the annual rental if payment is made in full at lease commencement. If payment is made by more than one cheque, the first cheque must be of current date and the others post dated.

3. Security deposit Ascertain the amount of the security deposit, which usually varies between Dhs2000 and Dhs5000. This is normally fully refundable at the time of vacating the premises at the end of the lease term. However, check on any stipulations by the landlord relating to the condition of the premises on handing over. Some landlords request outgoing tenants to repaint the property internally and will withhold this cost from any refund due, although this is not common practice.

4. Agency fee This is 5 per cent of the annual rent, payable by the ingoing tenant/company to the real estate agent.

5. Municipality tax There is a tax of 5 per cent of the annual rent payable annually and this amount may vary from emirate to emirate. This is paid by the tenant/company.

6 Utilities deposit There is Dhs1000 refundable security deposit payable for the supply of electricity, water and sewerage services to the property. This is refundable on vacating the property once the final bill has been paid.

Property Information

1. Maintenance This is normally the responsibility of the landlord, but confirmation of this should be obtained and specified on the lease agreement. It is also useful to know that the landlord or his appointed agent can be easily contacted in the event of an emergency.

2. Schooling When looking for an apartment, it may be useful to take into account the proximity of schools and travel time involved.

3. Surrounding vacant land If the property is surrounded by vacant land, if possible it is prudent to try and ascertain the use to which this land may be put in the future i.e. construction of a mosque, school etc.

4. Facilities Many apartment blocks provide facilities such as pool, gym etc., and maintenance of these facilities is the responsibility of the landlord.

5. Parking Dedicated parking is usually provided of one space per apartment free of charge.

6. Internal repainting Normally the landlord will pay for the internal repainting of an apartment every three years.

7. Cleaning of water tanks This is normally the responsibility of the landlord. As per UAE municipality regulations, water tanks should be cleaned once per year.

8. Location of power points/venting for dryer Some apartments are very poorly serviced in this regard and it is advisable to check the number of points provided, especially in the kitchen, and venting for dryer either in kitchen or laundry room if provided.

9. Satellite TV This is usually provided by the landlord; otherwise it will be the tenant's cost for the dish installation, de-coder and programme subscription costs

Abu Dhabi

The Abu Dhabi residential property market is dominated by apartments, due in the main to the island nature of the capital. The apartment sizes tend to be larger than in Dubai. However, unlike Dubai, very few buildings offer in-house facilities such as swimming pools and gymnasiums.

Abu Dhabi also differs from Dubai and Sharjah as there is much more intermixing of nationalities within buildings. Again this is attributed to the reliance on apartments as the primary source of accommodation.

Due to a previous oversupply of apartments, rents have fallen over the previous two years and have now 'bottomed out'. This is applicable to the newer and quality apartment buildings as tenants have upgraded accommodation from older housing stock. Older buildings and property in the lower middle to low price ranges still suffer from quite high vacancy rates.

The villa market is much more limited than either Dubai or Sharjah and, due to the shortage of availability, rental levels remain quite high in comparison to its neighbours.

There is a furnished apartment market that provides accommodation on a hotel style weekly/monthly basis. Many companies utilise this facility whilst seeking long-term accommodation.

Table 10.1.1 Apartments in Abu Dhabi

Type	*Average rents Dhs/annum (US$)*
1 Bedroom	20,000–30,000 (5400–8150)
2 Bedroom	48,000–55,000 (13,000–15,000)
3 Bedroom	55,000–70,000 (15,000–19,000)
4 Bedroom	80,000 plus (21,750 plus)
5 Bedroom	Up to 140,000 (to 38,000)

Table 10.1.2 Villas in Abu Dhabi

Type	*Average rents Dhs/annum (US$)*
3 Bedroom	150,000–190,000 (40,750–51,750)
4 Bedroom	180,000–250,000 (48,900–68,000)
5 Bedroom	250,000 plus (68,000 plus)
6 Bedroom	250,000 plus (68,000 plus)
7 Bedroom	300,000 plus (81,500 plus)

Dubai

The residential property market in Dubai offers a wide range of accommodation with the standard for apartments comparatively very high when combined with either Sharjah or Abu Dhabi. Most of the middle to upper range of apartments offer in-house swimming pools, gyms and sometimes squash courts.

Supply of apartments has historically always fallen slightly behind demand. However, during the last 12 months this appears to have equalised and, in turn, a previous pattern of rising rental levels has ceased, with rents levelling off throughout the different apartment types.

The villa market had seen dramatic increases in rental levels due mainly to ever increasing land prices, with a fall in demand for high end villas and a readjustment of land prices. Villas are now becoming available at more reasonable rates. Whilst there are several high quality villa compounds offering central facilities such as a swimming pool, stand alone or small groups of villas dominate the market.

Table 10.1.3 Apartments in Dubai

Type	*Average rents Dhs/annum (US$)*
1 Bedroom	35,000–40,000 (9500–10,900
2 Bedroom	45,000–55,000 (12,200–15,000
3 Bedroom	60,000–70,000 (16,3000–19,000)
4 Bedroom	70,000 plus (19,000 plus)

Table 10.1.4 Villas in Dubai

Type	*Average rents Dhs/annum (US$)*
2 Bedroom	50,000–60,000 (13,500–16,300)
3 Bedroom	75,000–90,000 (20,300–24,500)
4 Bedroom	110,000–130,000 (29,850–35,350)
5 Bedroom	150,000 plus (40,750)

Sharjah

Sharjah has for a long time been seen as a dormitory town to Dubai, due in the main to rental levels ranging between 20 and 40 per cent below that of its neighbour, Dubai. Whilst this may seem advantageous to companies operating in Dubai, consideration must be given to travel time between the emirates. There are two primary access routes between Dubai and Sharjah and these become heavily congested during peak times with delays of up to one hour.

The standard of apartments varies greatly but in the main is dominated by the middle to lower end of the market, the exception being those constructed around the lagoon. The provision of parking is not mandatory in Sharjah and this causes obvious problems.

Villas are readily available in certain locations, offering good value for money. However, the high water table and associated flooding during the rainy season, combined with a generally lower level of maintenance, should be taken into consideration.

The previous two years have seen a boom in the construction of all types of residential accommodation which has now outstripped demand. It is likely that existing rent levels may fall between 10 and 20 per cent during the coming year.

Table 10.1.5 Apartments in Sharjah

Type	*Average rents Dhs/annum (US$)*
1 Bedroom	15,000–18,000 (4050–4900)
2 Bedroom	20,000–35,000 (5400–9500)
3 Bedroom	40,000–45,000 (10,850–12,250)
4 Bedroom	45,000–70,000 (12,250–19,000)

Table 10.1.6 Villas in Sharjah

Type	*Average rents Dhs/annum (US$)*
2 Bedroom	40,000 to 60,000 (10,850–16,300)
3 Bedroom	50,000 to 70,000 (13,500–19,000)
4 Bedroom	75,000 to 90,000 (20,3000–24,500)

Although the U.A.E. economy is historically perceived as being relatively stable the recent construction boom has signaled the first true downturn in the economy. Dubai in particular has shown significant touristic growth, and continues to demonstrate growth in passenger arrivals.

The apartment market in Abu Dhabi is over supplied and occupancy levels are declining, however there is frustrated demand for quality villas.

In Dubai for the first time a landlord is offering substantial free rent periods to incoming residential tenants although frustrated demand exists in the medium price range, whilst the up market category is becoming over supplied as developers are trying to compete in the provision of leisure facilities. The demand for reasonably priced villas on compounds is good and homes in the Dhs. 70,000/per annum price range are popular.

In Sharjah the districts of Al Khan and Al Taawuun on the border with Dubai are currently showing high occupancy rates in apartment buildings which are often let to expatriates working in Dubai but prefer to live in Sharjah due to lower rentals. Similar to the apartment units, a large number of villas are rented by expatriates working in Dubai. There is a frustrated demand in Sharjah for villas in the rental range of Dhs. 45,000 to Dhs. 55,000 p.a.

The office market in Abu Dhabi is also overdeveloped, however new quality high spec office accommodation is in significant demand from international companies. The planned development of Sa'adiyat Island, Trade Zone which is expected to be developed as a major corporate and free trade financial centre, provides an alternative future supply of possible expat owned accommodation but the project is still in its early planning stage and further details on this opportunity are not yet available.

The current oversupplied office market in Dubai will continue to see softening rentals with an expected 1.8 million sq. ft. coming onto the market in the next 18 months set against an historical annual average absorption of about 600,000 sq. ft., and speculative development of office buildings in the short term is not recommended. We would expect long term development opportunities to improve as new supply is being absorbed in the ever expanding market. Alternative consideration could be given to the development of small office parks with standalone units, some on a design and build basis, set within an attractive environment which could command higher rentals than elsewhere in the market.

MARKET DATA

	Abu Dhabi	**Dubai**	**Sharjah**
Normal Lease Duration (Years)	1	1	1
Municipal Charge	0%	5%	2½%
Rental Payment Frequency	Half Yearly	Half Yearly/Annual	Quarterly to Annually
Rental/Security Deposit	Yes	Yes	Yes
Repair Responsibility-Structure	Landlord	Landlord	Landlord
Repair Responsibility - Internal	Landlord	Landlord	Landlord
Repair Resp. - Interior Decoration	Tenant/Landlord	Landlord/Tenant	Landlord/Tenant
Insurance (Not Contents)	Landlord	Landlord	Landlord
Rental Indexation	No	No	No
Termination Notice (months)	1	1–3	2
Tenant Pay Commission (5% first years rent)	Occasionally	Yes	Yes

Several proposed new retail projects are currently under construction in Abu Dhabi including the Marina Mall complex. When current projects are completed the city will be adequately supplied to serve the current population base.

Dubai is over retailed and the major viable developments are large mega-malls such as Deira City Centre which provides sufficient pull to divert demand from other retail centers.

Sharjah's shopping needs are to some extent met by the large malls in Dubai. Persuading international retailers to open outlets in Sharjah after Dubai is difficult, however, several new shopping malls are under construction to serve the local population.

APARTMENTS

	Abu Dhabi	Dubai	Sharjah
Average Rental Levels			
Unfurnished (2 bed, Dhs/Annum)	49,000	53,000	35,000
Furnished (2 bed, Dhs/Annum)	75,000	80,000	60,000
Serviced (Studio, Dhs/Day)	450	250	200
Villas			
Average Rental Levels (3 bed, Dhs/Annum)	190,000	90,000	68,000
Offices			
Rental Levels (Dhs/m2)			
Prime	700–810	700–915	375–485
Secondary	485–600	485–600	300
Anticipated Fall in Rents (2 years)	10%	10–20%	Nil

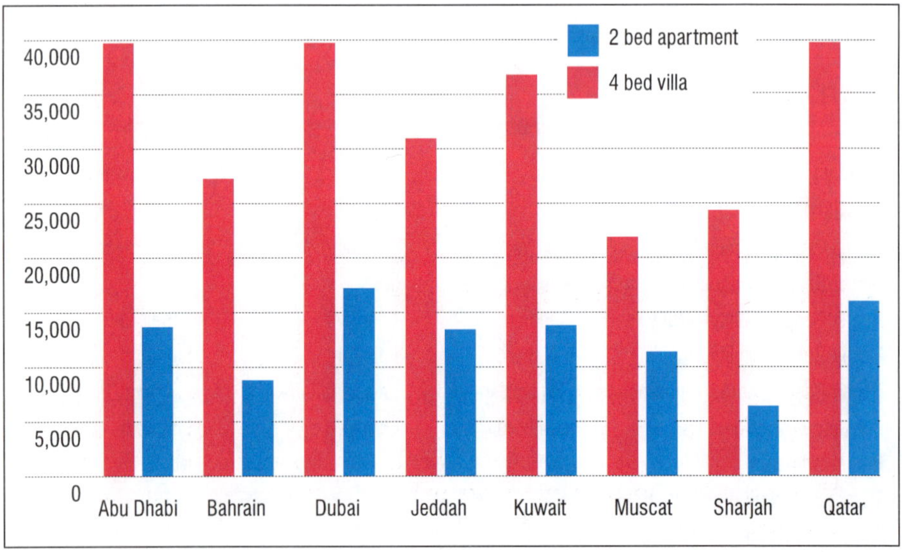

GCC indicative residential rentals in US$ pa. Source: Cluttons

10.2

The Commercial Property Market

Ian Albert, Cluttons, Dubai

The UAE is in general experiencing an oversupply of commercial office space. This is mainly due to a downturn in the economy combined with overbuilding of new space and a fall in demand. This is good news both for existing companies and new companies entering the property market. With a tenant's negotiating position much stronger than it was, say, two years ago, better deals are available and companies should negotiate hard to achieve the best possible deals as landlords are keen to fill buildings.

Traditionally the UAE economy rebounds from any recession over a two/three year period.

Therefore consultation with a reputable real estate company can help the tenant achieve the best terms. Particular attention in negotiation should be placed on capping rent increases at rent review/renewal.

Summary of practices

The following are guidelines for the renting and operating of office space in the three primary business emirates, Abu Dhabi, Dubai and Sharjah. Local variations apply and enquiries should be made to identify any pertinent issues.

Commercial lease structures

The majority of leasehold agreements are for a short term period of one to five years and the standard 'Municipality' lease agreement (i.e. one that is acceptable to the pertinent local municipal authority) traditionally contains nine or ten clauses. Disputes between landlords and tenants are dealt with by the local municipality under the auspices of a rent committee or similarly named body.

Long leases, i.e. of up to 15 years, are very rare in the UAE; these tend only to apply to pre-lettings to large space occupiers, mainly on a design and build basis.

Where outside consultants are involved in the management and letting of a building, then the lease agreements tend to be more detailed with less possibilities for disputes. There is no landlord and tenant legislation in the UAE and leases prepared by consultants for example, which are usually more detailed, tend to be viewed as a contract and fall under the Commercial Code (Federal Statute) and would be dealt with by the courts in the usual manner. Court decisions take precedence over rent committee decisions.

Payment terms

Rent is paid annually in advance, normally by means of two cheques. The first cheque is payable (first six months of the lease) upon lease signature; at the same time a second cheque is presented to the landlord dated six months later for the second half of the first year. During the negotiation stage the number of rental payments (post dated cheques) can be discussed as part of the overall terms and conditions.

Service charge

Service charges in the UAE tend to be included within the rent and not separated, as they are in, say, the United Kingdom. The landlord will therefore maintain the upkeep of the building, i.e. maintenance etc. as part of the rent paid by the tenant. You should clarify whether the landlord will also replace light bulbs within your leased area as this practice varies from owner to owner.

Utility charges

The tenant is generally responsible for the cost of water and electricity, which are usually separately metered to the tenant's property. The landlord will usually pay for the air conditioning and costs associated with maintaining the common parts. Some building owners will include all utility charges in the rent and clarification should be obtained on this point prior to lease commitment.

The costs for utility charges in the UAE vary dependent upon the local service provider. As a budgeting guide, occupants should allow for UAE Dhs3 to Dhs5 per square foot per annum. These costs are likely to increase in the near future to reflect the increasing costs to the local authorities.

Leasing/agency fee

The in-going tenant is responsible for the agent's fee, being 5 per cent of the first year's rental. The tenant is liable to pay the agency fee regardless of whether the involved agent is appointed by the landlord.

Insurance

As part of the lease agreement, the landlord will be responsible for insuring the buildings. The tenant will normally insure the office contents separately.

Fit-out/tenant's improvements

For commercial premises the landlord will sometimes allow a period for fitting-out works. Traditionally this does not normally extend beyond one month, although this can often be negotiated with the landlord for larger space requirements. Tenant's improvements are taken into account as a landlord's benefit at renewal, i.e. open market rental value for the subject premises at the renewal date.

There are many suitable office fit-out contractors in the UAE and many offer a full service from the supply of furniture to installation and supervision of partitions and carpets etc. Negotiate a rent-free or grace period to carry out any fitting-out works; a rule of thumb would be two weeks for every 1000 sq. ft, up to a maximum three months.

Termination procedures

Dependent upon the lease expiration clause, the tenant should inform the landlord in writing one to three months prior to expiration of lease term. The landlord does not have to provide a valid reason for refusal to renew a lease, although upon appeal to the appropriate municipality authority, they may request the same from the landlord. Valid reasons would be the landlord's self-occupation (no evidence is required to substantiate this), and breaches of contract may have to be substantiated before the authority.

Dilapidation procedures

The tenant is responsible for returning the premises to the same condition as at the date of occupation, subject to wear and tear.

Redecoration costs, if required, will be deducted from a holding deposit which is taken from the tenant at the lease commencement date.

Review/renewal and options to terminate

Renewal clauses are subject to initial negotiations. Renewal clauses for similar terms and conditions can be negotiated subject to a maximum 10–15 per cent maximum increase/decrease. Landlords are unwilling to accept rent capping for periods in excess of three years. Termination options prior to lease expiry are usually restricted to diplomatic clauses only, i.e. if the company can no longer operate within the UAE, but this can be subject to a three month penalty clause. Options to break are not common practice, although some tenants have requested and obtained the same in recent years.

Rent reviews are generally by negotiation and often more favourable to the client where an outside agent is involved. The negotiations are not necessarily related to the current market trends. The Abu Dhabi Municipality allows the landlord to increase rentals between 15 per cent and 20 per cent every two years, much like its neighbour Dubai. Sharjah allows 17 per cent every two years. If the market is stagnant, which it is at the moment, then negotiations can be more favourable to the tenant rather than the landlord.

Measurement of space

The general rule in the UAE can be related to the RICS Code of Measuring Practice 'Gross Internal Area', specifically all that area solely occupied and secured by the tenant including: w/cs, kitchens, internal staircases/lifts and office subdividing partitions. Facilities located along a lift corridor separated by full height block walls from the tenant's secured area will not be 'rentalised'. Basement and exterior parking areas, even if solely occupied by a tenant, are generally not rentalised.

Transportation/parking

All locations in the UAE are heavily reliant upon cars. Public transport is limited to taxis, which are in very good supply, and fares are very low in comparison to other modern cities. Buses are in use but are very modest and tend only to be used by labour workers etc. Car ownership is cost effective, with low purchase prices both for new and used cars. Running costs are low, particularly with the price of petrol. With this in mind, car ownership is very high and has an impact on the volume of traffic on the roads and space required for parking. Parking at and around buildings is a problem in the UAE and the volume of traffic exacerbates the situation.

Temperatures during the summer months can reach up to 50 degrees Celsius, and whilst underground parking is therefore desirable, it is generally limited. Prime office buildings in particular tend to offer a number of covered parking spaces as part of the rent and the number is dependent on the amount of space being leased. For example, common ratios are one space per 750–1000 sq.ft. We consider one space per 500 sq.ft to be adequate. Additional parking for staff and visitors is restricted to public parking that tends to be at the perimeter of the building. This can be very limited, particularly during busy peak periods. Negotiate the number of car parking spaces to be allocated solely for your use; these should be stated in your lease.

Specifications

The UAE has seen some dramatic development changes in the past few years, the result being an increase in the specifications of most office buildings. New office buildings tend to be of international standards, particularly for prime space, secondary space with marble lobby areas, high speed lifts (elevators), three compartment trunking/raised floors, screed flooring, suspended ceilings with air conditioning/lighting, fire detection/suppression in place. Carpeting, furniture and partitioning are generally the responsibilities of the tenant.

The commercial property market – general market overview

Abu Dhabi has traditionally had perhaps the strongest real estate market in the UAE. Only a few years ago, finding an office or apartment was difficult and many tenants ended up paying rent several years in advance just to secure a place to live or work. The majority of buildings were fully leased well before completion of the construction and finding tenants was not really an issue.

Abu Dhabi has since seen an intense period of new build construction throughout the city and this has resulted in a substantial increase in supply in nearly all sectors. Rents have now softened to accommodate the over supply and are now at best on a par with Dubai and in some sectors below. There is, however, still a shortage of good quality, well maintained office buildings within Abu Dhabi. Presently a large number of offices in Abu Dhabi are found on the first floors of apartment buildings. The result has been high levels of occupation of the purpose-built office buildings.

The main types of companies operating in Abu Dhabi are either local or foreign. Local companies, due to their size and importance, tend to have their own purpose-built buildings. Therefore new speculative office buildings are contracted to appeal mainly to the various foreign companies.

Offices are generally located on four main roads within the Central Business District (CBD) of Abu Dhabi. These are:

Corniche Road Also Known as West 1, this location commands the highest rental values of any office space within Abu Dhabi. It is the main road along the prestigious coastline which is the main focal point of the city. Parking is generally a problem, with insufficient space being allocated to each property. A relatively large car park is, however, in the process of construction and is located next to the 'Silver Tower' building, which is about half way down the Corniche, directly in front of the CBD.

Khalifa Street Also known as Third Street, located in the heart of the CBD, one road behind the Corniche. Many of Abu Dhabi's banks tend to have branches on this stretch of road, which is also home to retail outlets and hotels. Apartments tend to be located above many of the offices and retail space.

Hamdan Street Also known as Fifth Street, which runs parallel with Khalifa, a further road away from the Corniche. Again this is a mixed use area with office accommodation, retail units and apartments. This area commands around the same rental values as Khalifa Street, depending on the quality of the building and the lettable space.

Electra Street Also known as Zayed The Second Street. This road runs parallel with Hamdan, one road back further from the Corniche. Still part of the CBD, many shops and hotels have chosen this location, but it is also home to large office developments. Rental levels for this area are on a par with Hamdan and Khalifa Streets.

Outside the CBD, offices tend to be located in the following areas:

Tourist Area At the end of the CBD adjacent to the coast is an area known as the 'Tourist Area'. This area is home to some of the popular hotels and is also where the new Abu Dhabi Trade Centre is under construction. This will add some 44,203 metres square of lettable office space on to the market when completed. Construction, at the end of 1999, was still in its very early stages.

Khalidiya Street This road is a continuation of Electra heading out of the CBD and is otherwise known as Zayed The First Street. Interestingly this continuation of Electra is now home to some prestigious developments which are now commanding similar rental levels to those in the CBD. The 'Al Muhairy Centre' is a prime example where office rental levels are actually higher than those in the CBD. Other secondary roads adjoin this street, which also house office buildings.

Accessibility/parking

Parking in Abu Dhabi is inherently limited, especially within the CBD and Corniche area. It is therefore important to consider the current traffic volume, road infrastructure and the availability of parking for both the tenant and the visitor. Some of the modern buildings offer basement parking, but this is limited to the space being leased. Additional parking for staff and visitors is restricted to public parking, which can be congested in certain areas. Abu Dhabi Municipality do, however, have plans for car parks within the city and some of these have now commenced construction.

Rental trends

Rental rates are usually quoted on a metre square basis in Abu Dhabi but, as with Dubai, the lease agreements tend to quote the annual rental figure rather than a rate per metre square so it is imperative that the correct floor space is advised prior to signing the lease.

For the purpose of this report, all measurements are referred to on a metre square basis.

Rental levels have stabilised, if not fallen, within Abu Dhabi over the last few months due to supply exceeding demand. Prime office accommodation, however, still remains quite high in comparison and tends to be let much quicker.

Table 10.2.1 Abu Dhabi indicative rental rates

Type of Office	*Rent per m² per annum (dirhams/US dollars)*
Prime	700–800 (US$190–220)
Secondary	500–600 (US$135–165)
Older Secondary	350–450 (US$95–125)

Rents for offices tend to include air conditioning costs, but exclude water and electricity, which are usually separately metered.

Due to the current levels of vacant secondary office space, rental levels are expected to fall between 5 per cent and 10 per cent, but for prime facilities it is anticipated the current rental levels will remain stagnant. This is due to a shortage of good quality, well-maintained office space in Abu Dhabi.

Dubai office market overview

The market saw a boom in the early part of 1998, with many speculative office and showroom buildings leasing quickly at rental levels not previously achieved. However, during 1999 after the traditional summer period slowdown in the market, there has not been the return to increased take-up associated with the periods post summer to December. In general, the market can therefore be currently typified as flat or stagnant/ or falling.

Offices are generally located in four main areas:

Sheikh Zayed Road Also known as the Abu Dhabi Highway, between Interchange 1 and 2, this location currently commands the prime rentals within the emirate. The parking problem associated with town centre offices has until recently not been an issue at this location. However, with the growth of development, it has now become an issue, particularly access during rush hour and visitor parking. Currently, high rise office towers dominate this area. The proximity of the Jumeirah/Umm Sequeem residential districts also adds to the choice of this location, as most managerial levels of staff reside within a ten minute drive from offices in this area.

Khalid Ibn Al Waleed Road, Bur Dubai Also known as Bank Street, most banking houses have a representative office or banking hall in this location, together with many multi-national companies occupying space. Purpose-built offices are of medium height, usually comprising of basement car parking with ground floor and mezzanine with seven further floors of office space. However, the height restrictions imposed in this area appear to have been extended to allow taller high rise buildings to be developed.

Parking can be a problem in this area. However, the buildings are very close to the Bur Juman and Karama residential districts which house lower level expatriate managerial and clerical staff, with many apartment blocks being situated within walking distance of the central business district.

Garhoud Bridge Road Area The Garhoud area has developed as a business district over the last eight years with service-related businesses occupying a majority of space. Major development has occurred within the last three years due to major road improvements.

The majority of purpose-built office buildings offer approximately 50,000 square feet lettable area and comprise a basement or covered parking, with ground floor showrooms being linked to the mezzanine floor and three floors of offices, which may be open plan or sub-divided into smaller units depending on which building is chosen.

Beniyas Road, Deira Traditionally the centre of Dubai, most government buildings will be found in this location. Chronic parking problems due to older narrow streets led to the development of the three areas mentioned above.

However, improvements have been made to the road infrastructure, together with the development of 'Pay and Display' and multi-storey car parks, particularly located between Beniyas Road and Dubai Creek.

Medium to high rise buildings dominate Beniyas Road on one side, with views afforded over Dubai Creek.

Rental trends

Rental rates are usually quoted on a metre square basis in Dubai, but the lease agreement may well show the annual rental figure as opposed to the rate per square foot, so careful analysis of the correct floor space is advised prior to signing of the lease.

There has been a continuous upward climb during the previous three years, with levels peaking at Dhs75 to Dhs85 per metre square for prime office space and Dhs55 to Dhs65 per sq. ft for secondary office space. Owing to the current downturn in take-up and increased supply, we anticipate rental levels falling by between 10 per cent to 15 per cent on prime and 10 per cent on the upper range for secondary. Evidence of falling rents in Dubai currently exists. This is particular evident in older buildings where tenants have favoured relocating to more modern premises, at relatively little increase in rental rates.

Table 10.2.2 Dubai indicative rental rates

Type of office	*Rent per sq. m per annum (Dhs)*
Prime	700–800
Secondary	500–600
Older secondary	350–450

Rents for offices tend to include air conditioning costs, but exclude water and electricity, which are usually separately metered.

Due to the current levels of vacant secondary office space, we anticipate rental levels falling between 10 to 20 per cent for prime.

Sharjah office market overview

Sharjah has not historically been the business centre of the UAE and as such there has been little demand for high quality offices due to the lack of demand from major corporate occupiers. Despite this, there has been a surge of new development within the emirate and part of this has been the construction of purpose-built office buildings.

The impact of falling rents in Dubai and the association of Dubai as the business (non oil) capital of the UAE has not led to any significant take-up of the new purpose-built office space.

Sharjah is generally viewed as the industrial capital of the UAE, with approximately 40 per cent of the total industry operating in the UAE located within its boundaries. Businesses in Sharjah tend to be of a smaller nature than in its neighbour Dubai, with many companies operating as branch offices.

Rents have already fallen to levels well below the emirate's counterparts (Dubai and Abu Dhabi) and we do not expect levels to fall any further.

One of the major problems with Sharjah, as with Abu Dhabi, is the lack of building-dedicated car parking, something that is mandated by the planning authorities in Dubai. As such, very few of the new buildings have tenants' car parking facilities and this impacts the tenants' choice for Sharjah. Additionally, the buildings tend to be of a lower finished grade than in either Dubai or Abu Dhabi. However, the very price competitive rental levels associated with lower residential (staff accommodation) rental rates and the position of many new buildings overlooking the lagoons should make Sharjah a matter of investigation for companies.

Offices (purpose-built) are generally located in three main areas. These are:

Buhaira Corniche/Lagoon This is the main and prime office location within the emirate, commanding the highest rental levels. Buildings in this area tend to be of more recent construction and are therefore generally constructed to a higher specification. Parking has been generally a problem with insufficient space being allocated to each property.

Borj Avenue Central to Sharjah and located between Al Rolla Square and Sharjah Creek. The location is dominated by smaller general trading companies and banks.

Parking has been recently improved due to upgrading in public parking facilities by Sharjah Municipality.

Jawazzat Street (Old Airport Road) Close to the main arterial routes and slightly off pitch from the main business districts. The undeveloped nature of the surrounding environment allows relatively good vehicle access. This location has been chosen by many banks who have relocated from Borj Avenue during the last three years.

Rental Trends

Rates are usually quoted on a per sq.ft basis, although the lease agreements do state the floor area and the annual rent. Rental levels have fallen to probably their lowest levels, although additional incentives such as long rent free periods may be available.

Table 10.2.3 Sharjah indicative rental rates

Type of Office	*Rent per square metre per annum (Dhs)*
Prime	485–500
Secondary	320–350
Older secondary	270–280

Part 11

General Aspects of the Business Culture

11.1

Cross-cultural Considerations for Life and Business in the UAE

Jeremy Williams, OBE – Handshaikh

Your company is considering you as the Gulf regional director to be resident in the UAE. Read on – and conclude that outstanding 'people skills' are vital attributes for anyone in this role. Are you the right person for the job? Do you have the necessary patience?

First, clear your mind of certain misconceptions in respect of Arab geography and terminology. The western boundary of 'The Middle East' is usually regarded to be that between Libya and Egypt, whilst 'The Gulf' is the six Gulf Cooperation Countries ('The GCC') of Kuwait, Saudi Arabia, Bahrain, Qatar, the UAE and the Sultanate of Oman. Take care with the expression 'The Arabian Gulf' since 50 per cent of the shoreline of the Gulf is not Arabian at all but Iranian (Persian) and the inhabitants of Iran are not Semitic but Indo-European and whose tongue is Farsi, not Arabic. Arabic, of course, is the language of the Muslim world – which spreads far beyond the bounds of 'The Middle East' or 'The Arab World'. The latter consists generally of three areas: The Northern (or Levantine) region, North Africa, and The Arabian Peninsula and Gulf States. Some commentators find that the categories of Rich/Poor, Old/New and Stable/Unstable are useful divisions for the countries of the Arab World.

Secondly, and importantly: do not give much credence to those who, having lived for a number of years in one part of the region – but not the UAE – now offer to advise you because they 'know all about the Arabs' because 'Arabs are all the same'. They do not have personal experience of the *part* of the Arab world in which you are interested – in this case, the UAE. And *part* is the significant word here; *nation* is not really good enough. For example, the business style of Abu Dhabi is different from that of Dubai, while Sharjah – just up the road from Dubai – is also different. All seven emirates that form the nation of the United Arab Emirates differ from one another in a number of ways. So, do your homework on *your* part of the Arab world – your part of the UAE – and do not mentally group it with other parts.

Thirdly, the expression 'The Arabs' is as unhelpful a demographic expression as 'The Europeans'. Some similarity may exist internally within each grouping in terms of, say, political systems or religion (e.g. Islam – an essential ingredient within the Arab world); do some research, but it is never wise to regard those who form 'The Arabs' (or 'The Europeans') as though they have the same personal characteristics. People are different everywhere: what is *normal* behaviour for you may be wholly *abnormal* behaviour elsewhere.

Your company has been sensible and has paid for you and your spouse to spend a week in the UAE some months before you are due to take up residence. You have assembled the facts that really matter to a family; schooling, housing, travel, visas etc., things are looking good. You have met someone who says he is your sponsor (see below) who is charming and knows all about your company and its expectations. The children are excited at the prospect of living abroad. Your spouse is content. You know what your company expects of you and you have a decent line manager to whom you report at head office. Both of you have worked well together before. You are reasonably content with the allowances and emoluments that will affect you and your family at your new destination. The goods and services your company offers sell well to the rest of the world so the Gulf will be much the same, presumably. You have high standards and high expectations. You now want the job. You are keen. You can apply the same marketing techniques in the Gulf as anywhere else. What could possibly go wrong?

You have only scratched the surface of the situation. Now address the *hassle factor*, the *personal* and the *personnel* elements. Do you have any idea of the way Arab nationals actually conduct their business? Does your head office really have the arrogance to believe that its own standards, habits and methods will just *reach across* to the Gulf? Why would that be? What presumption! Even though the UAE has had considerable exposure to the West (from the UK formerly – but now the US) it has its own methods of reaching decisions; methods that may seem wholly illogical to you and your head office, but are, nevertheless, perfectly effective in the UAE.

Focus urgently on your *sponsor*. Do you understand what sponsor means in UAE terms? Does your company understand that a relationship with a sponsor is effectively a *Catholic marriage* because severance is not normally possible regardless of the performance of the individuals concerned? The selection of the company sponsor is the single most important act of any company new to the UAE (or to the Gulf generally). Who is he? Who knows him? What is his reputation? Who else has offered his services as your company sponsor? Has any relationship between your company and a sponsor been decided? Who in your company has been involved in the process? Do you trust that person's judgement in terms of his or her knowledge of the importance of the subject? Has an agreement actually been signed? Be clear and robust on this next point: if there is the slightest doubt in your mind that the process of sponsor selection has been casually handled by your company, and if – fortunately – there is no agreement in place, demand that your company delays closure until the whole subject has been closely examined and approved at Board level. If an agreement is already in place, then ensure that your line manager at home understands the details of the relationship and the risks involved.

Gulf law, regulations and practice are generally very much on the side of the Gulf national and national company. Outside certain free zones, all companies are owned or controlled by Gulf nationals or Gulf companies; exclusive foreign ownership is as good as unknown. Increasingly young Gulf Arabs[1] are expecting employment by right and their laws demand – for good reason – that all companies take on more nationals. For example, the banking sector in the UAE is required to employ 4 per cent more nationals each year. Many nationals – who form the minority[2] of Gulf populations – are excellent employees (and managers) but many if not most come from a family where great wealth has been the norm for perhaps two generations. The *work ethic* has therefore not been a prominent Gulf Arab characteristic, nor has *good timekeeping* – always a favourite cross-cultural subject noted by Westerners whose watches and diaries usually dominate their lifestyle.

The problems of gaining access to local decision takers will come to govern your endeavours in the UAE. It will be essential that you have a genuine friend at head office who understands the way of life of the Gulf. You need protection from those back home who believe that you have somehow, in western terms, *gone funny*, e.g. you cannot even accomplish the simplest of tasks, such as obtaining from the customer a straight answer to a straight question, or obtaining a timely programme for the CEO's UAE visit. Without such a friend, your stature in head office may well plummet and your promotion prospects may suffer unfairly since your former colleagues have no idea of what you are undergoing, or how to judge it. 'I managed to speak to Shaikh Abdullah in private for five minutes today about our project; I'm very happy. He said he would think about it all' might be a remark you might make in innocence on the telephone to head office. Your remark will only confirm to many there that you really have become *odd* – whereas the remark should have demonstrated that you have managed to gain the most respectable access to a most powerful person. You are not odd at all; you deserve the highest congratulation from the Board. To gain access needs good luck – and good exposure to, and understanding of, local practice. *Access* is the key to everything in the Gulf. It takes time and effort to achieve.

---

1 50 per cent of the nationals of the Gulf countries are under 15 years old.

2 The expatriate population of the UAE is close to 80 per cent. Most are from the sub-continent. A similar pattern is found in all Gulf countries.

Things are different in the UAE. Things can happen very quickly after perhaps months or years of waiting. Once an important person has focused on a topic, instructions are given that cause actions to occur that can astound western expatriates by both their speed and their nature. Gulf Arabs are dismayed that others – Westerners – cannot behave with the same flexibility and speed as they can. The solution is to understand the *culture* of *your* part of the UAE and to have the grace and personality to adapt to it accordingly.

Material things – housing, hotels, swimming pools – are usually more than satisfactory; this is not the main point to bear in mind when considering employment in the UAE. The mental stresses and strains must be discovered, since it is these that can ruin careers and break marriages. So, do your homework on more than just the *facts* of the UAE; look behind these to the more important cross-cultural factors and decide if you have the character (and company back-up and funding) to stay the pace. Pack *Patience* and *Resilience* in your hold baggage and happily pay the excess baggage charge for these essential Gulf items.

Memo to all HR departments: Don't send impatient people to the Gulf. If there is no choice, then start the re-selection process again ready for about a year's time. This is about when the current – impatient – incumbent will blow up and have to be replaced.

About the author: Jeremy Williams OBE has spent more than 14 years in five Gulf locations: Sharjah, Dubai, Riyadh, Abu Dhabi and Bahrain. He was the Defence, Naval, Military and Air Attaché in the British Embassies in Abu Dhabi and Bahrain. He remains in contact with many government and commercial organisations, both Western and Arab. His company, Handshaikh Ltd is based near Winchester in England, and Dubai in the UAE, and offers induction seminars, advice and negotiation training that focus on the cross-cultural aspects of life and work in the countries of the Gulf. He has counselled more than 200 companies.

His business book *Don't they know it's Friday?* (£17.50, ISBN 1–86063–074–X, Motivate Publishing, Dubai) addresses the cross-cultural aspects of Westerners' experiences with Gulf Arabs in the Gulf countries of Kuwait, Saudi Arabia, Bahrain, Qatar, the UAE and Oman. It deals with the realities of business practice, and the mental stresses and strains of operating in the Gulf as a Western visitor or expatriate. It encourages a bond of understanding between managers at home and their staff in the Gulf. It describes, in a straightforward manner, the effects of Islam upon the daily life of the expatriate, and is a useful reference book even for people who might think they already know how to behave in the Gulf. Handshaikh Ltd: UK: tel 01962 771699, fax 01962 771814, Dubai: tel 3366272, fax 3521033. Web site: http://www.handshaikh.com. email: mail@handshaikh.com

Part 12

Useful Addresses

All telephone numbers in the UAE are changing from 6 to 7 digits, a process to be completed by the end of May 2000. If in doubt, all the new telephone numbers can be accessed on the Internet at the following site: www.etisalat.co.ae/7digits.

Chambers of Commerce and Industry

Federation of UAE Chambers of Commerce and Industry,
PO Box 8886,
Dubai.
Tel: (9714) 2952977 Fax: (9714) 2955498

Abu Dhabi Chamber of Commerce and Industry,
PO Box 662,
Abu Dhabi.
Tel: (9712) 6214000 Fax: (9712) 6215867

Dubai Chamber of Commerce and Industry,
PO Box 1457,
Dubai.
Tel: (9714) 2950000 Fax: (9714) 2951646

Sharjah Chamber of Commerce and Industry,
PO Box 580,
Sharjah.
Tel: (9716) 5541444 Fax: (9716) 5541119

Ras alKhaimah Chamber of Commerce, Industry and Agriculture,
PO Box 87,
Ras alKhaimah.
Tel: (9717) 2333511 Fax: (9717) 2330233

Ajman Chamber of Commerce and Industry,
PO Box 662,
Ajman.
Tel: (9716) 7465177 Fax: (9716) 7467591

Fujairah Chamber of Commerce, Industry and Agriculture,
PO Box 738,
Fujairah.
Tel: (9719) 2222400 Fax: (9719) 2221464

Umm AlQuwain Chamber of Commerce and Industry,
PO Box 436,
Umm AlQuwain.
Tel: (9716) 7656895 Fax: (9716) 7657056

Embassies, Consulates, High Commissions and Legations in the UAE

The following list is not complete but provides information solely on those countries with commercial interests in the UAE.

Austria,
PO Box 3095, Abu Dhabi.
Tel: (9712) 6267755 Fax: (9612) 6267133

Belgium,
PO Box 3686, Abu Dhabi.
Tel: (9712) 6319449 Fax: (9712) 6319353

Canada,
PO Box 6970, Abu Dhabi.
Tel: (9712) 6263655 Fax: (9712) 6263424

India,
PO Box 737, Abu Dhabi.
Tel: (9712) 6664800 Fax: (9712) 6651518

United Kingdom,
PO Box 248, Abu Dhabi.
Tel: (9712) 6326600 Fax: (9712) 6341744

United States of America,
PO Box 4009, Abu Dhabi.
Tel: (9712) 4436691 Fax: (9712) 4435441

Russia,
PO Box 8211, Abu Dhabi
Tel: (9712) 6421797 Fax: (9712) 6488731

Germany,
PO Box 2591, Abu Dhabi.
Tel: (9712) 4435630 Fax: (9712) 4435625

China,
PO Box 2741, Abu Dhabi.
Tel: (9712) 4434276 Fax: (9712) 4435440

Finland,
PO Box 3634, Abu Dhabi.
Tel: (9712) 6428927 Fax: (9712) 6425063

France,
PO Box 4014, Abu Dhabi.
Tel: (9712) 4435100 Fax: (9712) 4434158

Italy,
PO Box 46752, Abu Dhabi.
Tel: (9712) 4435622 Fax: (9712) 4455873

Japan,
PO Box 2430, Abu Dhabi.
Tel: (9712) 44435696 Fax: (9712) 4434219

Spain,
PO Box 46474, Abu Dhabi.
Tel: (9712) 6269544 Fax: (9712) 6274978

Norway,
PO Box 47270, Abu Dhabi.
Tel: (9712) 6211221 Fax: (9712) 6213313

Sweden,
PO Box 2609, Abu Dhabi.
Tel: (9712) 6215444 Fax: (9712) 6332904

Holland,
PO Box 46560, Abu Dhabi.
Tel: (9712) 6321920 Fax: (9712) 6313158

Consulates in Dubai

In addition, a number of countries also have Consulates in Dubai, including the following:

United States of America,
PO Box 9343, Dubai.
Tel: (9714) 3313115 Fax: (9714) 3314043

Australia,
PO Box 9303, Dubai.
Tel: (9714) 3313444 Fax: (9714) 3314812

United Kingdom,
PO Box 65, Dubai.
Tel: (9714) 3971070 Fax: (9714) 3975750

Canada,
PO Box 52472, Dubai.
Tel: (9714) 3971717 Fax: (9714) 3977722

India,
PO Box 737, Dubai.
Tel: (9714) 3979666 Fax: (9714) 3974453

Italy,
PO Box 24910, Dubai.
Tel: (9714) 3314167 Fax: (9714) 331746

Japan,
PO Box 9336, Dubai.
Tel: (9714) 3319191 Fax: (9714) 3319292

Holland,
PO Box 7726, Dubai.
Tel: (9714) 3978700 Fax: (9714) 3970502

Switzerland,
PO Box 9300, Dubai.
Tel: (9714) 3313542 Fax: (9714) 3313679

France,
PO Box 3314, Dubai.
Tel: (9714) 2232442 Fax: (9714) 2270887

Germany,
PO Box 2247, Dubai.
Tel: (9714) 3973352 Fax: (9714) 3978138

Norway,
PO Box 8612, Dubai.
Tel: (9714) 3933833 Fax: (9714) 3933915

Sweden,
PO Box 9219, Dubai.
Tel: (9714) 3987716 Fax: (9714) 3982439

Foreign Trade Centres

As a major international centre of trade, Dubai also boasts a number of foreign trade centres including the following:

Belgium,
PO Box 53280, Dubai.
Tel: (9714) 3312200 Fax: (9714) 3311822

Cyprus,
PO Box 11294, Dubai.
Tel: (9714) 2282411 Fax: (9714) 2275700

Denmark,
PO Box 2988, Dubai.
Tel: (9714) 2227699 Fax: (9714) 2225751.

Hong Kong,
PO Box 7434, Dubai.
Tel: (9714) 2988255 Fax: (9714) 2989764

Italy,
PO Box 24113, Dubai.
Tel: (9714) 3314951 Fax: (9714) 3314279

South Korea,
PO Box 12859, Dubai.
Tel: (9714) 2220643 Fax: (9714) 2226330

Taiwan,
PO Box 3059, Dubai.
Tel: (9714) 3968176 Fax: (9714) 3968180

Singapore,
PO Box 14970, Dubai.
Tel: (9714) 2229789 Fax: (9714) 2231515

Spain,
PO Box 9350, Dubai.
Tel: (9714) 3313565 Fax: (9714) 3313944

International Airports

Abu Dhabi,
PO Box 20, Abu Dhabi.
Tel: (9712) 5757500 Fax: (9712) 5757285

AlAin,
PO Box 1554, AlAin.
Tel: (9713) 7855555 Fax: (9713) 7855278

Dubai,
PO Box 2525, Dubai.
Tel: (9714) 2245555 Fax: (9714) 2244074

Fujairah,
PO Box 977,Fujairah.
Tel: (9719) 2226222 Fax: (9719) 2224205

Ras alKhaimah,
PO Box 501, Ras alKhaimah.
Tel: (9717) 2448111 Fax: (9717) 2448199

Sharjah,
PO Box 8, Sharjah.
Tel: (9716) 5581111 Fax: (9716) 558105

Hotels in the UAE

There are numerous hotels in the UAE, Dubai alone having more than 250, many bearing well-known international names. Among these are the following:

Hilton
Intercontinental
Le Meridien
Sheraton
Rotana
Holiday Inn/Crowne Plaza
Best Western
Howard Johnson
JW Marriott
Quality Inn
Radisson SAS
Ramada
Kempinski

UAE Overseas Representation

Austria, 1190 Vienna, Peter Jordan Strasse 66 (tel: (01) 361455; fax: 362341)

Belgium, 73 ave FD Roosevelt, 1050 Brussels (tel: (02) 6406000; fax: 6462473)

France, 3 rue de Lota, 75116 Paris (tel: 45539404)

Germany, 5300 Bonn 1, Erste Fahrgasse 6 (tel: (0228) 267070; fax: 2670714)

Italy, Via S Crescenziano 25, 00199 Rome (tel: (06) 8394839)

Japan, 9–10 Nanpeidai-cho, Shibuya-ku, Tokyo 150 (tel: (03) 5489 0804)

Spain, Capitan Haya 40, 28020 Madrid (tel: (91) 2701004)

United Kingdom, 30 Princes Gate, London SW7 1PT (tel: 020 7581 1281; fax: 020 7581 9616); Consular Section: tel: 020 7589 3434)

United States, 600 New Hampshire Avenue, NW, Washington DC 20037 (tel: (202) 3386500)

Federal Ministries and Institutions

Ministry of Agriculture and Fisheries,
PO Box 213,
Abu Dhabi
Tel: (9712) 6662781
e-mail: maf@uae.gov.ae

Ministry of Communications,
PO Box 900,
Abu Dhabi
Tel: (9712) 6651900

Ministry of Economy and Commerce,
PO Box 901,
Abu Dhabi.
Tel: (9712) 6265000 fax: (9712) 6272390
e-mail: mec@uae.gov.ae

Ministry of Water and Electricity,
PO Box 629,
Abu Dhabi.
Tel: (9712) 6274222
e-mail: mowe@uae.gov.ae

Ministry of Finance and Industry,
PO Box 433,
Abu Dhabi.
Tel: (9712) 6426000 Fax: (9712) 6485999
e-mail: mofi@uae.gov.ae

Emirates Industrial Bank,
PO Box 2722,
Abu Dhabi.
Tel: (9712) 6339700 Fax: (9712) 6326397

UAE Central Bank,
PO Box 854,
Abu Dhabi
Tel: (9712) 6812220 Fax: (9712) 6818483

Abu Dhabi Government

Government of Abu Dhabi,
Saadiyat Free Zone Authority,
PO Box 5688,
Abu Dhabi.
Tel: (9712) 6463333 Fax: (9712) 6411888
www.saadiyat.gov.ae

Dubai Government

Department of Economic Development,
PO Box 13223,
Dubai.
Tel: (9714) 2959922 Fax: (9714) 2955577

Department of Tourism and Commerce Marketing,
PO Box 594,
Dubai.
Tel: (9714) 2230000 Fax: (9714) 2230022

Dubai Electricity and Water Authority,
PO Box 564,
Dubai.
Tel: (9714) 3968888 Fax: (9714) 3969345

Dubai Municipality,
PO Box 67,
Dubai.
Tel: (9714) 2951141 Fax: (9714) 2951795

Dubai Ports Authority,
PO Box 17000,
Dubai.
Tel: (9714) 8815000 Fax: (9714) 8816093
www.dpa.co.ae

Jebel Ali Free Zone Authority,
PO Box 17000,
Dubai.
Tel: (9714) 8815000 Fax: (9714) 8816093

Dubai International Airport,
PO Box 2525,
Dubai.
Tel: (9714) 2245555 Fax: (9714) 2244074

Dubai Airport Free Zone,
PO Box 2525,
Dubai.
Tel: (9714) 2027000 Fax: (9714) 2995500
e-mail: freezone@dca.gov.ae

Business Services

Abu Dhabi

Audit and Accountancy Services
Arthur Andersen & Co.,
PO Box 46477,
Abu Dhabi.
Tel: (09712) 6425262 Fax: (09712) 64778197

KPMG,
PO Box 7613,
Abu Dhabi.
Tel: (09712) 6323476 Fax: (9712) 6327612

Ernst and Young,
PO Box 136,
Abu Dhabi.
Tel: (9712) 6722224 Fax: (9712) 6722968

Legal Consultants
Hadef Al-Dhahiri & Associates,
PO Box 3727,
Abu Dhabi.
Tel: (9712) 6276622 Fax: (9712) 6276556
e-mail: hadalaw@emirates.net.ae

Al-Sayejh Richards Butler,
PO Box 46904,
Abu Dhabi.
Tel: (9712) 6313010 Fax: (9712) 6312155
e-mail: algt@richardsbutler.com

Afridi and Angell,
PO Box 3961,
Abu Dhabi.
Tel: (9712) 6329134 Fax: (9712) 632690

Trowers & Hamlins,
PO Box 45628,
Abu Dhabi.
Tel: (9712) 6345411 Fax: (9712) 6393123

Management Consultancy (Marketing/Investigations)
SSS Corporate Research,
PO Box
Abu Dhabi.
Tel: (9712) 6263455 Fax: (9712) 6263466
e-mail: corres@emirates.net.ae

Management Consultancy (Business to Business/Marketing)
ASA Consulting,
PO Box 238,
The Ridings,
Cobham,
Surrey KT11 2WP,
United Kingdom
Tel: (44) 1372 844317 Fax: (44) 1372 844437

Management Consultancy
(Industry/Business to Business Marketing and Business Development)
The Philip Dew Consultancy Limited,
PO Box 11836,
Bahrain
Tel: (973) 790886 Fax: (973) 790729
e-mail: pdew@batelco.com.bh

Insurance Services
Abu Dhabi National Insurance Co.,
PO Box 839,
Abu Dhabi.
Tel: (9712) 6343171 Fax: (9712) 6211358

Norwich Winterthur Insurance (Gulf) Ltd.,
PO Box 245,
Abu Dhabi.
Tel: (9712) 6774444 Fax: (9712) 6722505

Dubai

Advertising Services
Impact/BBDO,
PO Box 19791,
Dubai.
Tel: (9714) 3987147 Fax: (9714) 3986394
e-mail: info@impactbbdo.com

MEMAC Emirates,
PO Box 60484,
Dubai.
Tel: (9714) 2825414 Fax: (9714) 2825150
e-mail: memacem@emirates.net.ae

Fortune Promoseven,
PO Box 6834,
Dubai.
Tel: (9714) 2989686

Saatchi & Saatchi,
PO Box 23252,
Dubai.
Tel: (9714) 3314731 Fax: (9714 3314215
e-mail: ssabates@emirates.net.ae

TEAM/Young and Rubicam Dubai,
PO Box 14129,
Dubai.
Tel: (9714) 3435444 Fax: (9714) 3436636
e-mail: ateam@emirates.net.ae

There are more than 100 other advertising agencies in Dubai

Audit and Accountancy Services
Arthur Andersen & Co.,
PO Box 11615,
Dubai.
Tel: (9714) 3971311 Fax: (9714) 3971312

BDO Patel & Co.,
PO Box 1961,
Dubai.
Tel: (9714) 2955077 Fax: (9714) 2954867

Deloitte & Touche,
PO Box 1222,
Dubai.
Tel: (9714) 3313211 Fax: (9714) 3314178

Ernst and Young,
PO Box 9267,
Dubai.
Tel: (9714) 3314035 Fax: (9714) 3314999

Grant Thornton,
PO Box 1620,
Dubai.
Tel: (9714) 2688070 Fax: (9714) 2694599

KPMG,
PO Box 3800,
Dubai.
Tel: (9714) 3310222 Fax: (9714) 3310202

PricewaterhouseCoopers,
PO Box 11987,
Dubai.
Tel: (9714) 3321919 Fax: (9714) 3321572

Property Consultants
Cluttons,
PO Box 3087,
Dubai.
Tel: (9714) 3348585 Fax: (9714) 3348362
e-mail: cluttons@emirates.net.ae

Legal Consultants
Al-Mehairi Legal Consultants/Brian Cave LLP,
PO Box 13677,
Dubai.
Tel: (9714) 3314123 Fax: (9714) 3318287

AlOwais and Manfield,
PO Box 16686,
Dubai.
Tel: (9714) 2219000 Fax: (9714) 2219700

AlTamimi and Company,
Advocates and Legal Consultants,
PO Box 9275,
Dubai.
Tel: (9714) 3317090 Fax: (9714) 3313177

Clifford Chance,
PO Box 9380,
Dubai.
Tel: (9714) 3314333 Fax: (9714) 3314565

Trowers and Hamlins,
PO Box 23092,
Dubai.
Tel: (9714) 3969201 Fax: (9714) 3969205
e-mail: *dubai@trowers-hamlins.com*

Public Relations Consultants
Jack Pearce Associates,
In association with Saatchi & Saatchi,
PO Box 54250,
Dubai
Tel: (09714) 3328838 Fax: (9712) 3318887

Exhibitions and Trade Fair Services
International Conferences and Exhibitions,
PO Box 29884,
Dubai.
Tel: (9714) 3980503 Fax: (9714) 3980498

Dubai World Trade Centre LLC.,
PO Box 9292,
Dubai.
Tel: (9714) 3321000 Fax: (9714) 3312173

Management Consultancy
(Industrial/Business to Business Marketing and Business Development)
The Philip Dew Consultancy Limited,
PO Box 11836,
Bahrain.
Tel: (973) 790886 Fax: (973) 790729
e-mail: pdew@batelco.com.bh

Management Consultancy (Business to Business Marketing)
ASA Consulting,
PO Box 238,
The Ridings,
Cobham,
Surrey KT11 2WP,
United Kingdom
Tel: (44) 1372 844317 Fax: (44) 1372 844437

Management Consultancy (Education and Training)
Stafford Associates,
PO Box 21764,
Dubai.
Tel: (9714) 3431112 Fax: (9714) 3431105
e-mail: staffdxb@emirates.net.ae
stafford.hypermart.net

Market Research (Consumer)
MERAC-Middle East Research and Consultancy,
PO Box 60992,
Dubai.
Tel: (9714) 2822688 Fax: (9714) 2822711

Management Consultancy (Human Resources)
Hay Management Consultants,
PO Box 30987,
Dubai.
Tel: (9714) 3247396 Fax: (9714) 3247395

The Select Consulting Group,
PO Box 6787,
Dubai.
Tel: (9714) 3341145 Fax: (9714) 3321147
e-mail: select55@emirates.net.ae
www.banktech2000.com

Insurance Services
Norwich Union Insurance Group (Gulf) Ltd.,
PO Box 290,
Dubai.
Tel: (9714) 3243434 Fax: (9714) 3248687

AlAlamiya Insurance Co. Ltd. EC,
PO Box 9215,
Dubai.
Tel: (9714) 2958080 Fax: (9714) 2950791

General Accident Insurance,
PO Box 7017,
Dubai.
Tel: (9714)2951819 Fax: (9714) 2955310

Management Consultancy (Cultural)
Handshaikh,
PO Box 7979,
Dubai.
Tel: (9714) 3366272 Fax: (9714) 3931033
e-mail: mail@handshaikh.com
www.handshaikh.com

Management Consultancy (Mergers and Acquisitions)
Redwood Partners,
PO Box 35267,
Dubai.
Tel: (9714) 3319212 Fax: (9714) 3319722
e-mail: dknights@forrestwood.com

Ajman
Ajman Free Zone,
PO Box 932,
Ajman
Tel: (9716) 7425444 Fax: (9716) 7429222
e-mail: info@ajmanfreezone.com

Fujairah

Exhibition Services
Fujairah Exhibition Centre,
PO Box 1550,
Fujairah.
Tel: (9719) 2231212

Ports and Free Zones
Port of Fujairah,
PO Box 787,
Fujairah.
Tel: (9719) 2228800 Fax: (9719) 2228811

Government of Fujairah,
Fujairah Free Zone Authority,
PO Box 1133,
Fujairah.
Tel: (9719) 2228000 Fax: (9719) 2228888
e-mail: freezone@emirates.net.ae
www.fujairahfreezone.com

Sharjah

Market Research (Consumer)
MEMRB Gulf Co.,
PO Box 6097,
Sharjah
Tel: (9716) 5740007 Fax: (9716) 5740008

Insurance Services
Norwich Union Insurance (Gulf) Ltd.,
PO Box 153,
Sharjah.
Tel: (9716) 5353186 Fax: (9716) 5626953

Ports and Free Zones
Sharjah Container Terminal,
PO Box 225,
Sharjah
Tel: (9716) 5284205 Fax: (9716) 5284513

Khorfakan Container Terminal,
PO Box 10326,
Khorfakan
Tel: (9719) 2385604 Fax: (9719) 2387212

Government of Sharjah,
Hamriyah Free Zone,
PO Box 1377,
Sharjah.
Tel: (9716)5263333 Fax: (9716)5263555
e-mail: hfz@emirates.net.ae
www.hamriyahfz.com

Sharjah Airport International Free Zone,
PO Box 8000,
Sharjah.
Tel: (9716) 5570000 Fax: (9716) 5571010
www.saif-zone.com

Exhibition Centres
Expo Centre Sharjah,
PO Box 3222,
Sharjah.
Tel: (9716) 5391888 Fax: (9716) 539288

Umm Al Quwain

Government
Government of Umm Al Quwain,
Economic Department,
PO Box 1333,
Umm Al Quwain.
Tel: (9716) 7652200 Fax: (9716) 7653322

Free Zone
Ahmed bin Rashid Free Zone,
PO Box 1333,
Umm AlQuwain.
Tel: (9716) 7655882 Fax: (9716)

Part 13

Contributors' Addresses

13.1

Contributors' Addresses

All telephone numbers in the UAE are changing from 6 to 7 digits, a process to be completed by the end of May 2000. If in doubt, all the new telephone numbers can be accessed on the Internet at the following site: www.etisalat.co.ae/7digits.

Audit and Accountancy Services
Arthur Andersen & Co,
PO Box 11615,
Dubai.
Tel: (9714) 3971311 Fax: (9714) 3971312

Dubai Government
Department of Tourism and Commerce Marketing,
PO Box 594,
Dubai.
Tel: (9714) 2230000 Fax: (9714) 2230022

Free Zones
Abu Dhabi
Saadiyat Market,
Government of Abu Dhabi,
Free Zone Authority,
PO Box 5688,
Abu Dhabi.
Tel: (9712) 6763333 Fax: (9712) 6711888
Website: www.saadiyat.gov.ae

Ajman
Ajman Free Zone,
PO Box 932,
Ajman.
Tel: (9716) 7425444 Fax: (9716) 7429222
Website: www.ajmanfreezone.com

Dubai
Dubai Airport Free Zone,
PO Box 2525,
Dubai.
Tel: (9714) 2027000 Fax: (9714) 2995500
e-mail: freezone@dca.gov.ae

Jebel Ali Free Zone Authority,
PO Box 17000,
Dubai.
Tel: (9714) 8815000 Fax: (9714) 8815601
Website: www.dpa.co.ae

Fujairah
Government of Fujairah,
Fujairah Free Zone Authority,
PO Box 1133,
Fujairah.
Tel: (9719) 2228000 Fax: (9719) 2228888
Website: www.fujairahfreezone.com

Sharjah
Government of Sharjah,
Hamriyah Free Zone Authority,
PO Box 1377,
Sharjah.
Tel: (9716) 526333 Fax: (9716) 5263555
Website: www.hamriyahfz.com

Sharjah Airport International Free Zone (SAIF-Zone),
PO Box 8000,
Sharjah.
Tel: (9716) 5570000 Fax: (9716) 5571010
Website: www.saif-zone.com

Umm Al Quwain
Government of Umm Al Quwain,
Ahmed bin Rashid Free Zone,
PO Box 279,
Umm Al Quwain.
Tel: (9716) 7665882 Fax: (9716) 7665444

Industrial Bank
Emirates Industrial Bank,
PO Box 2722, Abu Dhabi
PO Box 5454, Dubai
Tel: (9712) 6339700 Fax: (9712) 6326397
Tel: (9714) 2211300 Fax: (9714) 2232320

Insurance Services

Norwich Union Insurance (Gulf) Ltd,
UAE Main Office,
PO Box 290,
Ground Floor,
Wafi Residential Centre,
Dubai.
Tel: (9714) 3243435 Fax: (9714) 3248687
e-mail: nuigdub@emirates.net.ae

Islamic Bank

Islamic Development Bank,
PO Box 5925,
Jeddah 21432,
Saudi Arabia
Tel: (9662) 6361400 Fax: (9662) 6366871

Journalist

Thomas Hussain,
1a Lawrence Road
London,
SE25 5AA
Tel: 020 8768 0395
e-mail: thomashussain@hotmail.com

Legal Consultants

Hadef Al-Dhahiri & Associates,
PO Box 3727,
Abu Dhabi.
Tel: (9712) 6276622 Fax: (9712) 6276556
e-mail: hadalaw@emirates.net.ae

Al-Sayejh Richards Butler,
PO Box 46904,
Abu Dhabi.
Tel: (9712) 6313010 Fax: (9712) 6312155
e-mail: algt@richardsbutler.com

Al-Mehairi Legal Consultants/Brian Cave LLP,
PO Box 13677,
Dubai.
Tel: (9714) 3314123 Fax: (9714) 3318287

Clifford Chance Limited Liability Partnership,
PO Box 9380,
Dubai.
Tel: (9714) 3314333 Fax: (9714) 3314565

Management Consultancy (Business to Business / Marketing)
ASA Consulting,
PO Box 238,
The Ridings,
Cobham,
Surrey KT11 2WP,
United Kingdom
Tel: (44) 1372 844317 Fax: (44) 1372 844437

Management Consultancy (Cultural)
Handshaikh,
PO Box 7979,
Dubai.
Tel: (9714) 3366272 Fax: (9714) 3931033
e-mail: mail@handshaikh.com
Website: www.handshaikh.com

Management Consultancy (Education and Training)
Stafford Associates,
PO Box 21764,
Dubai.
Tel: (9714) 3431112 Fax: (9714) 3431105
e-mail: staffdxb@emirates.net.ae
Website: stafford.hypermart.net

Management Consultancy (Human Resources)
Hay Management Consultants,
PO Box 30987,
Dubai.
Tel: (9714) 3247396 Fax: (9714) 3247395

The Select Consulting Group,
PO Box 6787,
Dubai.
Tel: (9714) 3341145 Fax: (9714) 3321147
e-mail: select55@emirates.net.ae
Website: www.banktech2000.com

Management Consultancy
(Industry / Business to Business Marketing and Business Development)
The Philip Dew Consultancy Limited,
PO Box 11836,
Bahrain
Tel: (973) 790886 Fax: (973) 790729
e-mail: pdew@batelco.com.bh

Management Consultancy (Mergers & Acquisitions)
Redwood Partners,
PO Box 35267,
Dubai.
Tel: (9714) 3319212 Fax: (9714) 3319722
e-mail: dknights@forrestwood.com

Market Research (Consumer)
MERAC-Middle East Research and Consultancy,
PO Box 60992,
Dubai.
Tel: (9714) 2822688 Fax: (9714) 2822711

Offset
BAe Systems Offset (Abu Dhabi),
PO Box 44891,
Abu Dhabi.
Tel: (9712) 6339600 Fax: (9712) 6314132

Property Consultants
Cluttons,
PO Box 3087,
Dubai.
Tel: (9714) 3348585 Fax: (9714) 3348362
e-mail: cluttons@emirates.net.ae

Public Relations Consultants
Jack Pearce Associates,
In association with Saatchi & Saatchi,
PO Box 54250,
Dubai
Tel: (09714) 3328838 Fax: (9712) 3318887

Index

References in italic indicate figures or tables

Index of Advertisers